THE REFERENCE SHELF

Volume XIV. $

WITHDRAWN

Volume XIII. $3.60

THE REFERENCE SHELF

Vol. 18   No. 4

PEACETIME CONSCRIPTION

Compiled by
JULIA E. JOHNSEN

THE H. W. WILSON COMPANY
NEW YORK   1945

PREFACE

Among the problems of the postwar period interest has for some time centered on the proposal that the United States adopt a system of universal peacetime military training. Peacetime conscription as a preparedness measure was tried for some months from 1940 up to our entry into World War II. The proposed drafting of young men for training in time of peace, however, as contrasted with conscription in time of imminent or actual war is so great an innovation to our national concepts as to have made the question a highly controversial one, and to have resulted in widespread discussion.

In this World War as well as in the earlier one it was necessary to give intensive training to unprecedented numbers of drafted men, a course that not only delayed the national war effort but gave rise, at times, to serious questioning of the adequacy of the preparation of the young men for the task before them. It was found, moreover, that large numbers lacked fitness for any service whatever, all of which caused widespread concern.

Leading officials of the Army and Navy Departments, the American Legion, and other organizations and individuals of prominence have urged or expressed a favorable attitude toward compulsory peacetime training. President Roosevelt at various times made known his approval of some system of nation-wide training for youth, and shortly before his death indicated his intention of sending a message to Congress setting forth his views. Bills were presented to the 78th and 79th Congresses, and a House Select Committee held hearings from June 4th to 19th last.

Many argue the advantages of a broader program than that of training for military purposes alone, ranging from general education to highly technical training or some form of national youth service. Opposition to the peacetime military training of youth is extensive; among its opponents peace organizations and churchmen are prominent, while educators range themselves on both sides. Many have counselled delay, and among other suggestions made have been those for a nation-wide referendum, for a national committee to give the question thorough study, and for the seeking of an international agreement for world-wide abolition of military service. The extent of the social background that would be affected by the proposed program, and the vital need today for the support of and implementing of the principles of world order, make the question a fundamental one in both a national and international sense.

This book has been limited to relatively recent materials and discussions bearing on military training as a postwar problem. Earlier numbers of the Reference Shelf, and other debate and general works, provide additional background material. Discussions have been presented here without bias, and from as varied points of view as feasible. The convenience of debaters has been kept in mind in classifying and arranging materials and bibliography.

Acknowledgment is gratefully made of copyright permissions and other courtesies which have facilitated the preparation of this book.

JULIA E. JOHNSEN

gust 22, 1945

CONTENTS

PAGE

CONTENTS

GENERAL DISCUSSION

MILITARY TRAINING [1]

With the end of the Second World War in sight, we are beginning to look forward to a drastic cut in the size of the armed forces and the return of millions of men to civilian life. We anticipate the day when the great majority of Americans now in military service will fold their uniforms for the last time and return to more peaceful occupations.

Yet the problem of military training will remain with us long after the fighting stops in Europe and the Pacific. If anything, it will become more acute. Public opinion polls indicate that the American people are prepared to support a permanent military establishment of a size never before contemplated. This prospect compels us to consider several questions, among which two are particularly important for educators: First, will compulsory military training be given in the public schools, or elsewhere? Second, what measures can we take to prevent the development of militarism, with its accompanying burden of high taxes, its incitement to rabid nationalism, and its corrosive effect upon our democratic institutions? As these questions reveal, the problem of military training is related, not only to the effectiveness of our defense against external aggression, but to the very organization of our economic and political life.

We may be sure that military men will argue in favor of compulsory military training for all boys. Since the early days of the nation they have called attention to the inequities of enlistment and the inability of those in command to plan effectively and to act immediately without a predetermined number of trained men under arms. In recent times the force of this argument has been strengthened immeasurably by the introduction of mechanized warfare. Even the man in the street now knows that

[1] By Lewis Paul Todd, Danbury State Teachers College. From article "Does the Probability of Compulsory Military Training Pose a Problem for the Public Schools?" *Educational Forum.* 9:341-8. March 1945.

it is not the potential strength of a nation, but the military force in being which must counter the initial blow of a resourceful and well-armed enemy.

Through the course of their history Americans as a whole have grudgingly come to admit that the power to conscript troops in wartime is a normal incident of the war power. As long ago as the War of 1812, Justice William Johnson of the Supreme Court predicted that conscription "will one day be adopted by the United States." Applied with limited success in the Civil War, introduced with initial misgivings in 1917-1918, the principle of a universal draft was adopted with only sporadic opposition in 1940, even before we formally entered the Second World War. Justice William Johnson's prophecy has at last come true. Compulsory military service in wartime—for men, at least, and perhaps for women—is here to stay.

But, although American citizens have accepted universal military service in *wartime*, they have never—with the single exception of the critical months from 1940 to 1941—shown any willingness to accept such service in times of peace. Nevertheless, this is precisely what they are going to be asked to accept. Public opinion is being prepared for this step in numerous statements emanating from highly placed officials in Washington. Representative of these statements were the remarks of Under Secretary of War, Robert C. Patterson, who, in an address at Norwich University, warned that because of aviation and other developments "our geographic isolation will continue to decrease. . . . The bulwark of our security must rest on well-trained and equipped forces of a strength to command the respect of unfriendly nations. In my own opinion we cannot maintain these forces and that necessary strength except by a system of universal military training for our youth." Three days earlier Mrs. Franklin D. Roosevelt, who holds no official position, although she has frequently acted as a sounding board for administration proposals, went even further. "If we're going to have compulsory military training after the war," Mrs. Roosevelt is reported to have said, "then it should be for boys and *girls*." The President has also expressed his general approval of some form of compulsory training, although, as yet, he has made no specific recommendations. Support has likewise been promised by the House Postwar Military Policy Committee. . . .

Forecasts are always dangerous. However, we have had in this country sufficient experience with the military training of schoolboys to predict with some probability of success that most informed military officials will emphatically reject any proposals to make such training a compulsory part of the public school program. Although the details which prompt this prediction cannot be given in an article of this scope, it is possible to support the forecast by recalling a few of the outstanding developments in the history of military training in the public schools.

Military drill in the public schools was initiated during the Civil War. Since that time the number of school-boys in uniform has risen and fallen with each armed conflict, reflecting the intensity of martial ardor. Two years after the Spanish American War, for example, more than 10,000 boys, or nearly 5 per cent of the male enrollment of our secondary schools, were engaged in some form of military training. Between 1900 and 1914, when martial enthusiasm was on the ebb, the number of schoolboy cadets actually decreased. By 1914 only 9,532 students were registered in military units of some eighty-two secondary institutions. With the outbreak of war in Europe, the tide turned once again, and by 1918 more than 112,000 high school boys, or one in every eight, were engaged in drill activities. New York State had even gone to the length of making military training compulsory for all boys between the ages of sixteen and nineteen. From the Armistice to 1939 there was another lull in the agitation, but as the Second World War began to press closely upon America demands were renewed for the training of high school youth. A bill to foster military education in the public schools of New Jersey was presented to the State Legislature in the spring of 1941. One year later the New Jersey Veterans of Foreign Wars adopted a resolution calling for compulsory military training for all high school juniors and seniors. At their annual encampment in 1944, the veterans from all parts of the United States unanimously adopted a resolution demanding that Congress enact legislation requiring a minimum of one year's training for every American boy. Such proposals, of which the preceding examples represent a crude and limited sampling, were similar to those which were made with great frequency during the years from 1914 to 1919.

An analysis of these developments reveals a pattern of behavior which we may reasonably expect to see reproduced, at least in its broad essentials, during the coming months. In the past, military training has been introduced most effectively into the public schools during the periods just before and after armed conflict, while the war spirit was at white heat. Mindful of this lesson, a number of Congressmen recently expressed their intention of pressing for the adoption of a compulsory peacetime draft *before* a wave of war-weariness engulfed the American people. Our experience to date also suggests that the movement for obligatory military service will have organized support.

In the past, the movement has been aroused and nurtured largely by veterans' organizations. As we have seen, the Veterans of Foreign Wars have taken a definite stand during the present conflict. In the years from 1914 to 1918 the movement was led by ex-army officers in general, and by the High School Volunteers of the United States in particular—an organization initiated by Howard K. Wheeler, editor of *Everybody's Magazine,* and endorsed by such prominent officials as Newton D. Baker and Franklin K. Lane, Secretaries of the War and Interior Departments. In the 1890's the Grand Army of the Republic sparked the enthusiasm. The War Department officially, and high-ranking military officers acting on their own initiative, have also encouraged these efforts to introduce military education into the public schools. . . .

President David Starr Jordan of Leland Stanford University protested against education "so blind, ignorant, insistent, and contemptuous of the values of human freedom." In his opinion, "only that training which develops individual initiative is worthy of the name of discipline. Collective discipline impairs individuality. The good citizen of America is not a chattel sheltered by a state he does not control." . . .

A CITIZEN ARMY [2]

Since the War of 1812, most of our military unpreparedness and most of our enormous military expenditures have been chargeable to two conflicting views as to the merits of two mutually antagonistic types of military organization. One of these may be characterized as the citizen-army type, the other as the standing-army type. In the War Department's plans for a postwar military structure, which of these two styles of architecture should the planners follow? This is a highly important question, for, in the absence of a decision on this fundamental point, the planners are almost certain to give us an incongruous hodgepodge of both systems, as they have invariably done in the past.

Fortunately, this fundamental question has been answered by Gen. George C. Marshall, Chief of Staff of the Army. In War Department Circular No. 347, dated August 25, 1944, he has directed the General Staff and all other planning agencies under his jurisdiction to adapt their plans to the citizen-army formula. It will help us to grasp the full significance of this important decision if we will consider the origins and places of these two military types in our past history.

General Marshall is not proposing anything new. He is simply directing his planners to make a modern adaptation of the plan which President Washington submitted to the First Congress in January 1790, as one of the essential foundations of the new American Republic. This 1790 plan was prepared by Maj. Gen. Henry Knox, our first Secretary of War, and was revised to meet the President's views before he transmitted it to the Congress. It was based upon the fundamental democratic principle that every citizen in a free state should be trained to defend his country. It contained simple and economical machinery for the orderly mobilization of all or any necessary part of the nation's manpower in ample time to meet any military emergency.

[2] From article "General Marshall Wants a Citizen Army" by Brigadier General John McAuley Palmer, United States Army. *Saturday Evening Post.* 217:9-10+. December 23, 1944.

Few of his countrymen realize that from the close of the Revolution to the end of his life, Washington gave continuous scientific study to the problem of military institutions suited to the needs of a self-governing free people. In 1783, shortly after the formal conclusion of peace with Great Britain, he transmitted his "Sentiments on a Peace Establishment" to the Continental Congress. This was a treatise on national military policy prepared after consultation with all the generals at his headquarters. Unfortunately, this important state paper remained in manuscript form for 147 years and was not printed until I found it among the Washington papers in the Library of Congress and published it in a book of mine in 1930.

In this 1783 treatise Washington had written: "It may be laid down as a primary position and the basis of our system that every citizen who enjoys the protection of a free government owes not only a portion of his property but even of his personal services to the defense of it."

After seven years of further study and mature reflection, he made this "primary position" the "basis" of the plans which he transmitted, as President, to the First Congress in January 1790.

In delivering his first inaugural address, nine months earlier, Washington revealed that he was deeply conscious of the world significance of the new American republic. He was a lover of peace, but as the founder of the modern democratic state, he sought to make it always strong enough to maintain its just rights in its cruise toward an unknown future. Unfortunately, a great majority of his fellow countrymen preferred to make it impotent. Therein lies the fundamental cause of the present world cyclone: A high barometer of overmilitarization in the regions of lawless aggression; a low barometer of undermilitarization in the regions of law-abiding democracy. Hence the inevitable storm. In their calculation of world conquest, the general staffs of the Axis powers counted primarily upon the continued military impotence of world democracy. They are now finding that this was a most disastrous miscalculation.

The Washington-Knox plan was very simple and may be outlined briefly as follows:

For a few weeks in their nineteenth summer, again in their twentieth summer, and finally in their twenty-first summer, all young Americans were to be trained as citizen soldiers in what Knox called camps of discipline. During these three years all these citizen soldiers in each community were to be enrolled in local units of what Knox called the advance corps of the national citizen army and held in readiness for a call to arms, if necessary.

In addition to his citizen soldiers, Washington insisted that there must also be enough regular officers and soldiers to do those things that obviously cannot be done by citizen soldiers. In Washington's day this meant the national military overhead, teachers in his military schools, guards for the national arsenals, and troops to garrison the posts on the Indian frontier.

In the event of an Indian war or other emergency requiring a temporary reinforcement of the normal regular army, each community was to furnish its equitable quota of citizen-officers and soldiers. If any community should fail to fill its quota with volunteers, the shortage would be filled by what we would call a selective draft within that community.

In the event of a great national emergency all citizen soldiers under the age of twenty-two would be mobilized immediately in their local units of the advanced corps.

Washington attached great importance to trained leadership. In an address to the Congress, less than four months after his inauguration, he urged that war-experienced veterans of the Continental Army should form the original officer corps of his new citizen army. These war veterans were to be gradually replaced by the graduates of a system of military schools. In his treatise of 1783, he proposed the establishment of "one or more" military academies. A year later he endorsed General Steuben's proposal that there should be three such academies, one in New England, one in the middle states, and one south of the Potomac —and this when our total population was less than 4,000,000. Later, Knox incorporated this proposal of Steuben's in his own plan. It is obvious that these three military academies would train many more officers than would be needed for the little regular army of about 2,500 men with which Washington proposed to guard the Indian frontier. A great majority of their graduates would therefore return to their homes to become the trained leaders of his citizen army.

Washington believed as a fundamental political principle that, in a free state, military promotion should be open to able citizen soldiers as well as to professionals—but subject to the imperative condition that no officer—professional or nonprofessional—should be intrusted with the command of any body of American soldiers, small or great, until he had demonstrated definite and positive qualification for that great responsibility.

If the First Congress had adopted the Washingtonian plan, and if subsequent Congresses had gradually adapted its detailed organization, armament, and training requirements to meet gradual changes in population, modes of transportation, and scientific progress, we would have been prepared for all our subsequent wars. To use Washington's language, it would have made us so "respectable in the eyes of our friends" and so "formidable to those who would otherwise become our enemies" that most of these wars—including the present global holocaust —probably could not have occurred.

But this was not to be. After two years of debate and agitation, the Congress finally adopted Washington's scheme for a nation-wide citizen army, but not until after it had carefully eliminated every provision for training its soldiers and for providing it with qualified officers. Washington had proposed a national citizen army in terms of gilt-edged bonds. Congress issued it in terms of watered stock. This is the origin of the notorious Militia Act of 1792, which got its inglorious try-out twenty years later in the War of 1812.

So Washington failed to secure the adoption of his most cherished plan for the future peace and welfare of the new American nation. His plan was rejected, not because it was bad from a military standpoint, but because it was obviously too good. The majority in Congress was influenced by a curious antimilitary complex which most American politicians had inherited from their English forebears. Back in the seventeenth century, Parliament had given Oliver Cromwell an effective army. Since then, anything savoring of military efficiency was regarded by most Englishmen with suspicion. And so, at the beginning of our Revolutionary War, their descendants in the Continental Congress were careful not to authorize an intelligent manpower policy for the Continental Army. If too easily victorious over King George, Washington might be tempted to follow Cromwell's example. This was the principal cause of an unduly prolonged war, with all its attendant economic and social distresses. On the whole, the Commander in Chief of the Continental Army encountered much more serious opposition from obstructionists in the Continental Congress than he did from King George's army.

After the adoption of the Constitution, the traditional antipathy to military efficiency took on a new form. Suspicion was now directed not against Washington, but against the government that he headed. Obviously, if the new Federal Union should be given effective military power in any form, it would be strong enough to nullify the divine right of secession. After the Constitutional Convention, a strong isolationist party had sprung up in each of the thirteen states. The isolationsists of that day regarded the proposed American Union much as their political descendants of the twentieth century regarded the League of Nations. They therefore did all they could to keep their respective states out of it. Failing in that, they entered the new government with their fingers crossed. They feared that the interests of a majority of the states might become fatal to the interests of a minority. They believed that, in that event, the minority could and should secede from the Union.

While large numbers of men, North as well as South, believed in the divine right of secession, they were not disposed to give the new Federal Government any effective military power. It might be used to preserve the Union as well as for national defense. It thus appears that the establishment of an effective military system, in any form, was not politically feasible in the United States until after interstate isolationism was finally wiped out in the Civil War. But by that time, Washington's legacy of military wisdom had long been forgotten by his countrymen.

It was the untrained militia of the act of 1792 that failed in the War of 1812. It may therefore be interesting to consider what the issue might have been if Congress had accepted Washington's plan for a citizen army composed of trained citizen soldiers under trained leaders. By 1812, his organized advanced corps would have numbered about 117,000. All able-bodied American citizens under the age of 40—about 600,000 in all—would have been graduates of Washington's camps of discipline. Practically all the veterans of the Revolution would have passed the military age, but they would have been replaced by younger officers who had been tested for each step in the ladder of promotion. Every company and higher unit would have had a commander accustomed to lead it in field maneuvers. Every divisional commander would have been familiar with the team play of infantry supported by artillery and cavalry. Could a little British raiding force have burned the capital of a nation organized like this? If Washington had had his way, Britannia might have hesitated before entering a second war against her wayward American daughter.

But if the untrained 1,792 militia failed completely in the War of 1812, our little regular army came out of it with the highest credit and prestige. Before the war, it had been little more than widely scattered constabulary on the Indian frontier. As war threatened, it was increased in 1808 and again in 1812. Under capable leaders like Brown and Ripley and Winfield Scott, the regulars became highly disciplined soldiers. At Chippewa and Lundy's Lane, they proved themselves a match for the best British troops. It was the gallantry of this new regular army and the brilliant exploits of our navy that redeemed some of the general disgrace of the war. The history of our modern regular army really begins with the War of 1812. Since then, it has never failed to give a good account of itself.

After the War of 1812, the War Department became the headquarters of this new regular army. Its leaders became the sole military advisers of the Secretary of War. They were neither military philosophers nor critical historians. They were hard-boiled, practical soldiers. To them, the lesson of the recent war was simple. The militia was utterly worthless. They had no knowledge of Washington's scientific plan to make it the source of an effective citizen army. In their minds there could be no effective military organization except with hired soldiers under professional officers.

When Monroe became President, in 1817, he made John C. Calhoun his Secretary of War. The new Secretary was fully indoctrinated by his generals. He therefore agreed with them that the existing militia was worthless. But instead of seeking to reform it, he proposed to replace it by what he called an expansible standing army. Here was a plan that Washington and his generals never heard of, and one that was the very antithesis of everything they ever advocated.

An expansible-standing-army bill was transmitted to the Congress by Secretary Calhoun in December 1820. It was based upon a radical conception entirely new in American history and foreign to American tradition. In time of emergency, instead of reinforcing the regular army by the mobilization of organized military units composed of citizen officers and soldiers trained in peacetime to defend their country, we should expand the regular army, as such, by drawing the national manpower into its lower ranks, there to serve under a permanent class or caste of professional officers.

Looking at the Calhoun plan after the lapse of one hundred twenty years, we are amazed that any group of intelligent men could have proposed an arrangement so utterly futile from a political standpoint. There was never a chance that it would be acceptable to the American people or their Congress. The trouble was that Calhoun's military planners—like many other distinguished practical soldiers since their time—were totally ignorant of the fact there is a political as well as a dynamic aspect of military institutions. They were proposing a type of military organization which later attained a high degree of efficiency in autocratic Germany and Japan. But they were unable to see that it was totally inapplicable to a democratic state such as the United States of America. Wise military statesmen like Washington are always inclined to improve or perfect existing institutions rather than to propose new or alien types. They appreciate that a national institution is a living organism, like a growing tree deeply rooted in the soil of national history and tradition. It can be pruned or guided or stimulated as it grows, but it cannot be replaced by a lifeless, artificial substitute such as a post driven in the ground. The trouble with the post is that, instead of taking root, it will rot where it enters the soil.

Notwithstanding its utter futility, the Scott-Brown-Calhoun conception of an expansible standing army became orthodox in the regular army for many years. It completely displaced the Washingtonian military policy. As late as 1876, General Sherman worked out a modern improvement of Calhoun's scheme. But he suggested a much greater coefficient of dilution. He proposed to expand a peacetime regular army of about 27,000 men into a wartime regular army of about 213,000. General Upton's coefficient of dilution was not quite so big. He proposed to stretch a peace establishment of about 23,000 into a war establishment of about 140,000. Under such a system, expansion for a great war would be impossible under the volunteer system, and none of the advocates of the expansible standing army ever dared to propose that its ranks should be filled by conscription.

While we officers of the old army were never able to say just how we proposed to expand our expansible standing army, we were all agreed that there was one infallible practical formula for national preparedness: Increase the regular army whenever you can. If Congress won't give you enough regulars, get as many as you can. We submitted this panacea to our friends in Congress and made it the theme of learned books and magazine articles whenever we could find a publisher. As General Pershing once said of his early days in the army: "Every army officer carried an army-organization bill in his vest pocket." I wrote one myself when I was a second lieutenant. I gave cogent reasons for a sufficient legislative increase to make me a captain of infantry. But while that highly commendable objective would have added $40,000,000 a year to the national budget, I can see now that my scheme would not have added a pennyworth to the solution of our national-defense problem.

It will be seen that there was one marked difference between the old army's military policy and Washington's. He wanted as many professional officers and soldiers as were needed for certain specific purposes, but no more. We disciples of Calhoun and Scott and Sherman wanted just as many as we could persuade

Congress to give us. And we were perfectly sincere about it.
We had been bred in the doctrine that citizen soldiers are worthless and that only professional soldiers are worth their salt.

This, of course, was due to a defect in our military education. There was a serious deficiency in the curriculum at West
Point. We had more mathematics than we needed, and no instruction at all in the history of our national military institutions.
How different our subsequent military history might have been
if some old superintendent of the Military Academy about a
century ago—when General Sherman was a cadet—had ordered
one of his bright young instructors to prepare and deliver a
course of lectures on that theme.

This increase-the-regular-army complex in the minds of
many regular army officers tended to vitiate their thought on
national military policy for many years. According to General
Grant, the superiority of the Confederate armies at the beginning
of the Civil War was due to the fact that the North did have
and the South did not have a standing army. The true problem
for each side was to develop its traditional citizen army as soon
as possible. The Confederacy concentrated upon this policy from
the start. Almost all the southern graduates of West Point and
other trained officers who resigned from the old army when
their states seceded were absorbed as leaders and staff officers in
the great citizen army of the Confederacy. As Grant said, "They
leavened the whole loaf." There was little such yeast for the
Federal citizen army, because the northern military authorities
wasted valuable time in securing their orthodox increase of the
regular army. Many trained and educated officers who should
have gone to the northern citizen army as leaders and staff officers
were, therefore, retained in new regular regiments, too few and
too small in total strength to exert any material influence
upon the progress of the war. It is well known that Calhoun's
political disciples in the South were powerful advocates of secession, but it is not so well known that his military disciples in
the North almost made it impossible for Lincoln to save the
Union.

Thirteen years after the Civil War, for the first time in our
history, the Congress made a constructive effort to establish a

sound military system. Now that the secession heresy was finally extinguished, this had finally become feasible from a political standpoint. A joint congressional committee, popularly known as the Burnside commission, comprising three Senators and four Representatives, was, therefore, appointed. All seven of its members had commanded citizen soldiers in the recent war, two in the Confederate Army and five in the Union Army. Here was a jury of seven soldier statesmen, highly competent to take up the light that had failed in Washington's administration.

And but for an unfortunate accident, Washington's message might have come to their hands. In preparing his military policy of the United States, General Upton had just finished a study of Sparks' *Writings of Washington*. Unfortunately, he overlooked the highly significant footnote in volume 8, which should have directed him to Washington's correspondence with his generals and his "Sentiments on a Peace Establishment," then among the voluminous unpublished Washington papers in the State Department. Lacking this essential key to Washington's constructive labors, he quoted most of Washington's denunciations of the untrained militia of the Revolutionary War, but failed to find any record of the scientific reforms that Washington, with the aid of his generals, had worked out after the war. In short, he found Washington's diagnosis of the national military disease without finding his sovereign cure.

Lacking Washington's own remedy, he then substituted his own, which was no less than a new version of Calhoun's expansible standing army. In this way, Washington was made the principal expert witness for a military policy which he never heard of and one which was the antithesis of everything he ever proposed. Strongly endorsed by General Sherman, then commanding general of the army, this was the gist of the military policy that the War Department submitted to the Burnside commission.

But even with the support of Upton's pseudo-Washington, the War Department was unable to sell its expansible standing army to the soldier-statesmen of the Burnside commission. They had all seen American citizen soldiers doing pretty well in a great war. As to the regulars being the whole show, the two Confederate veterans — Generals Butler and Dibrell — probably recalled that Lee and Stonewall Jackson had managed to do fairly well without any regulars at all. And so another great opportunity passed with nothing done.

After the Spanish-American War, the War Department again had an opportunity to present a solution of our national military problem to a receptive Congress. The result was a material increase of the regular army, but no effective step toward the development of our traditional citizen army. In 1903, upon the recommendation of Secretary Root, Congress authorized a new planning agency known as the General Staff and a new educational system for the training of prospective General Staff officers. But unfortunately, just as he was launching his new planning agency, Mr. Root gave it a bad start by publishing Upton's *Military Policy of the United States*, in an official War Department document, as a critical and exhaustive study of our national military system since Washington's administration.

In a message to the Congress shortly after the outbreak of World War No. 1, President Wilson proclaimed that the traditional foundation of our military system was a "citizenry trained and accustomed to arms." This pregnant hint from its commander in chief made no perceptible impression upon the General Staff, for it immediately proceeded to make plans for an expansible standing army on a large scale. As a result, when a great war army of citizen soldiers was required a little later, it had to be extemporized, as in the past. Again, as at the beginning of the Civil War, many trained professional officers who should have become leaders and staff officers in the wartime citizen army were tied up in new regular army regiments.

After World War No. 1, there was a widespread popular opinion that the citizen army, developed at such enormous cost during the recent war, should be perpetuated as a permanent national institution through a system of universal military training. This policy was advocated by the citizen army veterans who were then establishing the American Legion, and was endorsed by many regular army officers, including General Pershing. Unfortunately, the War Department recommended another policy based upon a large standing army, with no provision for the development of our traditional citizen army. But for these divided counsels, the National Defense Act of 1920 might well have contained a complete legislative solution of our national military problem based upon universal military training.

Failure to establish a sound system after the last war found us in dire straits at the beginning of World War No. 2. Again it became necessary to extemporize the national citizen army with which we have fought all our great wars. In accomplishing this tremendous constructive task, General Marshall and his assistants are demonstrating on battlefields throughout the world that the American army of the people is superior in sheer military might to the much-vaunted armies of the Axis Powers. In his recent War Department circular, he therefore directs all planning agencies under his jurisdiction to make that army the basis of their plans for a future peace establishment. As Washington did before him, he bases his military policy upon the democratic principles that in a free state every able-bodied citizen should be trained to defend his country and that every citizen soldier should be eligible for promotion to any rank for which he is able to qualify under sound and equitable standards.

The army of the future envisaged in the War Department circular would comprise a relatively small regular army, subject to prompt reinforcement when necessary from a great citizen army reserve composed of trained citizen officers and soldiers. The officer corps of this national army, as a whole, would comprise relatively few professional officers and a relatively great number of citizen officers. But the efficiency of the whole would depend primarily upon the efficiency and the disinterested devotion of these professionals. There can be no effective citizen army without them. It would be their indispensable task, as General Grant expressed it, to leaven the whole loaf. Within the limits of his true mission, as defined by Washington and Grant in the past and more recently by General Marshall, the highly trained professional officer would thus become one of the most invaluable servants of the modern democratic state. The plans now in preparation in the War Department contemplate that the National Guard shall continue to be an essential component of the Army of the United States. Under the provisions of section 5 of the National Defense Act, representative officers of the National Guard are now participating with regular army officers in the preparation of these plans.

The citizen army advocated by General Marshall would meet our military requirements, whatever the future world organization may be. It would not be provocative of war, as great standing armies are. It would be organized for the prompt reinforcement of a relatively small regular army in the formation of such expeditionary forces, great or small, as would enable us to do our part in suppressing lawless aggression. It would thus assure our friends and warn our potential foes that hereafter America will be not only willing but able and ready to do her part in maintaining a peaceful world order. On the other hand, if the organization of world peace should, unfortunately, break down, it would put us in a position to mobilize all, or any necessary part, of our total manpower in a minimum of time and with maximum effectiveness for war.

It would also form the basis for a military system of maximum economy. Under a system of universal military training, the money required to maintain one officer or man on the permanent establishments of our armed forces would maintain several trained reserve officers or reservists. With such a reserve system, our peace establishment would be capable of rapid expansion and, therefore, a relatively small and inexpensive permanent establishment would meet our needs. Without such trained reserves, there would be no such power of rapid expansion, and a much larger and more expensive regular establishment would be necessary in order to give us a reasonable degree of security. It may therefore be laid down as a fundamental principle that whenever we maintain one officer or man on the permanent establishments of our ground, sea, or air forces to perform a duty that can be performed effectively and in time by trained reserve officers or reservists, we increase the per capita cost of our national-defense system unduly and reduce its ultimate capacity to meet the nation's requirements in war.

HISTORICAL BACKGROUND [3]

Compulsory military service in the modern sense began with the French Revolution, though the French monarchy had taken some steps toward it as early as the late seventeenth century. In 1793 the French Convention decreed that all able-bodied men between the ages of 18 and 25 were liable to military service. The plan was not successful, says Major General J. F. C. Fuller, prominent British officer in World War I and writer on military affairs, until Napoleon seized power, when it became the means by which he "forged . . . his tremendous armies." In 1800 France provided him with 30,000 men, in 1813 with 1,140,000. Thus, the system which was begun as a step toward equality became an instrument of "conquering militarists."

General Fuller points out in the article already cited that "the cheapness of the musket as a weapon coupled with the democratic spirit of the age threw nations back to the primitive idea of military power, namely, the nation in arms." This theory "colored the entire strategy and tactics of the wars of the nineteenth century."

In the Treaty of Tilsit with Napoleon in 1807 Prussia accepted the limitation of her army to 42,000 men. Conscription was then decreed; the number of men allowed were trained, sent home, and another group called. By 1813, 270,000 men were well trained.

After the Napoleonic wars France gave up universal military service until the rise of the Third Republic after 1870. Prussia, however, maintained it. General Fuller comments that in that country conscription "consolidated the nation. . . . The army became the national university in which was cultivated a common spirit." It "reached the apex of its perfection in the sixties and swept all before it in the victories of 1866 and 1870." As a result all the important European countries, except Great Britain, adopted peacetime conscription between 1870 and World War I. Japan adopted it in 1873. Both the United States and Great

[3] From "Conscription for Military Training—Pro and Con." *Information Service* (Federal Council of the Churches of Christ, in America) 23:1-2. November 11, 1944.

Britain adopted conscription during World War I and gave it up after the war, to return to it again for World War II.

A number of less powerful countries also adopted conscription purely as a defense measure, e.g., Switzerland and Sweden. The Swiss system is best known. Harry L. Binsse, writing in *Commonweal* (New York) for August 25, explains that the Swiss Constitution forbids the maintenance of a standing army. All male citizens are called to military service at the age of 19. Often in peacetime less than half of those available pass the examinations, though standards may be lowered in an emergency. The totally disqualified must, "until they reach the age of 48, pay an additional annual tax." Clergymen and those in certain other occupations are exempt. (For most branches of the service training lasted in 1938 for 116 days.) The trained men then become members of the First Line until they are 32 years old, and may be called upon for active duty up to 60. There are "refresher courses" of 18 days each. They own their uniforms and rifles. Officers, commissioned and non-commissioned, are all reservists, except for the instructors and general staff members.

From 1910 to 1929 Australia had Citizen Forces for home defense only which required men from 18 to 22 to take four days' home training and eight days' camp training yearly. Boys of 17 were given "only . . . sufficient" military training in school to enable them to enter the Citizen Forces. It was abolished in 1929 and adopted again for the present war. But the decision had already been reached to drop it after the war.

DRAFT AFTER THE WAR? [4]

An armed force of from 2,000,000 to 2,500,000 men is being planned as the permanent, or at least semipermanent, military establishment of the United States. This force is in addition to the 900,000 men who may be trained each year under a national military training proposal now before Congress.

A force of this size is to be necessary to fulfill commitments made and obligations assumed by this country. The United

[4] Reprinted from the *United States News*, an independent Weekly magazine on national affairs published at Washington, D.C. 18:13-14. June 29, 1945.

States today is the No. 1 military power of the world. Its people have helped to win one war, and are taking the lead in winning another that will add to the nation's responsibilities. Large forces of occupation are to remain in Germany and Japan for a number of years. There is agreement to back up with force the new United Nations organization and the regional organization for this hemisphere. New bases already won, or to be acquired in the Pacific, must be manned.

Then, too, in an uncertain world, as the nation with the greatest riches and the most productive industries, the United States cannot rely for safety entirely on the good will of others at a time when oceans no longer are protection from airplanes and rocket bombs. This explains efforts to prevent a return after this war to conditions of the 1930's, of having an army of 120,000 men, including air units, and a navy of 100,000 men, maintained at a yearly cost of around $1,000,000,000 for the whole defense establishment.

Instead, the problem now compelling attention is where and how the United States is to raise, by voluntary service or draft, forces of the size that will be required after Japan is beaten. That problem, in brief, is this:

Germany must be occupied for a period of from four to five years, maybe longer. A force of 400,000 men is contemplated for this task.

Japan must be occupied for an indefinite period after this war. If Japan should be unwilling or unable to bring about the surrender of all forces scattered through the Pacific islands and the Asiatic mainland, American troops in substantial numbers may be needed to help wipe them out.

New island bases in the Pacific, taken or to be taken from the Japanese, will require large numbers of men to install airfields, build barracks, improve harbors and man guns, ships and planes.

Defense forces at home are planned to be in complete contrast to the condition in the 1930's. Then, they were merely token forces. In the future, powerful, mobile fighting organizations are contemplated for sea, air and land. They are to be kept equipped with the latest weapons. If universal military training is approved by Congress, the young men of the nation will provide a trained reserve for any needed expansion of the regular forces. About 200,000 experienced men will be needed to instruct the army trainees alone.

Also, to enforce world peace, the United States is expected to be ready to assign army and navy units to the world security organization. This will not necessitate an increase in this country's military forces. But, in case of need, the United States may make available up to one third of its navy and 40 per cent of its army ground forces and air forces to back the peace.

Sizing up this country's future defense problems, officials say it is impossible to make an exact forecast of the number of men who may be needed, until the nature of the peace is known. Thus far, officials do not foresee how as many men as are to be needed can be obtained. The figures, except as to the postwar navy, are only in the discussion stage. Here is about the way the estimates of needs are shaping up:

For the navy, a total permanent strength of 550,000 officers and men is proposed officially. This manpower would operate the regular fleet force of 15 modern battleships, 25 large carriers and 300 cruisers and destroyers. A large number of other ships would be kept as a reserve. In addition to the permanent personnel, the navy expects to add to the naval reserve 200,000 trainees each year under the national military training program, if that is approved.

For the army, exclusive of the air force, a strength of 750,000 to 1,000,000 men is being discussed. Army officials decline to make definite estimates until the nature of conditions to be faced after the war are clearer than at present. One million men would not be enough if the United States forces must occupy both Germany and Japan for a long period. In addition to permanent personnel, the army expects to add 500,000 trainees each year to the reserve under the proposed national military training act.

For the air forces, which would be the third branch with the sea and land forces in a proposed three-way Department of National Defense, present unofficial discussion centers on a total personnel of 750,000 men. But, because any future war would be expected to start with violent air action, this country is planning a powerful, mobile, well-equipped air arm for the future, nothing like the neglected force of five years ago. The air forces count on building up a substantial reserve from trainees.

The cost of maintaining such military forces has been estimated unofficially at $6,000,000,000 to $8,000,000,000 a year. This would be four to five times the nation's defense bill for 1940, after rearmament had begun.

But, over and above all questions of the size of forces needed and of the probable financial cost, there is the big problem of where the 2,000,000 to 2,500,000 men are to come from. The fact is that there now is no legislation, enacted, pending or proposed, that would enable the United States to raise and maintain a postwar combat force of such size. The pending universal military service bill provides only for training men, not for their use in combat, as occupation forces or other regular military service. At least in theory, there are several ways in which the men might be obtained.

Delay in proclaiming the official end of the war is one way. Men now enlisted or inducted for six months beyond the duration of the war may be surprised to learn that they will not necessarily go home six months after the last gun is fired in the war with Japan. Legally, troops can be kept in service six months after the end, not of the fighting, but of the war emergency as proclaimed by the President or Congress through joint resolution. But there is no evidence that either the President or Congress contemplates extended postponement of such a proclamation to keep these troops in service for a long time after the shooting stops.

Voluntary enlistment is another method. By increased compensation and special inducements, men in large numbers could be enlisted. But it will be difficult to get volunteers while the country is prosperous. General of the Army George C. Marshall told Congress that, at prohibitive cost, a maximum of only 250,000 volunteers could be obtained.

A postwar draft would be a third possibility. But this would be an unprecedented move that is certain to encounter strong opposition in Congress.

The future military standing of this country is being decided right now. The problem is to get men now in service to remain, and to provide for future recruits in sufficient numbers to maintain the necessary permanent strength. The national military training program is recommended by the President and his advisers to provide a general pool of trained manpower from which volunteers for permanent service can be drawn, with the rest comprising a reserve for use in emergency.

If compulsory training is defeated, what is regarded as the basic step in keeping strong forces cannot be taken, and officials will be stumped as to what to do next.

If compulsory training is adopted, officials say they can work out rest of answers for raising necessary manpower.

All military branches expect to offer opportunities to keep officer personnel up to strength. As for enlisted men, the chances of getting adequate numbers may be best in the navy, with world travel, and in the air forces, with a new and developing type of activity.

The army faces the biggest problem, and expects to meet it partly by scaling down occupation forces in Germany as rapidly as it can safely do so, and by holding such forces in Japan to a minimum. The army plans definitely to rely on volunteers from its present ranks and future trainees to keep up its strength.

If these steps fail to obtain enough men for the permanent forces, then the question of a peacetime draft will have to be faced, or the country will have to get along with a substantially smaller force than now thought necessary.

TRAINING FOR MILITARY SERVICE [5]

From the Revolutionary War through the Spanish-American War, and even into the early stages of the World War, this country was addicted to the almost fatal delusion that an army animated by patriotism needs neither instruction nor discipline to prepare it for battle. In Lexington and Concord days a cap-

[5] Prepared by the Bureau of Public Relations in collaboration with the Operations and Training Division, War Department General Staff. Written by First Lieutenant B. N. Harlow, Bureau of Public Relations. *Annals of the American Academy.* 220:29-49. March 1942.

8998

tain's commission was given to anyone enrolling a company of fifty-nine men; a colonel's commission was given to any man organizing ten such companies. The sole qualification for command was the ability to recruit men. The use of raw troops was resorted to everywhere during the greater part of our military history.

These mistakes perhaps are to be expected from a nation which traditionally has opposed large standing armies as inimical to democratic institutions. The repetition of these mistakes for more than a century after the War for Independence probably may be traced to American pride and confidence in the fact that the United States never has been defeated in a war. As John Adams pungently observed, "We follow success and not skill." Yet, this confidence in American strength, this reliance upon American ingenuity to solve crises *after* they appear, has resulted repeatedly in military fiascos, in the futile shedding of torrents of American blood on battlefields both in this country and abroad, and in the dissipation of American wealth and resources garnered through generations of travail.

If, as Socrates said, military training was important in the days of Greece, its importance today in a technological world is beyond overemphasis. The foot soldier today must have more technical knowledge and professional skill than the captain of 150 years ago, in order to operate effectively the highly intricate military mechanisms under his control. The captain today must have more technical and tactical ability, more initiative and adaptability, than the colonel 150 years ago. Honorable Robert P. Patterson, the Under Secretary of War, recently summarized the demands on the modern American soldier as follows:

The modern soldier is more than a mechanic or a truck driver in uniform. He is a two-fisted fighter who can give it and take it in the mud and the sand, who can ride in a tank or a truck for hours, under grueling conditions, and then stand up and fight it out, hand-to-hand if necessary. The American soldier of today must be skilled in the use of his weapons and must be able to assume responsibility if his commander is put out of action. He not only carries a field marshal's baton in his knapsack, but he is likely to have to take it out and use it.

The "two-fisted fighter" endowed with qualities of leadership and endurance, as described by Under Secretary Patterson, is not developed through a haphazard training scheme. He is the product of infinite patience and a meticulously planned program. His character, as well as his physique and technical skill, is a subject of concern and study, since soldierly traits must be developed in addition to manual dexterity. Each phase of his development into the self-reliant, capable soldier is conducted under the advertent scrutiny of military leaders. And all this care and attention is justifiable and necessary, because, as stated in the Army Training Manual, "the ultimate purpose of all military training is the assurance of victory in the event of war."

It is with that objective of "victory in the event of war" in mind that great care is taken to develop an aggressive, inflexible spirit in American soldiers, so that they will have the desire and the ability to close with and destroy the enemy. This aggressive attribute is not necessarily inherent in an army, but requires the careful and persistent instilling of such qualities as initiative, leadership, and discipline. A popular but mistaken belief exists that because our citizens individually possess courage, fortitude, and self-reliance, they must necessarily possess the same qualities when aggregated as soldiers; but brave though Americans are individually, they, as all soldiers, require intensive instruction in military subjects, a thorough acclimatization to military life, and must become instinctively responsible to military discipline before they are prepared for battle. Skill and confidence, initiative and discipline, coupled with an aggressive, resolute spirit, are the attributes desired in the American soldier. They are the major objectives of the military training program of the army of the United States.

In general, the traits desired in our modern American soldier are fostered through military schools and troop training. Which of these methods is employed depends primarily upon the purpose for which the training is conducted. When the purpose is to qualify men for appointment as officers, to augment the training of those already commissioned, or to train noncommissioned officers and specialists as instructors, military schools are utilized for instruction. This type of training, which is the method of all army service schools, gives uniformity in training standards, and requires fewer instructors and less time for training.

When the purpose is to develop leadership and teamwork, initiative, judgment of combat leaders, and the confidence of their subordinates, the method employed is troop training. This method makes use of all the officers and noncommissioned officers for instruction of their subordinates. It places emphasis on the combat role of each subordinate military unit, as well as that of the unit as a whole in an integrated military team, in order to develop the teamwork so imperative in modern warfare.

The army school system originated with the establishment of the United States Military Academy at West Point, New York, in 1802. It has since expanded to include a great number of specialized schools providing instruction for the Regular Army, the National Guard, the Officers' Reserve Corps, the Organized Reserves, and the Enlisted Reserve Corps. Various army schools and army extension courses afford a variety of training to the individual without regard to his membership in any particular military unit, insuring uniformity in doctrine and methods of instruction, and providing trained specialists. The formulation of plans and policies for this extensive school system, excepting the Army Industrial College and the air force training program, is under the direction of the War Department General Staff. These training policies are effectuated by the Adjutant General, the chiefs of the various branches of the army, territorial and troop commanders, superintendents and commandants of army schools, and the presidents of and professors of military science and tactics at civil schools and colleges. . . .

In addition to the army educational system, a large organization has evolved since the World War to provide instruction for civilians who volunteer for military training. The principal agencies for civilian instruction are the Reserve Officers' Training Corps (known as the R.O.T.C.), the Citizens' Military Training Camps (known as the C.M.T.C.), and Army Extension Courses. Certain civil schools receiving federal aid, and rifle practice provided by the National Defense Act are secondary educational agencies for civilians. This civilian educational system teaches national defense needs, including citizenship obligations, and qualifies civilians for the National Guard, the Officers' Reserve Corps, the Organized Reserves, and the Enlisted Reserve Corps in time of peace. It is also a source of trained manpower for the expansion of the Army of the United States in time of war. . . .

Reference previously was made to agencies providing military education to civilians: the Reserve Officers' Training Corps and the Citizens' Military Training Camps. Each of these agencies has been of great value in meeting the emergency situation of the past two years. On October 8, 1941, 76,000, or 67 per cent, of the 113,000 officers on duty were reserve officers, and approximately 29,000 additional reserve officers are available for active service. In the school year 1940-41 the Reserve Officers' Training Corps has approximately 198,000 members undergoing training at 276 high schools, colleges, and universities distributed across the entire United States. These units have averaged approximately 6,500 graduates during the past several years. The college R.O.T.C. units probably will graduate 9,000 seniors this year, who will receive their commissions as second lieutenants in the Officers' Reserve Corps. Reserve officers are serving today in every branch of the army from the General Staff to small scattered troop units, and roughly 90 per cent of the lieutenants with regular army units are reserves, most of them recent graduates of R.O.T.C. units.

The R.O.T.C. has been the fertile source of reserve officers since 1920. This training program cannot produce fully qualified officers, nor does it attempt that goal; but its military drills, classroom work, and lectures provide the students with the most important fundamentals of military training, which can be utilized to great advantage in a time of national emergency.

R.O.T.C. units are divided into junior and senior divisions, the former composed of students in high schools and other secondary schools, and the latter composed of college and university students. The junior division, consisting of three years of training with three hours of work per week, corresponds to the first two years' work in the senior division. The last two years of the senior course, known as the "advanced course," is elective to all but the purely military colleges, and consists of five hours of work per week on military subjects. The senior division is not restricted to infantry, but has units corresponding to the various branches of the army. At the end of the third year of college R.O.T.C. training, or after completing the first year of the advanced course, the students receive six weeks' training at a summer camp; and after the fourth year of college R.O.T.C. training they are presented their reserve commissions as second lieutenants in the Officers' Reserve Corps.

Another form of civilian military training leading to a reserve commission was afforded by the Citizens' Military Training Camps, which provided military training to young men who had no opportunity for instruction in the R.O.T.C. Due to the scarcity of instructors and equipment and the lack of training areas, the operation of these camps was suspended by the War Department in the 1940 fiscal year.

The complete C.M.T.C. course consisted of four summer camps of one month each, held in successive years and called the "Basic," "Red," "White," and "Blue" camps. The course included training in leadership and other military fundamentals, and in citizenship. The training was progressive from year to year, and only those considered good material for reserve officers were sent to the final Blue camp. Those who completed the four annual camps and met other requirements, including a full physical examination, were commissioned second lieutenants in the Officers' Reserve Corps.

The C.M.T.C. student was furnished transportation to and from his camp by the government, and fed, clothed, equipped, and given medical care during his attendance. About 35,000 young men were trained annually at camps all over the United States. The number of individuals trained in the C.M.T.C., 1920 to 1940 inclusive, is 367,592. The figure includes only those who completed the full thirty-day period in one or more camps.

The military educational system, according to army regulations, prepares "every individual and organization in the Military establishment for efficient service to the nation in peace and in war." How this objective is achieved has been the subject matter of the foregoing discussion. Educational agencies alone, however, cannot produce a well-rounded combat leader. Theoretical schooling must be supplemented by hard, practical experience in field training and with troops. Skill in strategy and fundamentals of administrative control may be taught in army schools, but teamwork and leadership, and the application of theoretical technique and tactical doctrines to combat situations, can be learned only through troop training.

Success in combat demands the subordination of the individual to the greater objective of the unit, and if individuals are to function as a unit, a feeling of unity must be achieved. Such a feeling is obtained by the careful training of the individual and the unit in the part each has to play as an element of the fighting team, and by the training of all elements in coordinated action toward a single goal. Teamwork is based upon the belief that the leadership is competent, and the confidence that each member of the team will perform his share of the task.

The military training of organizations, known in the army as "unit training," is the direct responsibility of unit commanders. By means of applicatory tactical exercises, drill, practice, physical training and athletics, and troop schools, the unit commander promotes the development of teamwork and leadership.

Drill is perhaps the best known of training expedients. It is practice in standardized procedure. Through its development of discipline, military bearing, and physical hardening of the soldier, it is a powerful aid in fostering self-control and a group spirit among the members of a military organization. Drill is supplemented by practice with weapons and equipment in order to render the soldiers proficient in their use. This process is continuous throughout the training period and is of utmost importance in the development of capable soldiers. . . .

The training of an army en masse poses an entirely different set of problems from those involved in training individuals. Leadership and teamwork are the goal of unit training; but the development of the skill of the individual to play his part effectively in the military team is the object of individual training. Modern battle, a maelstrom of noise and confusion, has enormously increased the importance of the training of the individual. He must acquire such skill in the technique of operating his implements of war, whether vehicles, weapons, or men, that he habitually follows correct procedure under any conditions which may be encountered. Modern warfare has also required the decentralization of the responsibility for making decisions. The increased tempo of war today, its rapid changes in local situations, and the great spaces it covers make it impossible for commanders to control the detailed action of subordinate units. Hence, the accomplishment of the will of the commander depends, in final analysis, upon the ability of the subordinates to make the proper decisions in unpredictable situations on the battlefield. These decisions require sound judgment and initiative—qualities which must be carefully developed and fostered in the training of every individual.

The training of individuals lacking prior military experience is one of the most difficult and important of the training problems confronting the army. On October 1, 1941, 705,000 selective service trainees had been inducted into the army. Awaiting them was a carefully planned training program to develop them into seasoned soldiers.

Since the recruit's first mental reaction to military life is almost certain to be confused, the first instruction for the inducted man is designed to orient him in his new surroundings. This orientation process begins at the induction station, where in a few hours' time the trainee undergoes a thorough physical examination and is sworn in as a soldier in the United States Army.

The process is continued at the reception center, where the trainee remains a few days (usually less than a week) and receives his first instruction in army regulations, military courtesies, sanitation, and the articles of war. It is also in the reception center that the neophyte soldier takes the Army Classification Test and is interviewed to determine his educational background, main occupation, secondary occupations, talents, hobbies, sports, previous military experience, leadership ability in civil life, and what type of army duty he prefers. All this information is entered upon the Soldier's Qualification Card, so that a Classification Officer may accurately channel the individual into the army organization for which his educational and experience background best qualifies him. Army clothing also is issued to the soldier-to-be in the reception center, and he is vaccinated, inoculated, and carefully examined by army doctors for communicable diseases.

This orientation and classification stage in the development of the soldier has been conducted for each of the 705,000 trainees in order to insure that each army organization will receive men whom it can use, train, and keep. Thirty-seven reception centers had been constructed for this purpose, with a combined capacity on October 30, 1941, of 50,250 men, who, as has been noted, may be routed through these centers in a period of less than a week. Through the reception center classification process, the army has been able, for example, to avoid training an air pilot to be a typist, or a typist to be an air pilot. Experts have been placed in assignments where their abilities could be utilized to the best advantage for the individual as well as the army. Moreover, and of vital importance to the development of the training program, army organizations have not been forced to trouble themselves over the deficiencies of useless or ineffective men, or to sacrifice training so as to complete initial records and administration of new soldiers.

From the reception center, the fledgling soldier is assigned to one of the replacement training centers, whose combined capacity on October 27, 1941 was 243,616 men. On October 11, 1941 there were 142,893 trainees receiving instruction in replacement training centers. . . .

At the replacement training center the recruit receives approximately thirteen weeks of basic training, concentrated on seven fundamental military requirements. The first of these, the understanding of the basic rules of military life and a knowledge of elementary training, is achieved partially in reception center training as well as in the replacement training center, and includes instruction in such matters as military discipline, military courtesy, hygiene, articles of war and army regulations, close order drill, and interior guard duty. The second requirement comprises the proper care and maintenance of arms, weapons, and equipment in the field. The third, proper physical condition for extended field service. The fourth, skill in the use of the weapon, which includes instruction in nomenclature of the piece, its stripping and assembling, care and cleaning, marksmanship training, and range practice. Next is instruction in the effects of weapons, the characteristics of toxic chemicals and projectiles, and the means and methods of gas defense. The sixth requirement is an understanding of terrain forms, cover, and concealment, and representation of terrain forms on maps. And the seventh, practice in the duties of an individual soldier on the march, in shelter, and in combat.

In addition to teaching these fundamentals of military life, which must become habitual with the soldier, replacement training centers conduct specialized training. Soldiers are taught a multitude of skills. They learn such specialized professions as automobile mechanics, radio operation and maintenance, and cooking. Many are developed into proficient clerks, since the daily operation of a huge army requires considerable "paper work." All trainees in this stage of their training receive instruction in the essentials of antiaircraft defense and defense against mechanized units.

Upon leaving the replacement training center, the soldier has become acclimated to his environment and is sufficiently skilled to participate effectively in the tactical training of units. The assignment to a tactical unit brings the trainee into the actualities of army life. "In the field," as the training process continues, he is under the close observation of his officers to discern qualities of leadership, initiative, and sound judgment. After four months, if he reveals "outstanding qualities of leadership as demonstrated by actual service in the army," he may become a candidate for a three-month course in an officer candidate school, which provides officer training in the latest techniques of the various arms and services of the army. The officer candidate schools, as the program now operates, afford an opportunity for one in each hundred soldiers to become a commissioned officer, the schools graduating approximately 14,280 men every year. This instruction is conducted in the special service schools.

The test of the training program is, of course, the performance of the soldier in combat, where the skills and initiative and physical endurance cultivated through the months and years may spell the difference between victory and defeat. What is to hap-

pen on the field of battle cannot be left to chance—the stakes
are too great, the investment too high. Consequently, the army
attempts to duplicate battle conditions as closely as possible in
its training program in order to train the officers and the men
in actual combat situations. This proving ground of the training
program is known as "field maneuvers." . . .

The men participating in these maneuvers had been given
complete basic training. The maneuvers initiated the advanced
phase of the mobilization training program—the actual tactical
and strategic exercises which simulated battle conditions. The
Chief of Staff, in an address to the National Convention of the
American Legion, stressed the importance, the purpose, and the
results of the recent maneuvers, when he said:

It is difficult to overemphasize the importance of the maneuvers.
You veterans who served in France will recall the fog of battle and the
utter confusion which often prevails when large military forces come to
grips; you probably remember the tremendous difficulties of ammunition
and food supply; the great strain placed on field communications and
the necessity of willing obedience and firm discipline. In actual battle
these matters are of decisive importance and they cannot be simulated
on the parade ground. The present maneuvers are the closest peacetime
approximation to actual fighting conditions that has ever been undertaken
in this country. But what is of the greatest importance, the mistakes
and failures will not imperil the nation or cost the lives of our men.
In the past we have jeopardized our future, penalized our leaders and
sacrificed our men by training untrained troops on the battlefield.

The maneuvers also constitute a field laboratory, to accept or dis-
card new methods of applying fundamental tactical principles. They
enable us to perfect close liaison between combat aviation and ground
units. They permit test of a possible solution to the secret of defense
against tanks. By actual field operations we are determining the proper
tactics for the employment of armored units. The development of our
mechanized reconnaissance units is being accelerated by experience with
the difficulties and uncertainties created by masses of troops operating
over wide distances. Opposing divisions are kept in the dark as to the
size, equipment, and other capabilities of their immediate opponents.

The results at times have been startling. In some cases divisions
would have been annihilated; in others they would have been captured.
On the field of battle, such events would be tragic. Today they are
merely mistakes. We can correct them, replace the ineffective leaders,
and go ahead. As an insurance policy against whatever operations our
troops might be called upon to perform, the cost of these maneuvers
represents a trifling premium to pay. Tremendous sums of money have

been spent on our national defense effort, but I know of no single investment which will give this country a greater return in security in the saving of lives than the present meneuvers.

NATIONAL SERVICE AND COMPULSORY MILITARY TRAINING [6]

It is recognized, generally, that the army and navy have planning groups working on the details of a comprehensive postwar plan which involves the following assumptions:

1. That some kind of universal military service will be forthcoming.

2. That the postwar army will approximate 1,000,000 to 1,500,000 men and that the navy will be twice as large as in 1940, or even larger.

3. That the areas released from the Japanese seizure and the new chain of Atlantic bases will require considerable forces, while the control of the disturbers of world peace will demand a much larger and more highly trained army and navy.

4. That it will be impossible to maintain an army of 1,000,000 to 1,500,000 men on a voluntary basis either from the standpoint of cost or of personnel, thus making universal service necessary. About 1,000,000 to 1,500,000 able-bodied boys would be of training age each year. It is thought that there will be need for an over-all peacetime force of about 2,500,000 with 1,000,000 or 1,500,000 in training and the remainder to maintain garrisons and to provide flexible reserves.

The program of training, as far as is now known, would be essentially similar to the general pattern which is now in effect for the making of a fighting force. After the basic general training, there would follow periods in the special service schools which would vary in accordance with the variety of special services needed. Aptitudes and abilities would constitute the chief considerations for assignments. Technical training would be greatly emphasized. This is borne out by the percentage of specialists in the various branches of the army: 21 per cent for the

[6] By Sidney B. Hall, Director of University Extension, George Washington University. *Social Science*. 20:83-92. April 1945.

infantry, 60 per cent for the engineers, 69 per cent for the signal corps, and 78 per cent for the air corps.

President [Roosevelt] . . . made favorable comments on the idea of a year of military training, and he . . . also expressed interest in accompanying special educational programs.

The Secretary of the Navy publicly stated in January 1944, that the nation should prepare immediately to set up a permanent universal military training system for American youth. He has emphasized the need for maintaining a large force abroad upon the cessation of hostilities, yet suggesting the desirability of making it convenient for those who have borne the brunt of battle to return home as quickly as possible. He pointed out that universal service, started in the immediate future, would provide the means whereby newly trained men could replace the veterans. Furthermore, he suggested that the ideal time for a boy to give a year to his country would be between 17 and 19 years of age. Then he revealed his thinking as to what the year's program should be, namely, the training of youth, *"physically, mentally, and spiritually for citizenshiip, the first duty of which is service in defense of his country in case of emergency."*

While the armed services have tended unofficially to comment that only military training would be involved, the Secretary of the Navy openly declared that a year of compulsory service would provide opportunities for developing occupational guidance, health habits, educational guidance, education in government, and the responsibilities of citizenship.

At the same time, it should be observed that at the New York *Herald Tribune* Forum in November 1943, Walter Millis, speaking as a substitute for Assistant Secretary of War McCloy, urged that the nation must try to conserve the real values of courage, discipline, technical progress, national unity, and military preparedness which have been discovered in the prosecution of the war. He argued that "the Selective Service System had given the selectees an incomparable physical education, a thousand skills of as much value in peace as in war, a toughness and self-reliance, a sense of individual purpose and of national duty that will stand both them and the country in good stead in the future years." Because of these values, Mr. Millis believes that a plan of national military training should be continued after the war.

Former President Neilson of Smith College, at the *Herald Tribune* Forum, suggested more extensive educational services, but through the regular channels of the established educational institutions.

President Lewis of Lafayette, at the same Forum meeting, urged that more attention be given in education to government service and suggested the possibility of special schools of citizenship. He felt that these schools might be operated for six months and attended by all youth during their seventeenth or eighteenth year.

Here they would be taught their duties as responsible members of a great nation; here they would be trained for national service, civil and military. Here they would study government—municipal, state, and national; explore the lessons of history; and consider what part they should play as loyal citizens in making our system of government function with the greatest effectiveness. Here also they would receive thorough instructions in basic military science.

For this type of program President Lewis suggested that the military camps and Civilian Conservation Corps camps scattered throughout the country could be used to house this new project.

In conjunction with these proposed ideas, by President Lewis and ex-President Neilson, attention should be called to the National Aviation Training Association and other similar organizations which have expressed keen interest in a permanent plan for the training of a large number of aviation cadets following the war.

Several "popular polls" have been taken among young *boys* and *girls* and, also, among farmers of different sections of the country. While these "polls" show certain sentiment for compulsory military training, it must be recognized that such opinions are being gathered under the influence and pressure of war, and obviously would tend to be favorable. It should be noted that a "poll" taken in 1940 showed the "farmer group" somewhat more favorable to compulsory training than the "poll" of 1944.

On the assumption that compulsory military training would be inaugurated after the war, the opinions of 1,000 representative school administrators was sought by the *Nation's Schools.* The opinions expressed by this group of schoolmen indicated a very definitely favorable opinion for one year of military training following the twelfth school year or on completion of the four years of high school training. (This group, however, seemed overwhelmingly against the establishment of a compulsory high school R.O.T.C.)

In view of the evidence presented in the foregoing sections, plus the constantly recurring statements in the press dealing with this matter and the tendency to give these items immediate consideration by Congress, it is quite obvious that the matters of *national service* and *compulsory military training* are now before the American people. Before these matters are settled either favorably or otherwise, it appears that certain questions as to the nature and character of compulsory military training should be raised.

Question I. Should national compulsory service be purely military in character, or should it contain methods and content ordinarily associated with the system of public education?

The traditional military point of view would favor all possible emphasis on strictly military training, but the line between military and non-military in any area of endeavor seems to be increasingly less distinct. The large use of standard educational methods and materials already currently made in the armed services, even in relatively short periods of time and under intense pressure, would seem to preclude a year of military training without extensive use of much that could be properly called educational rather than military.

The inadequacies of adolescent knowledge, habits, skills, attitudes, and functions are such that the leaders of public education have long urged the extension of the secondary school to cover the nineteenth and twentieth years as a part of public education for all youth (now incorporated in the commission's latest report of the Educational Policies Commission of the National Education Association with a new and stronger emphasis).

Therefore, any scheme for national military service which did not provide for continued desirable schooling would either seriously interfere with the system of public schools already projected, or else make desirable a still longer period of public education. Such statements as those made by Secretary Knox would indicate that certain educational obligations, such as civic, moral, technical, and physical training, hitherto assumed to be a part of education proper, will become a part of the military program.

Question II. Should the proposed national service be primarily concerned with the specialized abilities, interests, and needs of youth rather than with purely military training?

The educational assumptions suggested in the comments on question one would seem to follow here, but with much stronger emphasis. Accordingly such assumptions could go much further into important functional activities such as guidance, occupational adjustment, placement, and preparation for advanced studies, and all of these in recent years have become increasingly developed as outcomes of public school education.

Under the educational inferences of questions one and two, a year of military service could become the cap sheaf in the field of public education. The implications of military administrative control, of federalized intellectual, civic, and moral determinism, and of what the national service system thinks is best as the final, formal education for youth, would appear to be of considerable importance. Thus is precipitated the question of emphasis. Should it be on military training with a minimum of educational provision, or should it be on the national service of youth with military training as the associated means or underlying base? A fair guess would be that the chief protagonists of the national service act will argue for military training as the dominating feature; but once the plan was in operation it would increasingly become educational in form and content, although accompanied by much regimentation and regulation.

Question III. Further consideration of the above questions raises the issue of whether a plan of universal compulsory military service should be under the sole control of the armed services or under a commission composed of military and educational authorities.

In all probability the armed services would not welcome the idea of such a commission, possibly in any capacity, much less with a provision for control. Judging by past performance, Congress, if favorable to compulsory service, would be inclined to accept the recommendations of the War and Navy Departments. On the assumption that the proponents of national service will demand *and obtain* legislation requiring a full year of training under complete military emphasis and control, what would be education's answer? There would be several choices.

A. Full support of the army and navy plan with recommendations for the recognition of certain educational relationships such as the following:

1. Opportunity for youths over 18 who have not finished the high school to complete courses, while in service, which could be accepted as credits toward the high school diploma.

2. Recognition of the interests, skills, and abilities of certain individuals that have been partially developed in the secondary school, but which need further training for occupational adjustment. In many instances such a provision during the year of service would not be sufficient to bring the skills of some individuals to the point of their satisfactory placement either for war or for peacetime industry. More training would be necessary. Either supplementary opportunities would need to be made available as a part of the military plan, or there should be a provision whereby the public schools would offer continued training.

3. Opportunity for those who have not compiled secondary school records sufficiently clear for college entrance to acquire additional preparation.

4. Opportunity for those who have demonstrated adequate achievement, suitable ability, and clear choice for the learned professions, at the time of their entrance into national service, to receive a time credit, adjusted perhaps, between the national service and the professional school. For example, six months of national service rather than a full year, and at some stage of

professional training the allowance of a time credit for six months.

5. Opportunity for those who have physical or mental limitations, too marked for combat military training, to receive a type of special training which would permit adjustment to limited military service as well as to occupational placement. National service need not be limited by the arbitrary physical standards which have been applied hitherto for military service. This would seem especially desirable if the opportunity is accepted to improve the health of all youth during the period of military service. Obviously certain limitations such as those now in operation for educationally exceptional youth would need to apply.

It might develop that certain camps for particular specialized services would prove desirable. In any case, it would be especially important that those who have either mental or physical limitations should feel that their contribution had not been minimized.

B. Support of the general proposal, as stated in A, but with the suggestion of an alternative arrangement which would be better for youth morale and that would interfere less with the most desirable educational procedure.

1. In time of war, or if war is imminent, intensively continuous training would be obviously desirable. But if war is somewhat remote, a year of continuous intensive training is likely to be far more difficult for American youth to take than seems now to be recognized properly. Those institutions which have had compulsory R.O.T.C. units, where every boy in a public school is required to participate, have had an experience that should be worth much on this point. The matter of morale becomes a difficult problem in a compulsory system. It is well enough known that camp morale, even on the eve of war, was a serious matter in 1940. It would seem highly essential that the trainees should believe heartily that the period of national service was of real significance to their experience as well as a worthy contribution to the country's welfare.

2. Possibly morale could be more successfully maintained in short periods of time than it could in a twelve months' term.

Assuming that secondary schools and higher institutions will continue long summer vacations, it would be possible to operate a plan for four summers of three months each within an age bracket of 16 to 23. This would avoid interference with the orderly procedure of education, save time for the individual, and gain for the armed services the increased maturity of the individual. This latter might well be a distinct advantage to the armed services.

Those who did not wish to continue formal education after graduation from high school could be given the choice of taking a continuous six months of military service immediately after high school, or a full year, depending upon whether they had elected summer terms following their sixteenth and seventeenth birthdays. The arrangement would permit the camps to be operated in the winter and would more nearly simulate the actual diversity in degrees of training which would obtain under war conditions. Voluntary officers' training could follow the required periods in either case.

The Army General Staff took the stand at the beginning of the war that the minimum training period should be eighteen months. Congress thought one year was sufficient. Under modern methods more and better training has been given in the twelve months' period than had been expected by the General Staff. The latter will likely insist that a full year is needed for the proper training of youth, and that because of the limited period, the major emphasis at all times should be of military character.

3. It is probable that such time as might be termed recreational or leisure would be available for various types of informal education such as: reading, audio-visual, discussion groups, lectures, extension courses, etc.

C. An alternative which would allow the choice of any year between 17 and 23. This plan would avoid interference with the high school but would seriously interfere with the standardized continuity of college. No suggestion from Washington seems to have gone further than 21. If the age limit were extended to 22 or to induction following graduation from college, the interference could be largely eliminated.

Question IV. Should national service be interpreted as applicable to constructive work in federal projects, national parks, federal highways, etc.?

Certain phases of desirable federal works might become a part of the military training program, for example, in the training of military engineers and in the training of construction battalions necessary to the development of various military installations.

There would be a considerable group of trainees whose abilities and inclinations would fall into the simple forms of manual labor rather than into the technical skills necessary for successful combat.

Question V. Should the national service program include young women as well as young men? . . .

The experience of the present war with the performance of women in uniform would argue apparently for the inclusion of young women. Judging by school experience there is a much smaller proportion of girls than boys who take kindly to the military type of training. Probably the chief problem created by the inclusion of girls would be that caused by the doubling of the number of trainees, thus adding greatly to the costs and to the difficulties of staff, organization, and of operation.

Should boys of limited service capacity be included they would need very largely to be given the type of training now given to girls who are members of the armed services. This would probably increase the difficulty of providing proper functional training for girl trainees.

The inclusion of girls would obviously broaden the character and content of the national service and would likely result in largely increased educational provisions.

Summary of the arguments for and against compulsory national service:

A. *Favorable:*

1. It is necessary as an adequate provision for national security.

2. It is a requisite preparedness for our future international obligations.

3. It is a sure method of improving physical fitness and the health of the nation. Proper health attainment rests upon federal action and is much larger than merely medical care

4. A generalized national training program is necessary as the base upon which a scientifically applied selective system could produce the highly professionalized army of the future.

5. National service could provide a new means for the recognition and development of the duties and obligations of the individual to his country, and to society, in contrast to the over-emphasis on personal rights and on the responsibility of the nation to the individual.

6. The national service program could inspire a deeper appreciation of our national heritage and motivate a more active understanding of local, national and world citizenship.

7. It could serve as a means for the proper encouragement of further training and education in public service in established institutions and by new and more specialized schools.

8. It could continue certain technical training opportunities which are often not adequately accepted by youth in the public schools.

9. Youth's opportunities for guidance, occupational adjustment, and placement could be largely enhanced.

10. Its directness and disciplines could reduce the immaturity and irresponsibility of many youths who ordinarily are left to aimless purpose and dubious activity.

11. For certain types of youth, national service could perform as well as, or better than, the Civilian Conservation Corps did for similar types.

12. National service could hasten the return of the veterans now in service and provide more equitably for the extended service which will be necessary for some years following the war.

13. It would make desirable utilization of the great system of army and navy camps, stations, and of their extensive equipment.

14. The distinctive success of the Swiss military system under democratic operation, and with an effective demonstration of

general functional citizenship, suggests the favorable possibilities for a democracy.

15. It would be an important factor in the creation of jobs.

B. *Unfavorable*:

1. It is foreign to the American ideal.

2. Many immigrants came to America to escape compulsory military service.

3. It will produce a military hierarchy which would be a dangerous element in American politics.

4. It will increase political patronage.

5. It will prevent the reduction of taxes.

6. It will prevent the long anticipated and proper extension of public education. There will not be sufficient revenue for both.

7. It will interfere with our system of higher education.

8. Its influence will react to a dictation of the method, content, and control of secondary education.

9. It does not necessarily guarantee national security (France).

10. It does not necessarily insure peace, or freedom, or democratic progress.

11. The actual need, or the desirable size of a standing military force is not known now.

12. The question of national service is too important to be decided emotionally in the fever of war.

13. A national program of health for young children is more basic and promising for the health of the nation than a system of physical conditioning for youth.

14. The Secretary of War has affirmed that, "The amount of military drill actually needed can be given in a relatively brief period of time. . . . " that, "The physical condition of a soldier is of prime importance." This can be done by schools.

15. The army of the future will be small and highly professionalized. It can be successfully recruited from specialists and from the better trained individuals. The voluntary military units in schools can be operated more thoroughly and can be extended into summer periods more completely. With such pay

inducements as might be necessary to obtain recruits the entire cost of such a plan should be less, and at the same time should prove more effective than the mass military training of all youth.

16. National military service would create a serious problem of morale. The proper motivation would be lacking in peacetime.

STATEMENT OF EDUCATIONAL POLICIES COMMISSION AND PROBLEMS AND PLANS COMMITTEE [7]

In our judgment it is unwise to commit the nation at this time to a year of universal military service for the following reasons:

1. *Present Military Necessity.* Under the Selective Service Act, the present personnel needs of the armed forces are being met so far as the nation's resources of manpower permit. It therefore follows that the proposed year of compulsory military service is to be conceived in terms of a postwar, not a current, undertaking. No basic change in the present Selective Service System is necessary to provide required military personnel, not only for the period of the war, but also for the period immediately following the defeat of our enemies.

2. *Long-time Military Necessity.* Since the proposed year of compulsory military service is not a question of immediate military necessity, it must be appraised in long-range terms. In these terms it is clearly impossible at this time to debate fairly and intelligently the question of whether compulsory military service is a national military necessity. No one can foresee the international situation which will exist when Germany and Japan are defeated. Neither the international political nor the international military situation can be calculated while the war is still in progress. Prophesies on this subject and debate thereon may prove detrimental to sound national policy and to the unity of the United Nations.

[7] Statement adopted by the Educational Policies Commission of the National Education Association and the American Association of School Administrators, and the Problems and Plans Committee of the American Council on Education March 13, 1944, and concurred in by the Executive Committee of the National Association of Secondary-School Principals. *National Association of Secondary-School Principals. Bulletin.* 28:5-7. May 1944.

3. *Policing the Peace*. When the war is over, it may be necessary to maintain a large standing army to police the peace, and this may force us to adopt compulsory military training. No one is in a position now, however, to forecast fully the international responsibilities of the nation after the war, and certainly not the responsibilities that relate to the occupation of foreign territories. Until the postwar national situation is clarified, it seems to us extremely unwise and even dangerous to commit the nation to such a revolutionary change in fundamental national policy as would be the establishment of compulsory military service.

4. *The American Military Tradition*. Our Anglo-Saxon democratic tradition is strongly set against a large standing army and a military caste. We, along with the great body of Americans, will support a year of compulsory military service when we are convinced that the safety of the nation demands it. We are unreservedly for adequate preparedness, but we see great dangers in any unnecessary break with our tested democratic tradition respecting compulsory military service in times of peace.

5. *The Opinion of the Young Men Now Fighting the War*. The year of proposed military service, if adopted, will directly affect the children of the men who are now fighting in our armed forces. These men should have a voice in determining the desirability and soundness of compulsory military service. Their opinions cannot, however, be determined until the war is over. This constitutes another strong reason for delaying decision until peace has come.

6. *The Nature of the Peace*. The American people are fighting this war with the high hope that it will eventuate in an enduring peace. We all look for measures of international cooperation which will reduce the necessity for large-scale postwar military establishments. If, against the background of these great expectations . . . a year of compulsory military service [is urged], many Americans will interpret such action as a signal for the return of the cynicism of the 1920's or an admission . . . that the world will continue to be an armed camp in which the hopes for a more peaceful world are not to be realized.

A proposed year of national service, as contrasted with a proposed year of military training, seems to us to be a similarly radical and dangerous departure from our national tradition. We, therefore, strongly urge that no decision be attempted during the profound disturbances of war. Among our reasons for believing that a delayed judgment is in the best national interest, are the following:

7. *Invasion of Education by the Federal Government.* Under the Constitution, the control and administration of education is the responsibility of the states, and through all our history, Americans have zealously upheld this constitutional principle. Federal aid to the states for education has been granted for many decades, and in the future more such aid will probably be necessary. To assist the states in their educational activities is vastly different, however, from establishing a federal enterprise which would be in large measure educational. To substitute direct federal participation in education in place of federal aid to the states will, we feel certain, be unacceptable to the American people.

8. *Conflict with State and Local Autonomy.* We are, of course, aware that a plan of national service would provide several months of outdoor life, valuable work experience, and a kind of discipline for young Americans. We also realize that for boys who have not attended a public high school and who have therefore not associated with a cross-section of their fellows in American life, such camp experience would exert strong democratizing infleunces. But, American education is now developing plans for a broadened educational program for all American youth, including camps and work experience, in which intelligent concepts of discipline will prevail. These will be under non-federal auspices and we feel strongly that these plans should be matured before the Federal Government preempts an area which has historically been within the sphere of local and state autonomy.

9. *The Probability of Military Control.* The contemplated plan includes, we understand, not only broad educational activities, but also an undetermined fraction of time to be devoted to military training. For such training army and navy officers would of necessity be employed, and they would of course be under the control of their superiors in Washington. Since these officers would constitute the only closely knit group at work in the na-

tional service camps, the control of the enterprise would soon inevitably rest with the military authorities. Thus, the year of national service would soon become a year of predominantly military service or a year of service dominated by the military. All the reasons we have cited above against making a decision concerning a year of compulsory military service at this time apply, therefore, to the plans for a year of national service.

10. *Dangerous Totalitarian Precedents.* The present war became possible in large measure because Germany, Japan, and Italy exploited national service for their youth. For the United States to follow such totalitarian hazards might lead to partisan exploitation of the national youth organization and to the spreading of doctrines inimical to our way of life. We submit that the perils in such a development are so great as to give one pause in endorsing a peacetime national service act, except as a matter of clear military necessity.

HEALTH OF THE NATION [8]

At this moment the quality of our youth, its physical stamina and mental adaptability, is being critically tested in the crucible of war. During the last four years, while this country has been creating, equipping, and training the greatest fighting force of all time, it has also been uncovering some hitherto unheeded national weaknesses. These weaknesses have been revealed largely through (1) Selective Service statistics which deal with the rejection of registrants; (2) the high rate of discharges from military service on Certificates for disability; and (3) setting up programs for rehabilitation and for physical conditioning of the men inducted and making great effort toward proper assignment.

With this problem of health and fitness we, the people, must deal now and in the future. In the solution of this problem, education must play a leading role.

The magnitude of the problem can largely be covered in three sentences:

[8] From article "Education and Medicine Can Improve the Health of the Nation." By Col. Leonard G. Rowntree, M. C., Selective Service System. *Education for Victory.* 3:5. January 20, 1945.

To date, more than 5,000,000 men have been rejected (4-F) and a large number discharged as unfit to serve advantageously.

To date, more than 1,500,000 men have been rehabilitated within the services for dental defects, illiteracy, venereal disease, and hernia.

To date, it has been necessary to give extended physical training even to the healthy inductees in order to render them fit for military assignment and service.

Lack of health and of physical fitness prevails among the youth of the country because the nation has failed to recognize the importance of these things and to make the necessary provisions for prevention and cure of unfitness.

The present situation is the result of indifference and apathy on the part of the public and, to some extent, of the government —Federal, state, and municipal; on the part of parents, teachers, churches, the medical and dental professions and, to a certain extent, of youth itself.

In a large measure it is the failure in our educational system and in our homes, where youth spends practically all of its time during the most formative 15 to 20 years of life. The fault is the combined one; it is a fault of society itself. Youth is the victim. Only the all-out concerted effort of all those concerned in this failure can bring about the cure or, what is still more important, the prevention in the future. Are we prepared to make the necessary sacrifices and take the necessary steps? No one group can change the condition by itself. A great cooperative social effort is necessary. Medicine and education must furnish the leadership.

Perhaps no better indication of the problem of unfitness is available than the figures of rejection of registrants called for induction by the Selective Service System. . . .

These statistics indicate the failure of the past and the need for preventive action now and in the future. This is a job in which all must participate—the parents, teachers, the doctors, dentists, but, above all, the youth of the nation. Education and medicine must supply guidance.

When President Roosevelt learned that the rate of rejection of registrants was high, 50 per cent, and that 1,000,000 of the first 2,000,000 men examined were denied military service because of physical and mental defects, he attempted to set up a rehabilitation program, for the correction of remediable defects of rejectees. For reasons that need not be stated here, his program was never established nationally.

Likewise, on learning of the prolonged physical training required by men taken into service, the President again took action and created, in April 1943, a National Committee on Physical Fitness in the Federal Security Agency under the chairmanship of John B. Kelly of Philadelphia. This Committee has worked assiduously at its national headquarters in Washington and in the field to educate the public concerning the current situation and to indoctrinate the people with a consciousness of the national need for improvement in health and physical fitness. In the space of a year it interested many national leaders and harnessed together the resources and efforts of more than 400 national organizations.

However, the National Committee found itself in need of more vigorous medical leadership. Hence, this Committee brought its problem to the American Medical Association, and the medical profession has assumed its natural place in the leadership necessary for success. This was done through the creation, in June 1944, of the Joint Committee on Physical Fitness which would serve to guide medical activities in this field.

One of the sections of the Joint Committee on Physical Fitness has to deal with the health and physical fitness problem of the schools and colleges of the nation. Their objectives have already been presented in the columns of the *Journal of Health and Physical Education,* November 1944.

The physical fitness of the people of the United States is fundamental to the safety, security, productiveness, and welfare of the nation. The experience of our nation in times of war and distress has established beyond question the vital necessity for developing and maintaining in each individual the utmost self-reliance, physical fitness, and mental and physical health. The program must include the following constructive steps:

1. Help each American to learn physical fitness needs.
3. Attend to correctable defects.

3. Attend to correctable defects.
4. Know how to live healthfully in body and mind.
5. Act to acquire physical fitness.
6. Set American standards of physical fitness at high levels.
7. Provide adequate means for physical development.

Some may argue that in this country education is concerned solely with the training of the mind and is in no way responsible for these bodily defects uncovered in the examination of registrants for military service or for the lack of physical fitness in inductees. If such an argument is advanced seriously, it certainly will not tend to aid the cause of education in the minds of the people of the country. But, supposing for the sake of argument, we grant that this is true. Then what is the situation as regards the mental fitness of our youth with which education is inescapably concerned?

The magnitude of the problem of mental disease and mental deficiency and their relationship to defects in general is also revealed in . . . the causes for rejection. From the figures presented it is evident that more than three fourths of a million rejectees were disqualified because of mental disease and more than 600,000 for mental deficiency. Many of the latter group were rejected because of illiteracy. If we add to these figures the rejections for neurological defects, then the total is well in excess of 1½ million men disqualified for mental and nervous dysfunction.

This, however, does not tell the whole story. Another 300,000, approximately, must be added to this figure since over 40 per cent of those released or discharged on Certificates of Disability for Discharge fell into the neuropsychiatric group. Thus it is evident that between 1,800,000 and 2,000,000 registrants failed to qualify or serve satisfactorily because of nervous or mental unfitness as compared with 2,500,000 for physical defects. It is significant that the United States has already pensioned 130,308 neuropsychiatric veterans of World War II and "nine out of ten never saw battle."

These statistics do not stand isolated and alone. They should be considered in conjunction with the long-known fact that more than one half of the hospital beds in the nation are devoted today to mental diseases which, at present, amounts to more than 700,000 beds. This fact signifies, of course, that the problem now confronting us is not new, but an old one, which the nation has failed to solve to date either in war or peace. It has never really faced the problem.

In addition much emotional instability and failure to adjust is revealed in the high rates encountered for diseases of psychosomatic origin, such as peptic ulcers, duodenal and gastric, and asthma. Such diseases were very prevalent as revealed in peacetime selection but with the advent of war, they have increased markedly. . . .

NATIONAL NEEDS AND NATIONAL SERVICE [9]

The Selective Training and Service Act of 1940 has been indispensable and successful. The armed forces assembled and trained under its provisions have made the difference between defeat and victory—a defeat that would have meant enslavement and degradation, a victory that will mean the opportunity for the maintenance and improvement of our national and international ways of life. The training undertaken under the Act has been characterized by two notable values which are of more than military significance: the general establishment of fine physical condition in the men who have been trained, and the establishment in them of the habit of discipline.

It is generally assumed that the emergency which led to the enactment of the Selective Training and Service Act will soon have passed; and it is somewhat less generally assumed that, despite current and continuous efforts for the establishment of an effective international organization, a similar emergency may occur again. This second assumption calls for some clarification and emphasis—clarification and emphasis which, however unhappy, should at least be realistic.

[9] By Ernest H. Wilkins, President, Oberlin College. *American Association of Collegiate Registrars. Journal.* 20:186-92. January 1945. This article was one of a symposium of four.

It is indeed perfectly possible that before many years have passed we may become involved in another war. The complete defeat of Germany in the present war will not suffice to convince her that she cannot conquer Europe and the world. It will convince her only that she cannot achieve such conquest *by means used hitherto.* She may be expected to attempt to develop other and unprecedented means of conquest. She may be expected to attempt not only to develop "secret weapons" more devastating than robot bombs and to plan the sudden dissemination of gases more lethal than any we now know, but also to attempt the development of means of conquest that can hardly be classified as "weapons," or as military means in the ordinary sense of the term. What is true of Germany is true also of Japan, though Germany would presumably be more intense in resolution and more fertile in invention.

It is perfectly possible that if we become involved in another war we shall lose that war; and that the loss of that war will in turn involve not only immense immediate destruction of life and property, but an enslavement and a degradation from which we could not recover for decades, and might never recover. It is, indeed, probable that we shall lose that war unless (1) we do all we can (and this is not a matter for the United States alone) to prevent Germany and Japan from attempting to use again the familiar means of conquest, and from developing unfamiliar means of conquest; unless (2) we develop an efficient preparedness not only against familiar means of conquest, but also against the sudden use of unfamiliar means of conquest; unless (3) we do all we can to strengthen our internal unity; and unless (4) we do all we can (and this is not a matter for the United States alone) to maintain and to develop an international organization and international spirit which would tend to prevent the outbreak of another war.

Under these circumstances it is natural and right that the question of our future national defense should be an active question; and it is natural that the first suggested solution should be the proposal that the Selective Service System should be succeeded by an essentially similar system, namely, a system of universal military training for one year under the exclusive control of the armed forces.

It does not follow, however, that the adoption of a system of universal military training for one year under the exclusive control of the armed forces would constitute the best solution, or even a valid solution, for the problem of our future national defense; and it does not follow that our total national policy with regard to our manpower should be conceived exclusively in terms of national defense. For we should be concerned not only with the strength of our national defense, but with the excellence of that which we defend.

Let us consider first the question as to whether military training for a year under the exclusive control of the armed forces would be the best solution, or even a valid solution, for the problem of our national defense. At this point, and before the more definitely military aspects of the question are considered, comment on the development of the values of physical condition and discipline is in order.

It is true that military training has produced these values. It is not true, however, that military training is necessary for he production of these values. They can be produced, they should have been produced, and they should hereafter be produced, by civilian agencies, civic and educational, operating not for a single year, but continuously throughout the period of youth. Such agencies have been at fault in not achieving these values, and the armed forces have shown them their failure; but the national answer lies still with the civic and educational agencies, which must undertake in this regard the responsibility they have hitherto failed to carry.

The question of the continuous civic and educational maintenance and development of fine physical condition offers no really major difficulties of either a theoretical or a practical nature. The question of the development of the habit of discipline is much harder, both theoretically and practically, but it is not insoluble. Military discipline is not identical in character or purpose with normal civic and educational discipline. But they have more in common than is ordinarily supposed; and it is quite possible that the normal civic and educational experience should be made to contain certain elements which in emergency could quickly be transmuted into the acceptance of full military discipline.

There is, then, no justification for the idea that a year of universal military training under the exclusive control of the armed forces is necessary for the development of fine physical condition or of discipline. Is it necessary, on other grounds, for the maintenance of our national defense? Military training given to masses of men for a single year under the exclusive control of the armed forces would have to be relatively simple in character, and would have to be mainly concerned with the customary drills and procedures and implements of war. But if any prophecy with regard to future warfare can be made with assurance, it is that future warfare will employ methods and machines vastly different from those now in use—as different, perhaps, as the bazooka is from the bow and arrow—and that its onset will be so sudden as to make the blitzkrieg of 1940 look like the lumbering of a stage-coach.

There must be at all times an adequate and highly intelligent military force, ready to use instantly the best known military means of any given day, and concerned, in its higher brackets, with the swift development of new and better means. The importance and dignity of the military career so conceievd is such as to warrant its appeal to many of the ablest men of the nation. It would be well also that a considerable—but still a limited—number of young men should each year be made familiar with the weapons then in vogue, so that they might serve as a pool of first reserves available in case of sudden need.

What we need in the vast manpower of the nation as a whole, however, is not the ability to use weapons of defense which will soon become obsolete, but, first, a large body of men so well trained in the basic principles of science and technology that they could apply their basic knowledge effectively not just to one particular process or one particular instrument, but rather to any one of a variety of possible processes or instruments; and, second, beyond that, a whole body of citizens equipped physically and mentally to be geared very quickly into whatever system of defense may be attained when the emergency arises. The production of such a body of citizens calls not for a single year of a type of soon-to-be-outmoded training under the exclusive control of the armed forces, but for a broad and continuing program of civic and educational development. Furthermore, in an efficient policy of national defense every man or woman should be so used as to take advantage of the highest special abilities he or she may have; and no man or woman who possesses abilities which are potentially of special value to the national defense should be allowed to divert his or her time for a year to training which is not in the line of those special abilities. It is said that it took one British physicist one night to discover the principle of the German magnetic mine. Every hour that went into his expert training was well spent—any hour subtracted therefrom might have been fatal.

The maintenance of our national defense calls, then, for research on the part of a relatively small body of men; for basic scientific and technological training on the part of a much larger body of men; and for excellence in physical condition and resourcefulness on the part of all young men—all this rather than the mass enlistment of all young men in a year of universal military training under the exclusive control of the armed forces. But an efficient over-all policy of national defense will include elements that are not primarily military—elements that are necessary for a strong national defense, and yet are rich in values that are not limited to the national defense, but are as great in time of peace as in time of war.

There are many such elements. Two of the most important, both of them so obvious as to need no discussion, are the maintenance of a strong system of productive industry and the maintenance of a very large number of well-trained physicians, surgeons, and nurses. There are two such elements, perhaps not quite so obvious, that do call for statement and for comment.

No nation can be really strong, for purposes of defense or for any other purposes, which is gravely weakened by internal tensions. There exist in our own nation, at the present time, economic and racial tensions which have impaired our effort in the present war, and which, if left to their own cancerous growth, might lead to civil passions and to civil strife which could make it impossible for us to achieve defensive unity in the face of hostile attack. Any alert enemy, indeed, would seek to exploit such tensions, and thus to "divide and conquer" us. For the sake of national defense, therefore, even if there were no other reason, we must mitigate and, if possible, remove the tensions that now beset us. This is a task of vast extent and of extreme intricacy. It cannot be carried through by a few people; it cannot be carried through by partisanship or by sentiment. It can be carried through only by a great cooperative effort, based upon study and field work as exacting as the techniques of scientific research. It cannot be carried through without the basic training of great numbers of persons, of whom a minority will thereafter go on to some measure of leadership in this field, while the majority will be in a position to follow with intelligence the leadership of the advanced minority.

Effort exerted toward the relief and the removal of tensions is important not only because of its direct bearing upon the problem of national defense, but also because it makes for the development of a finer and a more complete democracy. This would be in itself an adequate and worthy end for such activity; and it would result in turn in the development of a reasoned national loyalty which would prove to be a positive source of strength in times of emergency as well as in times of peaceful growth.

The best way to avoid defeat in a future war would be to avert the possibility of the occurrence of a future war. The endeavor to avert that possibility is a double task. In its more immediate and more negative phase it is the task of national and international defense. In its more continuous and positive phase it is the task of establishing, maintaining, and improving a viable international organization.

No nation, from this day forth, can possibly live in isolation. Whether we like it or not, we are driven into close and indissoluble association with the other great powers, and with many of the lesser nations of the earth. The question is not whether we are or not closely associated with them: the question is simply what the nature and the quality of that association is to be. Radio has already put an end to distance in so far as verbal communication is concerned; and the increasing speed and range of aerial transportation, which have already reduced the oceans to mere lakes, will soon reduce them to mere rivulets. International organization and our participation therein are utterly inevitable. International organization is arising mainly because of the need of all the nations concerned for their own defense: for no one nation, now, and no small group of nations, can suffice— however large and powerful they may be—to avert the danger of sudden war and defeat at the hands of some aggressor nation or group of nations. In union there is strength, and there is no adequate strength without union. Some type of international organization is being created at this very moment through the urgency of a common international need; and the world for which we are planning will be a world marked by the existence of a new international organization.

But the mere creation of such an organization will not guarantee its continuance. It is, moreover, inherently improbable that the international organization now to be established will be in any considerable degree perfect or definitive. The task of the making of a truly effective international organization is far too difficult, far too complex for the achievement of any quick finality. The best we can hope for is the establishment of an organization strong enough to survive its own infancy and flexible enough to have place for and to encourage modification and development. This is a task, then, not for a single group of conferees, but for the continuous activity of a vast number of international civil servants and of a very great number of persons qualified to engineer constant improvements in international relations. This task is one that calls for the basic training of great numbers of persons in the understanding of other nations and in the first principles of international relations. The majority of such trainees will be qualified to follow intelligently the guidance of the minority who advance to leadership in this field. In this case also the efforts to be made are not only good as a means of lessening the danger of war, but are good also in and of themselves as a means of creating a higher measure of true freedom than has yet been attained in this or any other land.

These great ends—the maintenance of our national defense, the development of our democracy, the attainment of an international relationship conducive to freedom for all nations—these great ends are of the highest importance for every American citizen of the present time and of all time to come. They are ends of such paramount importance that every American citizen, now and hereafter, should be expected and should be willing to devote a substantial part of his or her life to their achievement.

The composite task thus suggested is not a task for the armed forces alone: it is a task for a national service system which will see the entire enterprise as a whole, and will assign to each of its branches such portions of the task and such quotas of the successive harvests of trainees as the growing and changing needs of the nation may require.

These considerations point to the conclusion that the adoption of a plan of universal military training for a year under the exclusive control of the armed forces would be futile, unwise, and inadequate; and lead to the conclusion that the maintenance of our national defense and the development of our national and international welfare call alike for the adoption of a broadly conceived and forward-looking plan of national service.

ROAD TO SECURITY [10]

On the other side of the argument for compulsory military training as a means of security there is of course the fact that our rapidly trained armies have proved in the end a fair match for the armies of nations that constantly put their major effort on preparation for war. Many of us, watching Germany in the last years, knew very well that at the time when we were putting our greatest effort into bringing back prosperity to our people the Germans had full employment because the government was preparing for war. We were devoting ourselves to the revival of business and farm prosperity while Germany was making the same kind of expenditures that we have been making since the war started over there.

I remember very well one lady who returned from Europe and praised both the Italian and the German governments for

[10] By Mrs. Eleanor Roosevelt. Two articles published in the *New York World Telegram*, June 16 and 18, 1945. Copyright, United Feature Syndicate.

the full employment she found there, apparently never realizing that it could only be there if production for war was continuous. The day would come when these trained youth and the piled up materials would have to be used or the break in the economy of the nation would be so serious that chaos would result.

It is quite evident that we want our economy to be based on peacetime prosperity, and we want that to be the same for nations all over the world. I think it is well for us to consider whether we will actually be more secure if our young men have a full year of compulsory military service under the army. I am not really afraid that our young people will become militaristic in the same sense that the young Germans became ardent and fanatical Nazis. We Americans are bored by military routine.

It seems to me that security rests on the best scientific research in every field that can be found anywhere in the world; on the most skilled people with the most original minds; on the healthiest people, mentally and physically, that we can produce, and on the best citizenry at home to back what we do both in the political field and the economic field, and, if need be, in the military field.

You might ask of every boy and girl in the country to give a year of training in the field of their choice to the good of the nation. In that year you might give a certain amount of military training to develop discipline, to check up on health and keep your records of what is available for military need at any time.

I have been trying in these articles to cover many points of view on this peacetime question. My own strong feeling is that before we decide finally the war with Japan should be finished and the youth of our country who fought the war have come home and have a chance to be heard.

* * *

For our future security, perhaps the first and most important thing we should think of is our obligation to see that every man able to work has a job, that every American family has a decent level of subsistence, and that every child has a chance to grow up without the physical and mental handicaps which arise out of bad housing, bad health and poor education and recreational conditions.

Our men have found, while fighting the war, that this country is the best country in the world in which to live. Yet during the depression years there were many people, even youngsters, to whom that would have seemed an impossible statement. We know that the things we want can only be secured if the other nations of the world have a rising standard of living and continuous desires which make the flow of trade more or less equal throughout the world.

A nation with a high standard of living is a nation with a high national income. This will enable us to spend all we need on our defense without hardship to our people. It will enable us to provide a navy which our experts will consider adequate for protection and which shall only be reduced as armaments throughout the world are reduced; an air force which shall also meet the requirements of our experts and which shall be reduced only as the rest of the world reduces its military equipment proportionately; and a research group that will at all times be abreast of every modern invention, so that no nation in the world shall be ahead of us in the knowledge essential to the winning or to the prevention of future wars.

If we do decide that compulsory military training is essential until our peace organization is functioning and until the various parts of the world which have been unsettled for years past are on a more satisfactory economic and political basis, then we must be very careful how we choose and allocate our young people to their various tasks. In addition, we must repay them—on their release from military service—by giving them training in their chosen fields which will make it possible to accelerate their entrance into productive life as civilians.

I would not be averse to seeing each and every citizen required to do something every year for his state and nation besides the mere act of employing his franchise. In every part of a great nation, some emergencies always arise in which trained people, young or old, are more useful than untrained ones.

We want to feel secure in a world where as yet force is the major weapon, but we also want to feel secure in a world where perhaps mental and spiritual force may grow to be the greatest force. We must not fall short in preparing our people to wield both kinds of strength.

SHALL WE HAVE ANOTHER LOST AND UNWANTED GENERATION? [11]

Compulsory national and public service divorced from military service.

1. Many people who are reluctant to accept peacetime military conscription believe that we should have a year of compulsory public service for both boys and girls as a means of developing their sense of social responsibility and of removing them from the labor market. They believe that this would have practically all the advantages of military conscription, and that it would avoid the dangers and undesirable features which they see in compulsory military service in peacetime. These proposals take many forms and exist in various combinations.

2. Some advocate that this service be given in national camps similar to the C.C.C. camps, and that the service be upon projects of significance and service to the nation. Benefits to health, development of discipline and habits of work, and growth in social consciousness are outcomes to be sought. Some opponents of non-military compulsory public service advance many of the same arguments against this proposal as against conscription. This plan, they say, would take boys and girls away from the influences of the home and the local community, and prevent the natural and healthful association of boys and girls in the restraining and normal atmosphere of the home community. The proposal would delay and make more difficult the easy and gradual induction of young people into the adult life of their normal communities. They doubt whether boys and girls would submit to the regimentation that the plan envisages.

3. Some advocates of a year of compulsory public service oppose national camps which would remove boys and girls far

[11] From pamphlet, "Shall We Have Another Lost and Unwanted Generation in the Postwar Period?" [Suggestions resulting from discussions at the School for Executives held at Jackson's Mill, West Virginia, August 15-24, 1944]. Arthur J. Klein. College of Education. Ohio State University. p. 5-7. [1944?]

from home, and suggest work on local public projects and activities. They believe that the work-learn-subsistence program of the National Youth Administration in schools and colleges provides a pattern that might be adapted as a work-subsistence program upon projects that would be of great value to home and local communities. Opponents believe that all public works should be constructed under private contract at going wages, rather than by forced labor with subsistence as the sole compensation. They take the position also that public services should be paid for at rates prevailing in the labor market. They say that these proposals for the profitable social use of youth make more difficult, rather than aid in, finding employment for the veterans of war and industry.

Opportunity without compulsion.

1. Many people are opposed to both military and non-military conscription of youth, on the score that America should not make regimentation and compulsion an objective or a normal process of our national life in the face of our strong tradition to the contrary.

2. They advocate provision of a rich variety of opportunities from which youth will freely select those desired and needed. They contend that we never have gone the whole way in providing educational and experience opportunities appropriate to the whole range of life interests and employments, and insured for all young people ease of access to them. Even our free public high schools have been out of reach of many because of the cost of living while they attended. The same restriction on college attendance is accentuated by the fact that even our public higher institutions charge fees. It would be easily possible at infinitesimal expense as compared with universal compulsory service, either military or non-military, to remove these financial restrictions. But the major failure in the past that must now be corrected is that of failing to provide in public school, in college, or elsewhere, a sufficient variety of programs to meet all the occupational, social, and cultural objectives of young people that can be served through educational means. Advocates of "opportunity without compulsion" believe that this too can be done at

a financial and social cost much below the cost of compulsory universal military or non-military training.

3. Advocates of conscription for military or non-military public service think that all this is vague, confused, and impractical. They call attention to our compulsory school attendance laws. They challenge the advocates of this proposal to produce a definite, understandable plan that could be put into operation speedily enough to take care of the youth emergency that is just around the corner. They ask, "If the established educational system believes in this attack, why was it necessary for the Federal Government to step in and set up special emergency institutions like the C.C.C. and the N.Y.A.? Why had education not been interested in, and made provision to meet, the needs of youth that these projects were intended to serve?" Educators reply that they were not the only responsible group that was asleep at the switch in the 1930's, but that they, along with many other of those sleepers, are now awake and ready to go. Besides, they add, society has never been willing to provide the funds necessary for them to tackle the youth problems of which they were aware even in the 1930's. They say that their plans are at least as definite and their resources as immediately available as those of the advocates of compulsory non-military public service, and more definite than those of advocates of conscription for military service, who have nothing clear to offer except training for undesirable military regimentation.

4. Those who favor "opportunity without compulsion" say that their proposal provides free opportunity for youth to choose military service and what it has to offer in comparison with other ways of life. Local and national public service of other types than the military may also be chosen if free preparation and opportunities are opened to youth. Many youth should and will choose to continue formal education leading to scholarly careers, technological education at many levels, or professional education, immediately after high-school graduation. Work-earn-learn programs may be as easily provided for all these young people under a free-choice plan as under the non-military compulsory public-service plan, and more easily than under the plan for military conscription. They point out that many young people from farm

families, from professional, industrial and other classes will be inducted naturally and easily into normal occupational and educational careers without the interruption and delay of conscripted service in either military or other forms of public work.

5. The advocates of "opportunity without compulsion" contend that the higher-level and more varied educational programs that they propose will multiply desires and demands for personal, social, and industrial services, so as to provide an ever-rising level of occupational opportunities for a constantly increasing number of people.

CONSCRIPTION FOR PEACETIME MILITARY TRAINING, PRO AND CON [12]

The most comprehensive general statement of the case for universal military training in this country is that by Frank Knox, late Secretary of the Navy, in *Collier's* of April 29. He declared that every American young man "not mentally deficient or immobilized by permanent physical handicap" should receive *"a minimum of twelve months continuous training"* at the age of 17 or 18. He believed that it would make the country "healthier, more unified . . . and more democratic." A "long-range, non-political, fixed policy of national defense" demands universal military training. "We have the military and naval establishments, the training camps and the instructors, ready and functioning. . . . Of necessity, the United States will have to maintain, for an indefinite period, armies of occupation and naval patrols and overseas supply lines, as the areas of occupation grow and expand to the final inclusion of Berlin and Tokyo. For years afterward, self-interest alone will dictate that we maintain military and naval police forces the world around. . . . The men who are doing the fighting . . . should be replaced in outpost duty by the younger men who are performing their year of military service, so far as numbers permit." The young men would be "helped to find a purpose in life, a place in society, and a rugged body." In the navy, at least, where "every man must

[12] *Information Service* (Federal Council of the Churches of Christ in America) 23:2-5. November 11, 1944.

become a specialist," personnel officers would help assign the recruit to the "job for which he shows the greatest aptitude." Illiterates would be taught to read and write.

Earlier, in an address before the Boy Scouts of Cleveland Secretary Knox had summarized the type of training he envisaged, saying that the young men would be "given physical training of the highest value, would be instructed in the expert use of fire-arms, would be taught how to live comfortably in the open and would be taught lessons in patriotism, love of country and devotion to flag. . . ."

There is sharp disagreement among qualified experts who write and speak on military affairs in regard to the value of peacetime conscription. Some consider it the only way to make sure of adequate defense; others go the opposite extreme and consider such huge armies well-nigh worthless for warfare as it is now developing.

For Conscription

Some writers on military affairs seem to believe that the United States could guarantee world peace by adopting compulsory military training now. Thus, a writer in the *Army and Navy Register* (Washington) commented on August 5: "Peace and goodwill amongst the nations can be maintained after the war if we maintain an adequate regular army, navy and trained reserve." Others, in view of the fate of France in 1940, argue simply (quoting from the *Army and Navy Register* of September 30) that "if and when war comes, it will assure us a better chance of victory."

The proponents of conscription stress the point that with a trained reserve a smaller standing army will be needed. Secretary Stimson in his letter of August 15, 1944, to the Citizens' Committee for Universal Military Training, wrote, "If we wish to protect our nation and our democratic way of life, we must have a state of military preparedness which will enable us to take effective military action in the shortest possible time. . . . The youth of the nation must have had the greater part of its military training before mobilization." Without a large standing army "this can only be done through a system of universal military training . . . under which all of the physically fit young men of the nation would be given continuous training for one year." The adoption of such a program "would be the strongest possible assurance to the rest of the world that, in the future, America will be . . . able and ready to take its part with the peace-loving nations in resisting lawless aggression and in assuring peaceful world order."

If, through such a system, Mr. Stimson wrote, "we have a great reservoir of trained officers and men in civil life, our peace establishment will be capable of rapid and a far more economic expansion than we have heretofore ever been able to accomplish." Otherwise, he said, a much larger regular army will be required in times of peace. Moreover, when we are analyzing universal military training in terms of cost, it should always be remembered that the greatest savings will be obtained through prevention or shortening of future wars. . . . "

General Marshall, in his directive on the postwar army (published in the *New York Times* of September 3) makes the same points and adds that the leadership of this system "is not exclusively concentrated in a professional soldier class. All citizen soldiers after their initial training are encouraged to develop their capacity for leadership to such an extent as may be consistent with their abilities, their tastes, and their civil obligations."

But no formal statement has yet come from the military authorities as to their interpretation of a "small standing army." It seems clear, however, that they are not speaking in terms of the small army the United States has depended on in the past. The size of the army that will be maintained depends, of course, on Congressional appropriations. The National Defense Act of 1920 authorized a standing army of 280,000 men but this was never reached in peacetime. During the late 'twenties and early 'thirties there were about 118,000 enlisted personnel. On September 16, 1944, the *Army and Navy Register* reported a broadcast "recently" made by Major General William F. Tompkins of the Special Planning Division of the War Department General Staff. He said in part: ". . . When we speak of a small standing army we do not contemplate falling back to the pitifully small army" of the period between the wars. "We believe that our requirements for national security in the postwar world will necessitate an army many times that size. This standing army would be supplemented by a much larger reserve force of citizen soldiers trained on a systematic and universal basis in peacetime." Judging from the scanty evidence available, the War Department will ask for a standing army of from 500,000 to 1,000,000 men.

How large would the reserve be? About 1,200,000 youths reach the age of 18 each year. If half or three quarters of them were trained yearly (the figure most often suggested), we would soon have a reserve force of several million men, even without the veterans of the present war. But not all military leaders or experts in military affairs are enthusiastic for a large conscript army.

Against Conscription

Some careful students of the problem believe that a nation like the United States which is not interested in conquest is not likely to maintain at all times heavy enough armaments to deter another powerful nation which is bent on conquest. Our history, they point out, is consistent in that respect. We have always reduced armaments between wars. The real solution, they say, is to be found in collective security. But collective security can be maintained in two ways: by uniting against the offending nation after the outbreak of war or by preventing the amassing of the armaments necessary for a great offensive. This can no longer be done secretly. If sanctions were used when it became obvious that such preparations were being made, then sea and air power with relatively small ground forces could prevent a great war from developing. Conscription may be necessary to fight a global war such as the present. But it will not be necessary if the united nations are ready to take preventive action, so the argument runs.

Writing on collective security as the only safeguard for defence, Major George Fielding Eliot, writer on military affairs for the *New York Herald Tribune,* said in his syndicated article on November 2: "Today, unless civilized man is to go underground and live the sunless life of the mole, he must think not in terms of defending his homeland against attack after attack has begun, but in terms of making it impossible for any one to attack at all. . . . What is now proposed is not war, but police action for the prevention of war. . . . In the world of the rocket and robot-bomb, if you wait until you are attacked it is already too late to do anything effective. . . . The only way we can keep from having to go to war because of things which will happen (in an unguarded world) in some other distant place of which we know little at present is by stamping out the sparks before the conflagration starts."

Some observers are concerned about the effect of so huge an army on our international relations. On the continent, as one country has increased armaments or lengthened the period of conscription others have taken similar action. Will Latin America regard it as an evidence of the Good Neighbor policy or as a new reason to fear the Colossus of the North?

Hanson W. Baldwin, writer on military affairs for the *New York Times,* in which he summarized the arguments for and against conscription, said in an article on January 20, that some military leaders fear that the training of a large number of men each year would keep the experienced officers so busy that they would not have time for the study of tactics and strategy that is essential if the army is to be kept at its best.

The essential question is, what kind of army are we likely to need in the postwar world? As yet, the advocates of compulsory training have not discussed that question to any great extent. B. H. Liddell Hart, well-known British writer on military affairs, points out that ". . . the Nazi movement was essentially a volunteer movement . . . and the most important sections of the German forces—the air force and the tank force—have been recruited on a semi-voluntary basis." "Conscription," he says, "does not fit the conditions of modern warfare—its specialized equipment, mobile operations, and fluid situations."

General Fuller, in [his] *Britannica* article . . . says that military power today "depends on the numbers of skilled mechanics, not only to manufacture war machines but to fight them. The advent of the motor-driven battle vehicle has reintroduced armor as an essential in tactical organization." Therefore, he believes, the tendency is toward smaller armies "in which quality will replace the quantity theory of the present cannon fodder masses."

Paul Mallon, Washington newspaper man, an advocate of a large standing army, carries the argument further in his syndicated columns of September 18 and 19. He writes: "Armies today are built on technicians. . . . Not only are the combat men now long-trained technicians, but so are the equally important men in radio communications, engineering, bridge construction, and practically every line. . . . For war your 17 year old graduates would have to be trained all over again."

Father Allan P. Farrell, a Catholic educator, summarizes the arguments for and against conscription in *America* of September 30. He comments that the question of "the role of manpower in modern fighting warrants further probing. In the plans drawn for the American army of the future, manpower is manifestly viewed as all-important; and not only manpower in general but GI manpower." He points out that some of those "closely connected with the technical side of the present war" challenge the assumption that we can "argue for conscription now in terms of the tactics of World War II. . . . Technicians rather than infantrymen . . . must be the backbone of manpower defense in any future wars. And technicians cannot be trained suitably in a year nor according to the program outlined by the military on a conscriptive basis. Further, youth of seventeen or eighteen would have neither the maturity nor the preparation required for this specialized type of training." The Swiss experience is often cited, but Father Farrell comments ". . . our military leaders will have none of the Swiss military ideal—they will have either a full year of compulsory training or nothing."

On October 17, 1942, General Marshall wrote to Representative Wadsworth opposing the proposal to keep in this country for one year the 18-year-olds who were drafted. He said that the length of training the individual needs before he can go into combat duty with "an experienced tactical unit," "varies according to the type of unit and the duties for which he is trained." An aviation mechanic is given from 18 to 36 weeks; a radio operator needs from three to five months (including his basic training); but the rifleman with 13 weeks of basic training "is prepared to take his place in an experienced squad at any time." For the immediate postwar years, the period for which many people are most concerned, there will be available a large reserve of thoroughly experienced soldiers. Is it, then, necessary or desirable to keep *all* trainees for the same period? Further, the rifleman can maintain his skill with "refresher courses." But with continual change in the designs of airplanes, tanks, and heavy artillery, could the technicians keep up their skill in civilian life? This is a question which seems to need more thought than has been focused on it in public discussions. . . .

Many people are raising the question of the effects of conscription on our cultural and religious life. Some think there is no danger that it would make us militaristic. A large standing army would be contrary to our democratic ideals, but training for every able-bodied young man would be quite as democratic a process as the selective service in the present war.

Others feel far less certain. Liddell Hart thinks that the advocacy of peacetime conscription in Great Britain can be traced to the years immediately before the war when "an influential section of the people . . . were more impressed by the social developments in the Nazi system than alarmed by its dangers." The more he has studied war and nineteenth century history the more convinced he has become that "the development of conscription has damaged the growth of the idea of freedom in the continental countries," and thereby weakened their efficiency, also, by undermining the sense of personal responsibility. He believes that conscription during World War I left "a permanent effect" in Great Britain "harmful to the development of freedom and democracy. . . . It is easier to adopt the compulsory principle of national life than to shake it off." It will spread to "all other aspects of the nation's life," including religious liberties.

Without a more elaborate study of European social history than has yet been made it is difficult, if not impossible, to say definitely what the effects of conscription have been. It seems to be generally accepted that conscription had a unifying, perhaps democratizing, effect on Germany in the first half of the nineteenth century. General Fuller insists, however . . . that this was true only before 1870. Without assuming, as some do, that conscription was one of the causes of the corruption in French political life in recent years, it is evident that it did not have an equally wholesome effect there. In Switzerland it is reported to have stimulated the reduction of illiteracy. The proponents of conscription here argue that it would have the same effect. But in a country where compulsory education has long been the law the strengthening of the public school system would seem the most effective method of reaching that aim.

European Quakers and Mennonites for the most part migrated to this and other countries after conscription went into effect in the nineteenth century. Some, particularly the Mennonites, gave up their historic pacifism. What would happen on that score here cannot be foretold, of course. Some observers fear that the number of conscientious objectors would greatly increase. Some pacifists fear that the historic pacifist churches and the objectors in other denominations would eventually forget their doctrine of non-resistance, as in Europe. One keen observer fears that the churches would be split over the issue and obliged to take a more negative attitude toward the state.

There are other aspects of the matter that trouble many of the opponents of conscription. They fear the use of the reserves against labor unions in tense situations. They point to the use of the National Guard in serious strikes in this country and to the breaking of the great railway strike in 1910 in France by mobilizing the reserves. Charles A. Ellwood, professor of sociology at Duke University, fears a different danger. In a widely reprinted letter to Senator Robert R. Reynolds, chairman of the Senate Military Affairs Committee, he wrote, "In this country we rightly fear . . . a civil war between classes . . . when the whole population has been trained to the use of armed force, they naturally resort to armed force as a political method. . . . Can one look with equanimity upon training to the use of arms of the lower elements in our own native laboring classes, both white and Negro? What will strikes become if the strikers are trained in military methods? Moreover, the growing restlessness and resentment of some elements in our Negro population makes the military training of this element a threat to the South if not to the whole nation." He is not, he insists, opposed to "an adequate and efficient navy" and air force, or to "a small, adequately trained, mobile army for defense and to preserve internal order."

Compulsory military training would "lessen the dangers of unemployment" by taking all the 17 and 18-year-old boys off the labor market and giving them "highly useful work to do," according to an article presenting the arguments for such training in the *Journal of the National Education Association* for November. But this, according to an article taking the opposite position in the same issue, is "defeatist" tending to "turn our attention away from the vital necessity of so arranging things that there may be full employment."

Still another point, about which no clear statement can be made at the present time is the effect on the higher education of the nation's young men. Some of the opponents of conscription fear that compulsory military training would result in putting too great a premium on technical training with a consequent draining off from other professions and occupations.

UNIVERSAL MILITARY TRAINING [13]

Our existing training program for new units has been tried and proven in combat. It has produced the Army Air Force squadrons which have bombed and strafed the Axis air, land and sea forces into impotency in every major combat of the war. It has produced the 85th and 88th Divisions which achieved glorious victories in their first battles in Italy. The 77th and 81st Divisions, with equally fine records in the Pacific, and the 11 new divisions that helped to conquer Normandy and then to sweep the Germans out of France and Belgium are products of the same program. The program has given us the new Army Service Forces units that are making possible the miracles of supply in every theater of the world where American troops are operating. Surely no one will suggest that in undertaking the training of our military forces of the future we should abandon or even materially modify so sound a program.

[13] *Army and Navy Register.* p. 26. January 20, 1945.

Based on our present training system for new units, with such minor modifications as would be necessary to fit a slightly different situation, an adequate training program would be divided into five phases.

The training proposed for the first phase would be the same for all trainees. The accurate information as to the mental and physical capabilities and aptitudes of individuals accumulated during this period would be used to revise the initial classifications. Based on the revised classifications, the permanent assignment of trainees to arms and services would be made.

The training of the remaining four phases would be that especially applicable to the arm or service to which the trainee would be assigned. For example, with the Army Ground Forces the remaining training would be divided in general as follows:

> 2d phase: Advanced individual and specialist training.
> 3d phase: Small unit training.
> 4th phase: Large unit and combined arms training.
> 5th phase: Extended field exercises participated in jointly by air, ground, and service units.

In determining how much time must be devoted to universal military training we must keep in mind the fact that the young men to participate in the program would be preparing for war, and graduating reservists would quite possibly be required to engage in combat with but little, if any, immediate refresher training.

Our precarious situation throughout the world during the months following the first atacks by our enemies in this war demanded that our units be prepared for combat with the least possible delay. We perfected our instructional methods. We gave special training to our instructors. With the assistance of the outstanding pedagogues and technicians of the nation, we were successful in designing and accumulating innumerable highly effective training aids. By such measures we succeeded in shortening the time required for effective instruction to an irreducible minimum. We reviewed our existing training programs. All subjects appearing to be nonessential were eliminated. Each subject adjudged essential was carefully analyzed to determine the minimum time in which it could be effectively presented. In order that no bungling of schedules by inexperienced personnel should delay the readiness of our units, every type of unit had a detailed training schedule. Every necessary hour of instruction in every essential subject was assigned to a definite place in the schedule. The training week was extended to include the maximum number of hours during which instruction could be effectively assimulated. These schedules became the Mobilization Training Program for new units. The operation of the program has been under critical observation through many months of training and its products have been battle tested. The training and combat experiences of three years of war have been utilized in its revisions and now we have, after long testing and successful achievement, a thoroughly sound program for universal military training and that time required for its completion is the absolutely minimum time in which units can be adequately trained for combat.

The total time required to complete satisfactorily the five phases of training under the Mobilization Training Program for new units is fifty-two weeks. If less time is devoted to the training of men who are to constitute units ready for combat, we shall send those men to battle without an average chance of survival and success.

The Reserve Officers Training Corps must be maintained at an increased number of suitable colleges and universities for the production of reserve officers and noncommissioned officers. Graduates of the universal military training program should be encouraged to continue their training in R.O.T.C. units. Students successfully completing the first two years of the R.O.T.C. course should be offered warrants as reserve noncommissioned officers. Graduates of the complete four-year course who are found physically fit and who are of acceptable character should be proffered commissions as second lieutenants in the reserve. With universal military training in operation, we shall be able for the first time to raise the R.O.T.C. courses to a real university level. Its students will enter the corps with their basic training completed. Basic subjects will, in general, be eliminated. The more advanced military subjects will be adequately presented. Student interest will be increased and the R.O.T.C. will acquire added dignity and prestige. Its graduates will constitute a more competent group of junior leaders than ever have been available to the reserve components of our army.

There will be young men with superior leadership potentialities who on account of financial or other unavoidable circumstances will be unable to attend any college or university. There will be others of superior ability who will enroll in colleges or universities where R.O.T.C. units are not maintained. The great reserve army will need the leadership of these young men and it would be an injustice to them as individuals to deny them an opportunity to qualify as officers. Correspondence courses should be made available to those who would otherwise be unable to attend the educational standards essential to commissioned personnel.

The army must provide combinations of military correspondence courses, courses at army schools, and tours of active duty with troop units for the purpose of qualifying reserve officers and noncommissioned officers for promotion.

The further military training of technical specialists must not be neglected. Trainees possessing special aptitude for technical work essential to the army should be discovered through appropriate observation and tests during their participation in the universal military training program. On graduation from the program, a limited number of these young men might well be given financial assistance to enable them to continue their technical education at civilian schools.

LEADING ARGUMENTS WITH RESPECT TO MILITARY TRAINING [14]

FOR:

In the 168 years of its existence the United States has had seven major wars, all undertaken with various degrees of unpreparedness. Realism demands that, in the future, we prepare continuously for whatever emergencies may come.

AGAINST:

There is no convincing proof that universal military training from the beginning of our national life would have prevented any of the major wars in which we have engaged and the outcome, in each case, has been satisfactory.

[14] *National Education Association. Research Bulletin.* 22, no 4:160-3. December 1944.

FOR:

In spite of any peace terms that may be made and any system of international cooperation that may be established at the end of World War II, compulsory military training is essential to the future security of the United States.

Universal military training is the only dependable way in which the United States can match the military strength of other world powers.

For defense against sudden attack, in undeclared wars, the United States should have at all times a large reserve force of trained civilians—perhaps a constant reserve of about 10,000,000 men. This would be more economical and more effective than to maintain a large, professional military establishment.

Because of technological advances, the geographic location of the United States no longer affords sufficient protection to permit adequate preparation for war after it has been declared.

AGAINST:

Universal military training will be entirely superfluous if suitable peace terms and a workable international organization can be developed. The introduction of universal military training now would be a retreat toward isolationism, would deny our faith in world cooperation, and would jeopardize any plan of international collaboration that may be developed.

Military training alone would be no guarantee of security, or of victory, if the United States were to come in conflict with a highly industrialized China or Russia with manpower and production in excess of our own.

For defense against sudden attack the United States should have, not an enormous reserve of common soldiers with training only more or less up to date, but a powerful navy, a large and effective air force, and a well-equipped mechanized army that is highly mobile and has plenty of striking power.

Assuming that the navy, air force, and regular army are strong enough to withstand the first shock of a surprise attack, a well-educated citizenry, together with a highly developed industrial and agricul-

FOR:

AGAINST:

tural life, afford the only basic protection that is needed in the United
States. Specific military training
"en masse" can be given after the
threat of war appears.

Military preparedness not only
affords safety in case of attack but
is the best way to prevent attack.
Thus, in a nonaggressor nation
such as this, it promotes peace.

Active military preparation stim-
ulates armament rivalries and tend
to provoke wars rather than prevent them. That compulsory training does not prevent aggression
witness the German attack on
France and Russia, particularly.

Universal military training would
give the United States greater stat-
ure in international affairs—create
greater respect for our international
policies and proposals.

Peacetime conscription would
cause other nations to regard u
with suspicion, particularly ou
Latin-American neighbors who
would resent this obvious threat
of interference in their affairs.

In the United States universal
military training would always be
regarded as a defense measure.
Committed as we are to the principles of democracy and the right
of self-government, our military
force—no matter how powerful—
would never be used in a war of
aggression.

A powerful military machine, to
military and political leaders, is
ever a source of temptation. I
could lead even in the United
States, to over aggressiveness in international affairs and perhaps ever
to imperialistic ambitions.

Postwar Military Needs

For several years after this war
ends, the responsibility which the
United States will have in policing

Although the size of the military
force needed after war ends cannot
be accurately determined now,

OR:

arious regions will require a large military force.

Because of the unrest and uncertainty which are sure to follow World War II, the United States should have a trained reserve ready for any emergency.

AGAINST:

every probable need can be met with those trained under the present Selective Service system.

The seven to ten million veterans and trainees who will return to civilian life at the close of this war will constitute a reserve adequate for any emergency for a period of at least ten years.

Military Effectiveness

Unpreparedness at the outbreak of a war always results in hasty, partial training, which in turn results in a large number of needless casualties.

In order to train a large reserve army the United States would necessarily have, at all times, a considerable stock of military equipment and supplies. In the absence of such a program, the tendency is to allow these stocks to dwindle.

Universal military training would give our reservists an "esprit de corps" which is never developed in a hastily-assembled civilian army. If called to combat duty the reservist would be a professional, not an amateur.

Training given when needed is up to date, not out of date. Without extensive retraining, a reserve army, too, would be subject to the "casualties of ignorance."

Existence of "standard" equipment and supplies may be a handicap rather than a help, leading to the use of obsolete materials. Without a large stock pile our armies must be equipped with new materials produced to latest specifications.

Much of the success of our armies in all wars is attributed, by some military authorities, to the fact that they have been composed of civilian rather than professional soldiers—men who were fighting to

FOR:

AGAINST:

defend their homes or their ideal rather than disinterested, well-dis plined regulars.

Compulsory military training would develop physical fitness, generally, and build the toughness and stamina which are essential to effective military service.

Most of the reservists, if away from training a year or more, would require essentially the same tough ening-up schedule as if they had never been in service. Military training would do nothing for those rejected because of defects.

After we are engaged in war there is not sufficient time to give a conscript army the training the men should have in basic military facts and skills.

Physical fitness, not specific mil itary instruction and drill, has been the outstanding training problem both in the present war and in World War I.

Economic Considerations

Preparation after war begins must necessarily result in extravagant outlays for the necessary military equipment and supplies. The step is too great in changing over from peacetime to wartime production.

A continuous program of mili tary training at an estimated annual cost of 2 to 4 billion dollars would in the long run, be less economical than periodic preparation which admittedly involves a certain amount of waste. In addition to the actual cash outlay, peacetime conscription would keep about a million men out of productive pur suits at all times.

Manufacture of the equipment and supplies used in the training program would provide employ-

Production for military purpose is economically unsound, since the output is focused on destruction

FOR:

nent for thousands of people and
thus add a substantial amount to
our annual national income.

The boys in training would be
off the labor market, out of competition with older men, and the
total number of gainfully employed
persons would be permanently reduced by narrowing the age range
of employment one year.

AGAINST:

Economically, from every point of
view, extensive military training
represents the choice of guns rather
than butter.

Because of the pool of unemployed persons which regularly
exists, a system of compulsory military training would have little influence on the labor market except
for the first year. About the same
number of "new workers" would
be seeking jobs each year, whether
at age eighteen or age nineteen.

Personal Values

Thru induction procedures health
defects would be discovered and,
in many cases, would be corrected.
Thus the whole level of health
would be materially lifted in the
United States.

Military training establishes good
health habits and teaches personal
health care. These are valuable as-
sets in civilian life.

Military training develops acquaintance with outdoor living and
independence in taking care of

Induction age is too late to check
up on health defects. This should
be done through an *adequate* school
health program beginning with the
first grade and extending through
the entire period of school attendance.

The health improvement claimed
for military training could be
achieved at lower costs and with
better results through adequate
school and public health programs.

The same degree of self reliance
in outdoor living which military
training gives can be acquired in

FOR:

one's self under whatever circumstances arise.

The proposed year of military training would include not only basic military instruction and drill but also, in a large per cent of cases, a valuable program of vocational education.

Military training is a valuable experience in citizenship. If universally required, it would increase patriotism and give each trainee a feeling of "personal investment" in the country's welfare. It would teach the responsibilities as well as the rights of citizenship.

Military training affords valuable lessons in cooperation, efficient teamwork, assumption of personal responsibility, and so on.

In their military training, many boys would find vocational interests and aptitudes and lay the foundation for their peacetime careers.

In military camps, many would be removed from a too-sheltered home life, would overcome homesickness, and gain that degree of

AGAINST:

nonmilitary activities, notably i well-planned camps for older chil dren and youth.

Vocational training, the same a education of other types, should b the function of the schools rathe than the army.

Citizenship in a democracy ca be taught more effectively in school and in civilian pursuits than in a army camp. Even a period of na tional service, if that were deeme advisable, might be required with out resort to military training.

Effective teamwork and grou loyalty can be developed—are be ingfi developed—by schools, camps and many other nonmilitary agen cies.

Compulsory military servic would necessarily interrupt eithe the educational or occupationa plans of young men and tend t postpone the time when they coul marry and establish homes.

The moral atmosphere of mili tary camps usually is not the mos wholesome. Probably the danger from this quarter are fully as grea

FOR:

personal self-reliance necessary to their own success.

Military training would often bring out qualities of leadership and administrative ability which had not been discovered and developed in civilian life.

The discipline imposed during military service would be a valuable asset to the individual all through life. Everyone needs a wholesome respect for duly constituted authority and the habit of prompt obedience to it.

Military training would afford opportunities for boys to travel about over the United States, becoming acquainted with the different regions, and to experience something of the frontier adventure once available but now virtually gone.

AGAINST:

as that of an excessive amount of "apron-string" control.

Those who would "find themselves" through military training must be balanced against those who, because of the delay, would not go on to college and whose vocational plans would be revised downward.

Enforced obedience, as exacted in military discipline, is not the conduct pattern needed in a democracy. Military life makes a small contribution to self-discipline and to harmony in personal relationships.

Due to improvements in travel facilities, we are well on the way toward the elimination of provincialism. Travel is neither an adventure nor a novel experience for a substantial number of American youth.

Relation to Democracy

Since volunteer military service is never adequate when the United States is at war, universal peacetime conscription is a logical national policy. Compulsory military train-

The fact that conscription in wartime is the fairest, most democratic way of meeting an emergency, nowise means that peacetime conscription is also democratic. On the

FOR:

ing in peacetime is just as democratic as universal conscription in wartime.

A year of military service would help young men to understand, and to revere, the principles of democratic government. It would help them to understand and appreciate the basic freedoms on which democracy rests.

Lack of preparedness at the onset of war makes it necessary to yield dictatorial powers to the executive branch of government in times of crisis. Because of the difficulty in recalling these powers, every war emergency is a threat to democracy.

Compulsory military training is democracy in action. In the training camp, rich and poor would live together and engage in common tasks. Boys from city and country, the sons of professional men and unskilled laborers, youth of all nationalities and creeds would live and work together.

AGAINST:

contrary, it is an encroachment on personal rights and freedom which millions of immigrants came here to escape.

Conscript armies have been the foundation of the totalitarian states. Schooled in the use of force and trained to unquestioning obedience, they have been ready to follow a strong leader. Democracy is not enhanced by training which makes "the voice of the drill sergeant louder than the voice of conviction."

Dictatorial powers must be given to the executive branch of government in wartime, irrespective of degree of preparation. The threat to democracy in peacetime conscription is fully as great as the threat arising from the wartime delegation of any additional discretionary powers to the President of the United States.

Military training, no matter if universal, is undemocratic. The officer caste system accentuates inequalities. Aside from accidental acquaintance little is done to bridge the gap between the rich and the poor. Military camp management is autocratic, not democratic.

OR:

A year of compulsory military service would increase the per cent of voting citizens. Through preparing to defend democracy, with their lives if necessary, the trainees would learn the importance of the ballot.

Through military training many competent leaders would develop their powers and afterward use them in the service of their country.

A reservist army would be useful in preserving the peace in case of any internal disturbance or emergency situation arising within the United States.

Those whose formal education ends with high-school graduation or before, need, especially, another year of educative experience and training. Even those who continue college would profit by a year of military instruction.

AGAINST:

Trainees would acquire a dangerous respect for, reliance upon, and skill in the use of force. This would soon be reflected in public opinion on international issues. Perhaps, also, it would result in greater violence in the case of strikes, more frequent attempts at mob rule, and other resorts to force instead of to the ballot.

Just as some of the most intelligent and aggressive young men from other countries have come to the United States to escape military service, so would military training here tend to drive out some of our best potential leaders.

Reservists, including union members, could be called into service and sent back to their jobs, in uniform, to break strikes. This was done in France.

It a system of universal military training all boys would come under complete federal jurisdiction just before they reach the present voting age. Yet federal control of education — which surely could never be so complete—is generally recognized as a hazard to democracy.

The Time to Decide

FOR:	AGAINST:
Universal military training should be introduced now while there are officers and camp facilities to handle such a program.	Facilities and training officer will be readily available for considerable time after the presen war ends. This is a secondar rather than a primary consideratior
Unless the issue is settled now, while there is a keen awareness of defense needs, the public is likely to take no action. In peacetime it is hard to dispel the sense of false security which is blind sometimes even to the most essential defense requirements.	If military training is a wise na tional policy, the American peopl can be trusted to make that de cision on the basis of cold fact without the strong emotions an hysteria of war. Also, those nov under arms should participate i any decision of such importance both to the nation they are defend ing and to their own sons.

EXCERPTS

The balance of good relations between nations is delicate at the best. As the price of preparedness to defend our security against any aggressor or combination of aggressors which might hereafter wish to attack us, we in America should not have to single out particular nations and talk about them as possible enemies.—*John J. McCloy, Assistant Secretary of War. Collier's. Je. 9, '45. p. 14.*

Safety is a basic and underlying consideration of every operation of your army. It is one of the major concerns—and one about which the public knows little. . . .

In the interest of clarity let me over-simplify the subject a bit by saying that the army's objective is to make war as safe as possible for our men and as unsafe as possible for the enemy's.

To me, the greatest advance in safety procedure in this war is preparation for the unexpected. This is accomplished by systems of training both for ground troops and air forces which attempt to duplicate under rigid control the actual conditions which men will face in combat with the enemy.

In military matters surprise is one of the most important factors, therefore we protect our men against this element so that our troops coming up against the veteran forces of the enemy will not have the danger increased by the unknown.

Our training efforts have, therefore, been greatly revised and they now duplicate as nearly as possible all the hazards of actual warfare. This is an intelligent recognition of the fact that a man's safety depends not only on his physical condition, but largely on his mental condition. . . .

Troops unaccustomed to battle sounds are inclined to become rattled in their first engagement, and, therefore, they become more vulnerable to enemy attack. In our training we now reproduce the sounds of battle through controlled explosions precisely like those heard on the battle field.

We reconstruct villages and our troops storm them. On entering them they find the same booby trap hazards with which our crafty enemy still kills our unwary soldiers. . . . Literally thousands of lives are saved by the modern system of training on the ground and in the air.—*Robert A. Lovett, Assistant Secretary of War for Air. National Safety News. N. '43. p. 14.*

The world of tomorrow, like the world of yesterday, is certain to be a world of power politics. Already, long before the last shots are fired, we can dimly see some of its complexion. Regions, and spheres of influence, are being established—by Russia in eastern Europe, and quite probably in Manchuria and Korea and northern Persia; by Britain in western Europe, the Mediterranean, southeastern Asia, southern Persia; by the United States in the Western Hemisphere, west-central Pacific, perhaps in the Middle East. The Italian and Greek troubles are previews of things to come. Ideological strife is not ended. Suspicion and economic rivalry are rife. The world of tomorrow will not be any bright new world, but the same old world with patches. But this is no reason for despair; world betterment cannot be measured in the life span of a generation. Americans must retain their hope but acquire a historical perspective.

American foreign policy in the near future will presumably try to provide some form of *international* security, while at the same time hedging and bolstering our position by *national* security. It is against the background of such a policy that the issue of conscription must be judged.—*Hanson W. Baldwin, Writer on Military and Naval affairs. Harper's Magazine. Mr. '45. p. 296.*

World War II has been a ghastly laboratory for military science. Amazing progress has been made in the art of destruction. It is enough to give our next possible enemy a basis for the belief that he might engineer a lightning stroke to win before we could start to fight.

The robot bomb, the rocket plane, electronics, and new amphibious operations have revolutionized warfare. It is no longer fantastic to envision the next war's swooping down on us in a hurricane of death-dealing, giant monsters of the sky, automatically and accurately loosed on our principal cities without warning from thousands of miles away.

In fact Rear Admiral J. R. Redman, director of naval communications, recently said:

"In future wars all natural barriers such as oceans, will be eliminated. We may be expected to be attacked from any direction and certainly by air without warning."

America then will have no time to mobilize to train or to mobilize to produce. It will have to mobilize to fight. It will really be total war. There will be no non-combatants.

With warfare thus revolutionized, America must revolutionize her entire policy of national defense. We must accept the grim fact that the age of electronics with its miracles is here and adjust our thinking to its vast potentialities.

After this war we must be in a state of constant preparedness or court sudden, swift national disaster. Weapons are complex machines today. They require experts to use them. It takes time to train men to use them. When the firing starts it will be too late to start that training.—*Milt D. Campbell, Director National Defense Division, The American Legion. American Teacher. N. '44. p. 16.*

We must accept a new and tough concept in world affairs— that the earth is not civilized enough to make world-wide disarmament practical for peace-loving nations. We wasted no time at Dumbarton Oaks, and we shall take our place in an international organization to attempt to keep the peace and to make secure the essential freedoms throughout the world. America's heart and mind will work intensively day and night to keep the world in peace. But that isn't enough. We can't take a chance. When this war ends, we must immediately prepare to defend ourselves, particularly to make sure that our enemies realize that if they dare to strike again, they'll lose again.

I have no doubt that powerful forces in Germany and Japan are preparing even now for their next attempt to conquer us. We will try to keep them impotent, but only a perpetual army of occupation would be able to prevent them from rearming eventually.

We don't know what new weapons will be developed. Robot bombs, armies landed from the air and from submarines, enormous bombing planes, and perhaps gas will be among the devices that might be used in an effort to defeat us quickly if we are not prepared. Before such an attack, attempts will be made to cause us to become careless and complacent.

With propaganda, fifth columns, and sheep's clothing, enemies preparing for attack will attempt—perhaps with some success—to convince us that they are lovers of peace, who are interested only in becoming our good friends and customers. They may try to persuade us to allow them to rearm—not, of course, for war, but only to keep up the morale of their people, to help prevent unemployment, to furnish a market for our steel, and to defend themselves, peace-lovers that they are, from bad nations *that might attack them!—Harry L. Hopkins, Special Adviser to the late President Roosevelt. American Magazine. Mr. '45. p. 104.*

Despite a lot of loose talk to the contrary, despite the great increase in the range, and power of the plane, we know that our geographical position is still our greatest *defensive* asset. There is no neighboring great power which might suddenly invade us by land. And although flying bombs and long-range rockets, planes, airborne troops, and new and perhaps revolutionary types of fighting ships which could span our defensive sea barriers are potential military threats, and fifth-column activities (which cannot, however, be met by military means) are potential psychological threats, the defense against these forms of attack is in the air and at sea, and in the mind—not on land. No great land army is needed for the defense of the continental United States, at least not in the initial year of war.

But no war can be won by defense. And our military obligations go far beyond the borders of the continental United States. We shall certainly oppose infringement of the Monroe Doctrine in this hemisphere. Whether we like it or not, we are morally obligated to ensure the security of the Philippines. Our commercial interests will take our flag to China and to other distant parts of the world; and already the government and private interests are committed to a continuing interest in the Middle East. Furthermore, strategically it would be against our vital interests and would represent an eventual potential threat to our economic and military security if any one power were to control all of the western coastline of Europe, or all of the eastern coastline of Asia.

These things, then, are some of the things for which we might have to fight—outside the continental limits of the United States. To enable us to fight successfully, and to protect the continental United States effectively—even against air or sea attacks —we shall require bases outside the continental United States, bastions for defense, springboards for offensive.

In the Atlantic, Greenland, Newfoundland, Bermuda, and the West Indian bases are a minimum requirement; we should also secure by treaty the *right* to use bases in Canada, Labrador, Iceland, the Azores, and Brazil. In the Pacific, we shall need connecting links to the Philippines; Alaska and the Aleutians must be guarded; and bases will be required also at Hawaii, Midway, Johnston, Palmyra, Canton, the Marshalls and the Carolines, the Marianas, the Philippines themselves, and perhaps the Nansei group—with the *right* to use bases (acquired by treaty) in Australia, New Guinea, New Britain, and possibly Singapore, China, and the Kuriles.

Our bases must be heavily defended and fortified against surprise attack of all kinds, including amphibious landings.

It is also clear from a glance at the map that the chief elements of our defense should be air and naval; the plane and the ship are the only elements that can link together outlying bases with the continental homeland and make the whole a strong system. Clearly, therefore, we shall need a sizable air force and a big navy for defense of the continental United States and its overseas interests, supported by small but well-equipped and highly trained land garrisons and small amphibious forces. We need no mass army in being at the *start* of a war (unless we intend to wage a war of aggression). . . .

However, we shall certainly need a large army to *finish* any major war. To which it may be argued, "The United States intends then to fight on foreign soil?" To which I say "Amen." The whole object of any sound defense policy is to ensure that any wars into which we may be drawn will not be fought on our soil. It will be too much to expect that in the next war our land can be kept inviolate from bombs or rockets; but our objective must be to make such air attacks as do penetrate our defenses militarily indecisive and to keep the land fighting on foreign fields.—*Hanson W. Baldwin, Noted Writer on Military and Naval Affairs. Harper's Magazine. Mr. '45. p. 297-8.*

The very day on which President Roosevelt told the press about his ideas for a universal training program came news from Argentina that President Juan Peron announced that country's decision to require army training for men and women from the ages of 12 to 50. Pre-conscription will begin at the age of 12 and continue until 20. Conscription will begin at 20 and last for two years. Upon their discharge from conscription training all males will be eligible to post-conscription duties until age 50. Girls will serve in a variety of women's auxiliary services.

The Argentine government explained that its pre-conscription plans for children aged 12 is aimed at improving "youth health standards," rather than forming "infantile battalions." The plan, the Argentine government said, merely would permit unification of systems of physical education now in the private and public secondary schools, and provide a program "which takes into consideration the physical and moral welfare of the child, and offers appropriate physical exercise, including rifle practice of the same kind which students of public high school now conduct after the third year." The new military statute probably will be put into effect early next year.—*Ohio Schools. D. '44. p. 416.*

What is needed is a fact-finding commission, after the pattern of the Morrow or Baker Board, composed of some of the most capable men in the country: a commission appointed by the President, or by Congress, or by both together, and made up of judges, lawyers, scientists, educators, and congressmen. It should have army, navy, and air force advisers, but probably no military members. Thorough hearings on the broadest possible basis should be started immediately, and the commission should continue its studies until such time as world developments and its analysis of the war's lessons permit it to make final findings. Only in such a way can the framework of a sound, integrated defense system, keyed to our foreign policy and to our social and economic and political life, be set up.

Whether or not such a solution is adopted, upon two things we should insist. First, that peacetime conscription is not a separate issue; it should be treated as part of a far broader problem—the whole problem of postwar defense. Second, that it must stand or fall on its military merits. If it is adjudged essential to implement our postwar military policy we must have it, but we must remember that the harm it may do to our political and economic and social institutions may well outweigh its incidental political, economic, and social benefits.—*Hanson W. Baldwin, Noted Writer on Military and Naval Affairs. Harper's Magazine. Mr. '45. p. 300.*

I went back to Europe in 1937. I visited every country in Europe a number of times. I went to all the Balkan countries, Turkey, and around the Mediterranean, and I have found everywhere exactly the same thing. I happen to have had the entree to military people and diplomatic people, members of different governments also.

I found everywhere a simple thing. They said, "If you, the United States, and other democracies want us to follow your ideas you have got to be prepared to meet the terrible military force which Germany now possesses. We have no illusion about it. We know on the ground and in the air what she can do. We know Germany's readiness to use it if we do not do what Germany wants us to do. If you and other democracies will not show you have got the force to meet that force, why should we, to use slang, stick our necks out? We will get them cut off and you won't be around to help us."

Now, certainly, that happened in the case of Norway, Denmark, Holland, Belgium, Luxembourg, Finland, Esthonia, Latvia, Poland, Hungary, Austria, Yugoslavia, Czechoslovakia, Rumania, and Bulgaria.

From the beginning of the war we have been talking about getting Turkey into it. Turkey kept out of it. The answer is very simple. The Turkish sympathy was with us, with the democracies, but she found out very quickly that the plan was that Turkey do the fighting, and, to put it roughly, we do the talking. The Turks told me, "When you and the other democracies will come here and furnish us with troops, the guns, the airplanes, the tanks, and everything which is necessary to enable us to face Germany, we will be glad to do it, and until you do it we haven't the slightest intention of going to war."

Now, when it comes to the other side of the earth, Japan, I happen to have been mixed up in the inside of things out there at various times in my life. My second tour in the Philippines was as far back as 1909. I was then in the Military Information. It is so far back there is no secret about it.

One of the things that I personally did was arrest two Japanese spies in the act of purchasing Corrigedor plans from a sergeant. There is no secret about the thing; that is just one of the thousands of things reported between the two wars. . . .

When I came back from Europe for a few months in 1941, I found no one that wanted to listen. No one wanted to publish anything except the service journals, the *Infantry Journal,* the *Cavalry Journal,* and one or two other service magazines. No news reel and no broadcasting company wanted anything about what was really going on from a military point of view in Europe, and you wouldn't believe for one instant there was any danger of war with Japan. . . .

We are being told once more that disarmament brings peace and armament provokes war. We accepted that propaganda after the last war. We accepted it for 25 years. In 1920, we passed a National Defense Act because the country was against universal military training. A citizens' army was raised by voluntary enlistments. They provided for the Regular Army, Reserves, Citizens Military Training Corps, Reserve Officers Training Corps, and all those things.

If it hadn't been for that act, some of it having been kept going, and if it hadn't been for General MacArthur and others insisting on mobilizing the National Guard, bringing the Regular Army up to war strength, taking the fullest advantage of the graduates of the Reserve Officers Training Corps, which we did have, we would have been caught in a much worse condition than we were when we finally entered the war in 1941.

Under the influence of pacifists and the disarmament advocates as a road to peace at the Washington Arms Conference, which I happened to have attended as a newspaperman, we gave away, among other things, six new battle cruisers and seven battleships. We haven't yet caught up on those 45,000-ton battleships with all the building which we have been doing. We are only beginning to get the strength at sea which we would have had if we had kept those ships instead of giving them away.

We gave away our position in the Pacific. We didn't get out of the Philippines and neither did we put sufficient force there to hold them. We didn't do anything with Guam except leave it with a few sailors and a few marines, just nice bait for the Japanese to take and boast about. We didn't do anything about the Japanese taking the mandated islands and violating every one of their promises.—*Brigadier General Henry I. Reilly. Statement Before the House Select Committee on Postwar Military Policy, June 9, 1945. Hearings. p. 266-8.*

AFFIRMATIVE DISCUSSION

FUTURE MANPOWER NEEDS OF THE ARMED FORCES [1]

From the days of the Revolutionary War to the years immediately preceding the present conflict, the military facts of life failed to attract the interest of the American people except in time of actual war. For a nation which in 150 years has fought five major wars, this is a curious situation. One reason for it is our experience when, as a British colony, relatively large standing armies were maintained here. In the main, however, the explanation lies in the reliance on geography—vast oceans and distances—which in the "horse and buggy" age provided us with a sense of security. It is also probable that other factors are the military good fortune which in the end has seemed always to rest with our arms, and that bubbling optimism and confidence in the military capacity of our people so characteristically American.

The fact remains that, generation after generation, we have paid an unnecessarily high price in blood for the doubtful privilege of military improvisation. It is a historical fact that until the time of World War II the United States has consistently failed to make adequate preparation, even on the eve of battle, for the military implementation of the national will. Our people, unregimented and relatively free to choose their own occupations and their own scheme of life, have, from the very founding of the nation, viewed with active or passive hostility the concept that the privileges of security are necessarily accompanied by equivalent responsibilities. Again, since most of us over the years have been amateurs in war, we have tended to accept two persistent fallacies characteristic of superficial students of military policy: the first, that by a process of improvisation military vic-

[1] By William F. Tompkins, Major General, United States Army. *Annals of the American Academy.* 238:56-62. March 1945.

tory can be achieved; the second, that military victory can be achieved cheaply by the employment of some particular arm, doctrine, or policy.

In the quarter of a century between World Wars I and II, the manpower needs of our armed forces, in both the professional and the reserve components, were consistently neglected. Part of this neglect may be attributed to an entirely laudable and humane hope that through the pledges of major nations the specter of major warfare had been banished from the earth. The confusion of those among our citizens who took an intelligent interest in the national security was added to, however, by the campaigns of sundry publicists in the field of military affairs who argued that due to technological advances great armies composed of the mass manpower of nations had had their last bloody fling in World War I. The exponents of this theory maintained that in the future it would be unnecessary and indeed disastrous to attempt to mobilize the massive forces of 1914-18. "Streamlined armies" of a few hundred thousand men at most, composed of highly trained technicians, would put to flight the awkward masses of the past. A storm of mechanized land forces, aided and abetted by a tornado of airpower, or perhaps airpower alone, would overwhelm the opposition in a matter of weeks. According to these writers, modern war involved the surgeon's knife rather than the club of mass manpower.

Few professional students of war, who had noted the increasing tendency to total war expressed in the "all-out" effort, accepted any such colorful theory as that outlined above. The rapid collapse of the French Army in the spring of 1940 under the attack of the German air forces and panzer divisions, heralded in the press as the triumph of mechanized warfare, did not convince those who looked behind the planes and the tanks. The military history of the past three years has proved once again that in modern warfare between first-class powers, every resource, human and material, of the nations will be mobilized for the battle. The penalties of defeat in modern war are far more terrible than in the days of the eighteenth century, when wars of limited objectives fought by limited forces were the rule of the day. It is possible by the use of exceptional new matériel or extraordinary organization and leadership for a sudden on-slaught to overthrow the military strength of a great power, but if for any reason the first aggressive move fails of its intended purpose, the war inevitably degenerates into an ever more bitter trial of the ultimate strengths of the nations involved.

The serious student of modern war, therefore, must assume that the manpower needs of the armed forces in time of war are limited only by the possibilities of the national population. The problem is not one of decision on limited employment of armed forces, but one rather of the selective allocation of the entire manpower of the nation to the direct needs of the military, the requirements of matériel production, and the minimum essential maintenance of the civilian economy. At one time it was theorized that approximately 10 per cent of the gross popu-lation of any country represented the maximum available military manpower. More detailed examination of both military and civilian requirements will indicate that such a generalization is of small value. Actually, the portion of the male population of a country available for military service is determined by a series of specific factors whose weight varies according to particular na-tional circumstances.

There are two principal drains upon the manpower resources of a country in time of war *other than the directly military.* The first of these is formed by requirements for labor in the produc-tion of war matériel to be employed by and in support of the soldiers. The second consideration involves the minimum neces-sary maintenance of the civilian economy. If the first limitation is not given proper weight, great armies may be raised but ade-quate equipment and matériel for their support will be lacking. In the second instance, military manpower, adequately equipped and supported, may be available but the nation will confront eventual if not immediate collapse of the war effort through de-terioration of the home front.

The situation is complicated by the necessary admission that for a relatively short period of time it is possible to reduce the standard of living of the civilian portion of a country's popula-tion below the figure necessary to maintain long-run production efficiency. To use phraseology made popular in the present war, "guns can be substituted for butter" to a very large extent, but only for a relatively short period of time. In the long run successful management of a war effort requires a careful balancing of needs and the optimization of the collective effort of all citizens of the country through a proper distribution of the national productivity. Accomplishment of such a distribution requires careful allotment of the national manpower. This problem on a nation-wide basis is exactly comparable with the question of distribution of military manpower between combat and support elements within a modern army. Recognition of both the military and the social-economic requirements of society in time of war is responsible for the age-old "division of labor" by which the younger men of the social order are held responsible for the fighting, while old men, women, and, if necessary, the older children are expected to supply the bulk of the effort toward the maintenance of munitions production and the necessities of life for the civilian population.

In September 1939 when Germany attacked Poland, the United States Army consisted of 190,690 officers and men; by 1941, on the eve of our entry into the present war, 1,644,000 officers and men were on active duty, and at the present time approximately 8,000,000 are in the land and air forces. In less than five years we have multiplied by more than forty times the number of men actually serving in the Army of the United States. The Navy has also experienced a somewhat corresponding increase in personnel.

The turnover alone in such huge forces amounts to a staggering figure. By August 31, 1944 more than a million men had been honorably discharged from the armed forces of the United States for one reason or another, excluding casualties. It is entirely possible that before the end of World War II, at one time or another, 15,000,000 men will have served in the Army and the Navy of the United States. . . .

The type of military system to be adopted for the future armed forces of America will greatly affect the nature of our manpower needs. Generally speaking, there are two basic types of military organizations which may be relied upon to guard the national safety. The first of these involves the maintenance in time of peace of very large professional or "standing" armies. From the strictly military point of view, the advantages of large professional forces are more or less obvious, granting that such forces are properly equipped, trained, and led. Such armies possess the virtues of the professional in any field, as opposed to the amateur. They are presumptively ready for immediate action and possessed of high uniform quality.

The alternative to large standing armies is the maintenance of a professional peace establishment "to be reenforced in time of emergency by organized units drawn from a citizen army re serve, effectively organized for this purpose in time of peace."

The traditions and institutions of our country have always been opposed to the idea of maintaining very large professional forces as our principal defense. The dangers to a free people in the necessary development of a powerful officer caste to lead such professional armies generation after generation are obvious. It is, therefore, the deliberate policy of the War Department to advocate principal dependence for our national security upon the citizen soldier in arms. It must never be forgotten, however, that such dependence is as on a hollow reed if provision is not made for proper training of such citizen soldiers in great number so that they may play their part in time of need. Failure to recognize this requirement has always been the primary source of military difficulty for the United States. Professional armies, it must be stressed, can be held to a minimum only where adequate provision is made for the training, equipping, and ready mobilization of large reserves of citizen soldiers to meet major emergencies.

It is totally erroneous, therefore, to conclude that if, following the present war, we expect to rely primarily upon citizen reserves to guard this nation and its interests, the direct and indirect manpower needs of the armed forces can be small. In order to provide the necessary degree of military security, to train adequately, and to provide professional cadres for the citizen in arms, our professional army, while relatively small, must be larger than was the case prior to World War II. Nevertheless, the officer corps of the national army as a whole ought to comprise comparatively few professional officers and a relatively large number of reserve officers.

Now, under what program are our citizen soldiers to be given the necessary training to fit them to defend this country from aggression? There is only one practical answer—universal military training. The consistent practical failure of the "volunteer" system in our past history is proof enough of its inability to meet the needs of the national defense; but in addition, it should be reflected that a volunteer system violates the very principle of democracy, in that the few are saddled with the responsibility of sacrificing to defend the many. In the past seventy-five years we have fought three serious wars, in no one of which victory was possible without the use of the draft to provide the necessary personnel. There is no reason to presume that it will be different the next time. If in time of war it is necessary to rely upon selective service to furnish the great bulk of our manpower, it should be evident that we are taking the obvious step forward when we propose to train in time of peace those who will be called to fight in time of war. Since all our great wars have been fought in the main by citizen armies (I refer to the Civil War of 1861-65, the First World War, 1917-18, and the present World War) "the proposal for an organized citizen army reserve in time of peace is merely a proposal for perfecting a traditional institution to meet modern requirements which no longer permit extemporization after the outbreak of war."

A universal military training act ought to provide that all the able-bodied young males of the United States should devote, as part of their democratic contribution to the welfare of the nation, a period of one year to military instruction given by the army or the navy. It is computed that this program would permit the training of approximately 800,000 young men a year, 600,000 for the army and 200,000 for the navy. At the end of a few years a reserve army would be in hand capable of being mobilized rapidly and effectively in an emergency to reinforce the shield provided by the regular army and navy and thereafter move decisively to bring the war to a speedy and victorious conclusion.

The force needed to train 600,000 army inductees a year in order to build our reserve army must be larger than that which existed before the present war. The personnel of this training force will not all be regulars, by any means. Reservists desiring active duty by which to qualify themselves for promotion would constitute the major number of those engaged in giving training. That number would be approximately 100,000. In addition, provision must be made for garrisons in our outlying bases such as Panama and Hawaii and those in the Caribbean area, together with some units ready for immediate action (especially by air) in the continental United States. These latter units must be prepared to reinforce threatened areas or to assist in maintaining the peace generally.

Obviously, the exact number of regulars and reservists required to implement these plans would depend on world conditions. The figure would approximate several hundred thousand.

There are those who oppose the principle of universal military training on the ground that it conduces to militarism. The answer to this is that the military organization of a country reflects the ideals and purposes of a people. Universal conscription in Germany and Japan unquestionably strengthened the spirit of militarism in those countries. There is no evidence that universal military training has encouraged militarism in Sweden or Switzerland. The outline of the military system including universal military training which is proposed for the United States specifically repudiates and rejects the militaristic form of service characterized as "the European conscript system."

The proposed American system of universal military training is in fact a modern adaptation of the democratic military system which President George Washington proposed to the First Congress *before any of the European conscript systems were established or even thought of.*

That universal military training may be expected to have an effect on the labor market is only logical. In the first place, there would be a direct effect through the removal for a year of some 800,000 young men from the labor market. In the second place, there are the indirect and beneficial effects which, it may be anticipated, would show up in the form of increased efficiency of our whole social-economic effort. Improvements in health, the values of intermingling of young men of all classes from all parts of the country, and lessening of illiteracy, all should assist greatly in unifying the peacetime purposes of the nation.

The objection has been raised that universal military training would injure or handicap America's youth by removing them from the labor market for a year or limiting their educational opportunities. Neither of these assertions seems realistic. It should be remembered that the time sacrifice involved will be equalized once a universal military system has been established. The economic competition of youth is with youth, and if all the able-bodied youth of the country take, age for age, such military training as is proposed, there should be no inequality of sacrifice involved.

As far as interference with education may be concerned, there seems at least as much reason to believe that exposure to the broadening influences of a year of common training would encourage a desire on the part of ambitious youths for college education as that it would lend discouragement. Once the universal military training system has been established, there should be nothing to fear on the part of the higher educational institutions of the land from the financial point of view. The lag factor will have been absorbed in the first year.

The intensity of modern combat is such that for direct participation therein a man is now considered old when he is past thirty. The limitations thus placed upon the age groups of militarily available males emphasize the necessity for maintaining the health of the country at a figure which will make the maximum possible number of young males fit for service. In this country we have long flattered ourselves that we possess the world's highest standard of living. Nevertheless, about one third of all the young men belonging to the age classes traditionally first called upon for military service have been rejected in the present conflict.

Medical figures indicate that proper attention to health in childhood would have prevented or easily cured a very considerable percentage of the causes for rejection noted in the records of the government. From the purely military point of view, considering the almost limitless demands on manpower in modern "all-out" war, any favorable results from the extension of physical examinations, sanitary medicine, curative medicine, improvements in the national diet and nutrition, and a broader program of healthful outdoor sports would be of the greatest value, and a national asset.

It is an interesting fact that, although the young men of today enjoy better average health than is recorded for previous generations and are taller and heavier than their ancestors, the increasingly artificial nature of our civilization, with the substitution of the use of mechanical devices in place of human muscles, requires us to devote a greater period of time to the physical conditioning of military trainees than was the case in the past. In short, the boy of today is better raw material for a soldier than his father or grandfather, but this raw material requires more extensive processing to meet the peculiar requirements of the energetic and outdoor life of a fighting man.

With a sound system of universal military training permanently established, a mass of trained manpower will feed the military reservoir of the country in the future in steady replacement of the age-stricken armies of the present war. Such a program would do more than any one other thing to assure the future military security of the United States.

COMPULSORY MILITARY TRAINING? [2]

I am in favor of compulsory military training for all able-bodied American young men as an essential basis for the protection of American interests and international peace in a confused postwar world. No one can prophesy how long it will take to evolve an orderly system of international relations. But we must surely expect a long transition period before we can hope that both order and law can be established in an international sense. During this period of indefinite length the United States must be in a position to exert its power promptly and effectively as may seem to us wise and necessary. International

[2] By Charles Seymour, President, Yale University. *Educational Record*. 26:9-16. January 1945.

peace will not be established the moment formal fighting stops, nor will international organization be accomplished by signatures to a treaty or treaties. The United States cannot divest itself of responsibility for the settlement of international problems, and this responsibility cannot be fulfilled except the nation dispose of organized force.

There are those who argue that no one can foretell at this juncture what the postwar situation will be like and that it is foolish to set up a system which may not be necessary or may provide more than our needs. "How can we decide now," asks a distinguished university president, "what number of soldiers and sailors will be required for 'national security' after the war?" The answer, in my opinion, lies in the certainty that unless we set up a system of guaranteeing complete adequacy for any reasonable contingency we shall, as in the past, find ourselves without any preparation at all. We may be sure that for many years the state of world confusion will be such that it is better for us to be overprepared than underprepared.

It seems reasonably clear from our historical experience that the postponement of a decision upon military training results not merely in underpreparation but in no preparation at all. It is natural that following vital military effort and victory, the immediate danger having been eliminated, the people should succumb to the desire for relaxation. We know from our history textbooks of the efforts which George Washington made, at the moment of the winning of independence, to bring the Congress to establish a plan of universal military training. Provision for the national defense which the preamble to the Constitution emphasized strongly was, in his opinion, a major task of the young government. Consulting with his most trusted military advisers, especially Steuben and Knox, he prepared his *Sentiments on a Peace Establishment,* unfortunately buried for nearly a century and a half. He demanded a small regular army and a "well-organized militia" based upon the principle of universal obligation to service. The specific plans which General Knox drafted under his supervision failed to meet the approval of Congress. Alternative plans calling for universal training were so far emasculated by Congress that finally the Militia Act of 1792 made no provision for the maintenance of a reservoir of trained youth.

The nation paid the price in the disasters of the War of 1812. Indeed we might have been spared the second war with Britain if the young men of the day had been trained by a system which according to Steuben "would make us more respectable with the powers of Europe than if we maintain an army of 50,000 men." As General Palmer has pointed out:

> We were provoked into war solely because we were not respectable with the powers of Europe. Both France and Great Britain treated us with contempt. With our soil impregnable against invasion, with power to seize Canada, or the Floridas, or Louisiana at will, and with a tight little navy having no thought but for the open sea, our weight must have been different in the councils of the world. In these circumstances, the impressment of American seamen might not have been such a harmless sport.

Everyone knows the heavy price we paid in World War I because of our unreadiness. Indeed it is possible to argue again that if we had disposed of a well-trained mass of citizens who could have been rapidly mobilized we should not have had to fight that war at all. Those familiar with the German documents are aware that the decision to launch the unrestricted submarine warfare in 1917 was taken in the light of our inability to strike swiftly and effectively. Once in the war, effective action against the German troops could not be undertaken for more than a year; and the heavy losses in the Meuse-Argonne can largely be traced to the lack of basic training in our army and to faulty staff work.

Following World War I, as after the Revolution, the natural desire for relaxation in succession to vital effort prevented the establishment of an effective system of military defense. People felt that the victory of 1918 gave us the assurance of a period of prolonged peace. The League of Nations had been founded. Even if another European war broke out it would not tempt us into intervention again. Then as now people asked why it was necessary to make sacrifices in preparation for national defense until it was clear that our security was actually threatened. How can we decide now what number of soldiers and sailors will be required?

As after the Revolutionary War, efforts were made in 1919 and 1920 to maintain a reservoir of trained manpower. Senator Wadsworth introduced an army organization bill which had as its foundation universal military training. It was based upon Washington's conception of an organized citizen army. It aroused the most widespread opposition. General Palmer reports:

> Every senator was overwhelmed by a flood of letters and telegrams from agitated constituents. The cost of the proposed training system was stressed by serious persons who were concerned by the existing burden of wartime debt and taxation. Other earnest persons pointed out that as we had just won a war to end war there would never be any need for great armies in the future; now that the world was at last safe for democracy why waste any more time and money in defending it—now was the time to get back to "normalcy." The objectors were reinforced by the usual small but vociferous minority of pacifists who believe that any form of military preparedness is militaristic and provocative of war.

The results have been written in the history of the past twenty years. Despite the improvements in our military system provided by the National Defense Act of 1920, we failed to maintain the vast reservoir of trained man power that emerged from World War I and made no provision for a future reservoir that might serve to protect us against the perils of a second world war. One can only guess how far Hitler and the Japanese, in the development of their aggressive plans, took into consideration the fact that the United States was incapable of immediate military action. We do know the price we have paid since Pearl Harbor for our willingness to postpone the decision in 1920. As the Secretary of War has pointed out, if we had been "prepared to mobilize quickly and efficiently millions of well-trained men, and if our production had been geared to equip these men during their training, millions of lives, ours and our Allies', might have been spared, untold suffering avoided, and huge extravagance prevented." Herein, it seems to me, lies the answer to those who once more would postpone decision as to preparation for military defense.

There are those now, as a quarter of a century ago, who argue that we are fighting a war to achieve a world in which we will not have to be constantly prepared for war; that we are at the moment engaged in setting up an international organization that will preserve the peace. Should we confess defeat in these efforts before they have been tried, by simultaneously setting up a system which will keep us constantly ready for war? I yield to no one in my enthusiasm for an international organization that may provide a political substitute for war and I believe that a great responsibility rests upon the American people for leadership in such an organization. It should establish not merely the mechanism for arresting an aggressor nation, but should also develop actively many institutions of international cooperation which shall foster the welfare of the nations and give them an incentive to follow a peaceful policy. We have before us not merely great international difficulties but also great international opportunities.

But the history of the past twenty-five years makes clear that men are far from eliminating force or the threat of force from their social relations. The League of Nations in the last instance failed to keep the peace because the peace-loving nations that controlled its policies themselves failed to maintain a force sufficient, in the emergency, to meet that of the nations who attacked the principles of the League. Underlying any machinery for the prevention of war there must be organized power, and the more effective that power the greater is the chance that it will not have to be used. The threat of force in the hands of an irresponsible maniac, whether an individual or a nation, is a firebrand; in the hands of the representative of law and order it becomes a weapon of insurance. Thus if the United States is actually going to assume a role of responsibility in protecting the peace of the world, it must have at its disposal an adequate military establishment to serve as the authority upon which our policy and our actions shall be based.

Today, as always, there are those who admit the need of an adequate military establishment but who insist that an army of the size that would result from universal military training is not merely outrageously expensive but practically unnecessary. The only alternative to a trained citizen army, however, if we admit the need of effective military force, would be a professional army, "expansible" as they say, to meet contingencies as they arise. Such a principle was accepted by our military leaders from the time of the War of 1812, in which the regular army achieved great distinction, down to World War I. It has been discarded. A large regular professional army sufficient to meet any contingency at any time is not merely expensive; it is unsuited to a democracy. It rests upon the doctrine that only professional soldiers are of value, a doctrine which has been proved to be false by every war in our history. The principle of the small "expansible standing army" has, when put to the test, been proved impracticable. As in the war with Mexico and the Civil War the small regular army had to be reinforced by a citizen army, but nothing could be done to organize such a force in time of peace. Both on political and military grounds the weight of authoritative opinion is against the expansible standing army.

The principle of a trained citizen army, on the other hand, is in accord with our political ideals and it is approved by the military authorities. Responsibility of the individual for the defense of the community is an aspect of our Anglo-Saxon heritage. . . .

This obligation is recognized without difficulty in time of national danger and war; it is incumbent upon us to recognize it also in a practical sense in time of peace, when preparing against the dangers of war. In all humility I submit that those who characterize universal military training as "un-American" should reread our history and ponder our American political philosophy. Of all methods of military defense it is the one closest to the democratic ideal.

Similar historical study should be urged upon those who oppose universal military training on the ground that it would create a military "caste" or tend to "militarize" the attitude of our youth. The assertion is quite clearly based upon confusion between that system of universal training suggested by General Marshall with the German system which has been characterized by placing the German General Staff outside the control of the civil government. The history of our great citizen armies in the Civil War and World War I offers clear evidence of the deep-seated nature of antimilitaristic feeling among these soldiers even after long service. If an example is sought abroad it may be found in Switzerland where universal military service has not only provided a force sufficient to warn all aggressors off, during the wars of the past eighty years, but which has served to strengthen the spirit of democracy.

In advocating a system of universal military training I do so as a citizen, hopeful that the nation will not allow its existing reservoir of trained manpower to evaporate and believing that there are sufficient dangers and uncertainties ahead of us to demand the continued maintenance of such a reservoir. My advocacy does not proceed from my interest in education but from military and political conditions. Indeed the question ought not to be blurred by the injection of educational factors. Judged by criteria of national military and political necessities the issue seems to me clear; judged by educational criteria it is exceedingly confused. I am quite frankly troubled by President Roosevelt's remarks at a press conference of last November in which he called for a year of "compulsory national service" with physical upbuilding for the boys and cooking for the girls. There is the suspicion that he was thinking in terms of some sort of Civilian Conservation Corps program. Others less highly placed have suggested the possibility of injecting "some education" into the program of military training apparently with the idea of sweetening the bitter pill of a year's service.

I am sharply opposed to any attempted mixture of military training and civilian schooling that extends beyond the existing principles of our Reserve Officers Training Corps. A year's military training cannot be made a substitute for a year of college. It is better to face the fact squarely and make our educational sacrifice honestly in the determination to improve our military establishment. If the sacrifice is effective in its results we can make it the more cheerfully, realizing that if the nation is not prepared to defend our freedom against sudden attack, liberal education itself is always in danger. We who are dedicated to education may gladly sacrifice convenience in the hope of assuring the very existence of free education.

That our educational system in schools and colleges would suffer inconvenience, perhaps serious disadvantage, if universal military training were introduced, is a fact that cannot be denied. I need not specify the problems which it would entail. It is the more important that earnest study should be devoted to the details of any plan, in order to discover means by which the system, without loss of essential effectiveness, might be adjusted to the main needs of education. Attention should be given to the age of induction, or the stage of the trainee's education, so that he might avoid untimely interruption of his education. Careful consideration should be given to the Swiss system of training, which was urged upon Washington by General Knox himself and which provides for short periods of training each year, for a series of years as may be necessary. In view of the speed with which the army and navy now train combat replacements, not selected for advanced specialized work, it is fair to ask whether in peacetime a full consecutive year is universally necessary. It is fair also to ask whether a distinction should not be made as to the training of the rank and file, the training of noncommissioned specialists, and the training of commissioned officers.

These and other questions demand prayerful and intellligent study. But there must first be answered the basic question as to how the essential reservoir is to be filled. The only answer in consonance with our needs and our political principles is found in acceptance of the principle of universal military service for men.

PEACETIME MILITARY TRAINING [3]

The people of the United States have been strongly idealistic ever since the Colonists first settled this country, seeking opportunity to live in accordance with their ideals of religious and political freedom. World War I and World War II were peak periods of the continued struggle to preserve these ideals.

Unfortunately people with the highest of ideals do not always follow the best procedures for bringing these ideals to

[3] By Karl T. Compton, President, Massachusetts Institute of Technology. Statement before the House Select Committee on Postwar Military Policy, June 8, 1945. *Congressional Record.* 91: (daily) A3022-4. June 11, 1945.

reality and effectiveness. Most of us will now agree that this was true of the extreme pacifist groups during the 1920's and 1930's, both in this country and in Great Britain. Many of us believe that the sad lack of military preparedness and the very strong sentiment against any move even to prepare for war were simply invitations and incitements to Hitler, Mussolini, Hirohito, and their followers to let loose their mad avalanche of armed aggression for conquest.

As long as the world contains selfishly ambitious groups who are unscrupulous and ruthless enough to try to gain their ends by force if given a chance, it will be necessary for peace-loving countries like the United States to prevent the would-be aggressors from having this chance. This can be done by an expenditure of only a very small portion of the effort and money which go into a war.

There are a number of things which the United States must do if it is to guard against the danger of future war. To be prepared in a military sense is only one of these things. To be strong in science, technology, and production is another requirement. Even more important, the United States must be just, reasonable, and cooperative in its dealings with other countries. And in order that the burden of preventing wars may not fall too heavily on any one country, it is important that all countries which are determined to have peace in the future should combine to insure it. But, in any case, I believe that a reasonable degree of military strength is one of the realistic essentials to the future peace of our United States.

Just how much military strength a "reasonable degree" calls for and how this "reasonable degree" can be most advantageously secured are very important questions. As to the first, it would seem to me that "reasonable strength" would mean a rather strong military establishment for such a considerable period after the war as may be required to establish an international plan to maintain peace and to evaluate its effectiveness. If, after this international plan has been given a convincing trial, it proves to be effective, then I should think that all the participating nations would be justified in a gradual reduction of their armed strength. But right now we would be well advised to establish our reasonable military program, and to let the world know that we mean business when we talk of preserving peace, and that we are ready to adopt strong measures to insure our safety against attack.

Technological developments have greatly changed the conception of an effective citizens' army. For one thing, war on land, sea, and air has become so highly technical that a much longer period of training is necessary than was true 50 or 100 years ago. The training itself must be largely technical. More important still, the speed of transportation and the development of methods for making powerful attacks with great suddenness and at a great distance mean that it is no longer safe to wait until war breaks out to begin the intensive training of our armies. These factors, I take it, have all been influential in leading the military experts to the conclusion that a year of military training is needed to provide a continuously replenished reservoir of men who could be quickly called to arms for effective military service at threat of war.

Some of my colleagues, impressed as I have been with the great value of scientific and engineering skill in contributing effectiveness to our armed forces, have argued that scientists and engineers should be exempt from any universal military training. They back up their argument by pointing out the very critical shortage of such personnel to meet both the military and peacetime requirements which we can see ahead. I recognize a real force in this argument, which can also be made for young men going into the medical profession, for men in agriculture, industrial production, and all other essential activities. The difficulty with this argument, as I see it, is that once it is acceded to for any one group, the pressure cannot be resisted to grant similar exemption to many other groups, and the military training program hence breaks down. It seems to me best therefore to carry out the program without exemptions.

On the positive side, a strong argument can be made for giving military training to scientists and engineers, for many of these are needed among the officer personnel in these days of technological warfare.

Another argument against the plan, with which I have little sympathy, is that the year spent in military training would be a waste of time, particularly for any young man who is planning to go ahead with a professional or other education. This objection seems to me ill founded on two counts.

In the first place, very many of the most successful and effective professional men—scientists, engineers, doctors, or what not—interrupted their educational careers for a year or more to work at some job to earn the money with which to proceed. On the whole I am convinced that they were strengthened by this work. I have often wished that far more of our young students in college could be induced or forced to put in an intervening year of serious nonacademic work. They would come out of it with greater maturity, more realistic social adjustment, and greater determination to make the best use of their future educational opportunities.

In the second place, the year of military training, as now outlined by the armed forces, incorporates a considerable amount of useful educational experience. To be sure, relatively little of it is of a classroom variety, but a large portion of it has to do with learning to understand technical equipment and how to use it, and how to work with precision in an organization, both of which are useful elements in any young man's education.

For these reasons I do not believe that a year's loss of time in getting through college or getting established in a job is a serious objection in comparison to the values of the year of military training from a national security standpoint plus the inherent educational values of the year of training as a partially compensating by-product.

One further argument against universal military training is that the methods of warfare change so rapidly that the training given in any one year may be obsolete a few years hence. This argument I believe to be illogical. The same type of argument would say that we should not train an electrical engineer at M.I.T. today because some of the techniques of engineering practice may be different five or ten years hence. Actually, details will change and new elements will be introduced into the picture, but the fundamentals do not change so much, and anyone with the fundamental training can pick up the developments of the next five years with relative ease and in a short time. In any case, an effective army could be mobilized and trained in far shorter time if it drew upon young men who had had the year of military training within the preceding ten years than if the whole military strength had to be built up out of raw recruits after the emergency was upon us.

While I believe that the basic argument for universal military training must be founded upon military value and aimed at national security, there are several educational values which are incidental but which still seem to be of considerable importance. I think, for example, of the concern which has steadily grown over the last twenty years with respect to the undisciplined character of many of our young men, particularly in the big cities and under the influence of the inevitable gangs. Not all boys' gangs are vicious.

Among my prized recollections of boyhood are my adventures as a member of the North End gang of a small city, where I believe that the things which we learned about human nature and team play far overweighed our nuisance value. However, the problem of youth in cities and towns is a serious one, especially since our increased technical productive power has resulted in leaving more and more leisure time. By and large, I believe that a year of military training under good officers and with a sound program could have a very wholesome influence on the succeeding generations of our young men. Since this is an important educational matter, I should like to discuss it in a little more detail as to discipline and ideals.

Discipline: To be a stable and effective citizen requires a nice balance between freedom and initiative on the one hand and discipline on the other. In the modern age we scarcely need to make an argument for freedom and initiative because certainly the youth of our country, by and large, have a great deal of both. The serious question, in fact, is whether they do not have too much freedom and too little discipline to be the most effective possible members of society.

It is only the man who lives entirely alone who has complete personal freedom. Every social contact requires some adjustment, and every effective adjustment is a discipline. I believe that one year in the stage between youth and manhood spent in the universal military training program would develop fundamental habits of promptness and precision. It would develop the ability to work as part of an organization with an attitude of teamwork, which I believe is what is meant by real discipline. A football team, for example, is disciplined down almost to the last reaction and motion. It is trained so that the most fundamental actions are gone through automatically, smoothly, swiftly, and without thought. It is this very discipline and automatic character of action which leaves the football player free to concentrate his attention on the new and unusual factors in the game where quick and intelligent handling determines the success of the play.

Discipline in the sense in which I am using it does not mean subjection of the individual. It means smooth and automatic action by the individual in his routine situation so that he can be free to give attention to the new and unusual problems which may face him. It is this type of discipline which is fundamental in an army and it is this element of training and character which I believe a year of universal military training would strengthen in our oncoming generations of citizens.

Character: If there is one feature which is important above all others in a soldier it is character. This word connotes many qualities, such as skill, accuracy, perseverance, promptness, efficiency, good sportsmanship, fair play, honesty, loyalty, and similar virtues. These are all important attributes of a good soldier. They are therefore, all of them, qualities which a competent program of universal military training would include as objectives in its training program.

Morale: Most important of all to a man, or to an army, or to a country, are the ideals which motivate them. It is these ideals, more than anything else, that determine what is commonly called morale. One of the most important aspects of successful military training, therefore, must be the inculcation of proper ideals. It is these ideals, for example, that a soldier means when he asks, "What am I fighting for?" or tells the world that he is fighting for such and such a cause. The most powerful military weapon ever devised in history has been the cause for which the army has fought. In America this cause would mean all of the things which we prize and cherish in American life and in the American ideal of a land of freedom and opportunity.

This subject of ideals and morale is so important to an army that it would have to be an important concern of those charged with planning and carrying out the program of universal military training. Of course, the background of morale is found in the home and in the public schools and in the church. These are essential and quite basic. Nevertheless, there is surely something which can be gained by a year of concentrated effort in which all the young men of a given age group in the country will be simultaneously working and training together for the basic purpose of defending something greatly important —their country.

Other educational by-products of the universal military training program have to do with literacy, a problem of some magnitude in certain sections, and with physical fitness. These are so obvious that I merely mention them for the record.

Putting all of the above things together, it seems to me that out of a program of universal military training aimed primarily at national security would come secondarily as a by-product an exceedingly valuable and wholesome development of attitude on the part of group after group of oncoming young citizens.

Implementation: Are these educational objectives practically capable of achievement, and if so, by what means? In my judgment all of these objectives are capable of achievement to a very worth-while degree. The procedures for doing this would have to start with the best ideas and experience which can be marshaled at the beginning, and would have to be improved with experience and further constructive study of the problem. The following thoughts are I think pertinent to these questions.

The army has had, during the past four years, some very intensive experience in the art of training. The nation can take justifiable pride in the results. I have personally had opportunity to observe some phases of this training in various army and navy radar schools and also as a member of an advisory committee on the ordnance training program as carried out in various ordnance training centers. I have here seen some very enthusiastic, skillful, and effective teaching. I do not mean to imply that these army methods should revolutionize our general system of education, but I do mean that the army tackled new and specialized educational problems and quickly demonstrated skill, imagination, and effectiveness in handling them. I have been struck with the morale and enthusiasm of both the teachers and the enlisted student personnel.

In my judgment there would be two elements essential to the success of the proposed military training program. The most important of these would be that it be put in the hands of absolutely top-notch officers, all the way from the top command down into the instructing ranks. If this training program were to be used to provide berths for ineffective officers it would be a colossal failure, but in the hands of able and inspiring men it could be an outstanding success. The other point is that the plan should draw upon the best educational talent in the country, both within and without military circles, for initial planning, continued evaluation, and advice.

Timing: I would say a word about the timing of the inauguration of universal military training. On this point I differ with certain of my very esteemed academic colleagues, for I do not believe that consideration of the subject should be postponed until we have settled down to peaceful pursuits after the war. I believe that the soundest decisions are likely to be made in times of stress when we are keyed up to the determination to deliver the best that is in us for a good cause. After every time of stress, whether in an individual or in a national group, there is a time of let down, and this in my judgment is the worst of all times in which to make an important decision, particularly if this decision should call for some exertion and perchance for some sacrifice. I believe, therefore, that the universal military training question should be faced now and not postponed until the time of let down after the war.

Whatever the decision on this question may be, there is one basic thing on which I hope we shall not fail. It is that we should have the courage to do whatever needs to be done after this war to insure, as far as possible and at almost any cost, that still another world war will be made impossible, and that we may strive for this objective with such determination that we shall not allow minor differences of opinion or complications to deter us from the main objective, which is a world with the greatest possible assurance of peace, opportunity, and freedom.

UNIVERSAL MILITARY CONSCRIPTION [4]

The American Legion wholeheartedly endorses the principle of universal military training for the youth of this nation, and we urgently recommend that such a system be placed upon our statute books without delay.

We realize there are organizations and individuals sincerely opposing a system of universal military training. Others oppose it but temporize with majority public sentiment by suggesting "Let's wait until after the war," and still other groups oppose it because they have always opposed this nation's national defense and security. In the latter class I place the pacifist groups and, unfortunately, some educators. I shall take this up in detail a little later in my statement. I used the phrase "majority public sentiment" because I base it upon all the public polls thus far taken.

On November 17, 1943, the Gallup poll announced the results of its survey as compared with 1939, as follows:

		1939	Today
Approve training	per cent	37	63
Disapprove	do	5	8
Undecided	do	5	8

According to the editorial polls of the country, so far as the ladies are concerned, we have picked up 1,005 editorials in the press of which 825 were for universal military training; 165, "No"; and 15 were neutral.

On November 6, 1944, it was announced in the *Washington Post* that a majority of the members of the United States Cham-

[4] Statement of John Thomas Taylor, Director, National Legislative Committee, The American Legion, before the House Select Committee on Postwar Military Policy, June 5, 1945. *Hearings*. p. 35-48.

ber of Commerce favored universal military training; and, on December 4, 1944, a report that 79 out of every 100 persons interviewed favored universal military training was announced by the National Opinion Research Center at Denver University (Colorado). There are others but it is unnecessary to detail them here.

On January 24, twelve American college presidents addressed an open letter to President Roosevelt urging him to reconsider his request that Congress enact during this war a law for universal military training. Their main contention was that it is hoped this is the last war and that we should do nothing to alarm our allies, and that we should wait for calmer times. . . . The open letter received nation-wide publicity and I believe the public may have obtained the impression that American college executives in general are in favor of a waiting policy. This is not the case. A few weeks after the aforementioned letter, fourteen other college heads sent him an open letter taking the opposite view. . . .

Later, the *Washington Times-Herald* published the opinions of 42 college presidents on universal military training and of these 24 favored waiting until after the war, 18 favored adopting such a law now.

It is most regrettable that college executives have seen fit to take such a position publicly because there are those that suggest possibly the educators might have been swayed in judgment by materialistic reasons. The further suggestion is made that the educators fear many boys of 18, finishing high school, and undergoing military training, would not desire to continue in college after the training. Rather than oppose universal military training, the college executives could perhaps increase the 6 per cent of our youth which graduates from colleges each year by making the college course more attractive.

It is needless for me to tell the members of this committee that since its birth in Paris, France, in 1919, the American Legion has labored only for the good of our nation. Legionnaires who fought in 1917-18 learned some harsh lessons. Their experience made them realists. We of the American Legion saw young boys leave their homes, go to camps, see as little as two weeks' training, be shipped overseas, and die on the fields of battle because of lack of knowledge and training which might have saved their lives. That is why the very first national convention of the American Legion recommended a system of universal military training for the United States.

We don't want any more untrained American boys sent to death. Our organization has wholeheartedly and consistently supported a preparedness program for this nation, knowing full well how much it was needed. Our only regret is that some of our proposals on national security and defense were not followed, thus avoiding the wartime costly scramble to make up for years of neglect and delay.

The American Legion prides itself on the recommendations it has made ever since its first caucus and national convention held in 1919 at St. Louis and Minneapolis. Commencing with those meetings and continuing through the years, we have advocated a sound, progressive, and intelligent program of national security. World War I taught the American Legion that war-provoking acts of aggression are likely or unlikely in the ratio to which the peaceful party is prepared to fight.

Our then new organization aided in the preparation of the National Defense Act of 1920 which was adopted by the Congress and approved by the President. However, in subsequent years appropriations were not made to give it effect. The military establishment was steadily reduced and for some years was obliged to exist largely on reserve stocks. Little was done toward replacement or keeping equipment abreast of developments. . . .

Year by year, the military establishment was cut until, instead of the 280,000 enlisted men prescribed by the National Defense Act, the standing army was reduced to the low of 118,750 enlisted men. Whether it was the feeling of confidence inspired by the belief the veterans of the World War were still fit for duty, or a return to the feeling of false security which has been a dangerous American characteristic, the fact remains that the lessons of the war were soon forgotten. The navy fared no better than the army. In a beautiful gesture, we extravagantly scuttled the advantage we had gained as a result of wartime naval construction and proceeded to sink battleships while rival maritime powers sank blueprints. . . .

It has been stated that organized labor will oppose the adoption of a system of universal military training.

The men who do the fighting in time of war are drawn principally from the ranks of the working people. Their families bear the principal burden of taxation and suffer most from the deprivations and hardships that war entails. Universal military training, as advocated by the American Legion, has a threefold objective that should appeal strongly to members of organized labor and other American citizens who earn their bread by toil and sweat. These objectives are:

1. To provide the men who will have to bear arms in time of war with a knowledge of the miltary art which will enable them to carry their country's program to victory and which will also equip them to protect themselves against the weapons and devices of the enemy.

2. To give the country such a strong background for the national defense in the form of trained reserves for the army, navy, and air force that aggressor nations will not dare to wage war against the United States.

3. To aid labor, who must supply the materials for defense; where labor itself knows the need for and the uses of that which they make, there is less difficulty in the making

Members of organized labor, like all loyal American citizens, desire peace. The American Legion, composed of veterans of two great wars, from every class, creed, and race of our citizenry, has declared in favor of an international organization to insure world-wide, long continued peace. Members of the American Legion sincerely believe that had its program of universal military training, put forward at the first Legion convention in 1919, been adopted then, the world would not now be torn by war in every quarter; that a strong United States, cooperating with other strong and civilized powers, could have checked the international outlawry that led to the present conflict. . . .

In this era, when oceans are no longer barriers behind which America can be safe, but highways for the air and sea fleets of the world, America can no longer expect to prepare for war while heroic allies keep the enemy at bay.

If any other war breaks, America will not be given the chance to become again the arsenal of democracy. The Germans made that mistake twice, the Italians and the Japanese once, and neither they nor any future outlaws among the world's family is likely to repeat it. America will be the first target, with air bombs, rockets, and the terrible robots of the future, along with airborne and amphibious troops, bringing the war to our homes, farms, and factories, unless America is so strong in its trained citizen reserves that an attack against us is foredoomed to failure.

Many proposals of this nature have been made, for the drafting of money, property, labor, and fighting men in time of war. The American Legion has long favored some kind of national universal service in time of war only. There has not been, and probably never will be, any proposal for drafting labor in time of peace. That is so contrary to fundamental American tenets as to be unthinkable.

Universal military training, as the Legion urges it for the United States, is for training purposes only. The citizen does not become a part of the regular services, except by voluntary enlistment. He cannot be sent upon expeditions or missions of conquest. His only contact with the regular services is that of training. After completion of his period of intensive training, he is placed in the reserve for a period of about 6 years and can be recalled to active duty only by an act of Congress after declaring a national emergency.

Now, that should dispose of the fear that men in training or in reserve could be used to coerce organized labor in times of industrial strife. These men can be employed in nothing but training during their active year, and they cannot be recalled from the reserve except by Congress after declaration of a national emergency, and it is inconceivable that Congress would declare a national emergency because of a strike or labor disturbance.

Of concrete benefit to organized labor will be the appreciation of organized effort that men will learn during their period of universal military training. Men from "both sides of the railroad tracks" will meet on common ground in the training camps, and the result should be a growing solidarity among

Americans and the gradual effacement of such class distinctions and prejudices as exist today. Young men from the homes of working people will undergo the same drills, eat the same food, sleep in the same beds as the boys from the homes of the well-to-do and the employer. Democracy will be genuinely at work, and the value of teamwork and cooperation will be a daily lesson.

Organized labor need have no fear that men of 18 to 20 years of age will be indoctrinated by a military caste hostile to the interests of working people. Training will be conducted mainly by reserve officers drawn from all levels of society, and the program is confined solely and solidly to military training. There is no time allowed for political or social indoctrination of any nature.

The only fear that organized labor need entertain with respect to universal military training is the fear of the consequences if it is not put into effect. Behind the bulwark of trained citizen reserves for the army, navy, and air force, organized labor will be free to grow and to battle for the rights of its members, safe from the destruction that would certainly be its fate if an invader could land successfully on American soil

The American Legion has in its membership many loyal members of organized labor; also many leaders of organized labor are supporting the American Legion and other proponents of universal military training. . . .

Until World War II had destroyed all previous concepts of international conflict, Americans rightfully thought themselves safe from invasion behind their great ocean barriers. Today, they see those same barriers and the air above them used by Americans to invade not only scores of islets in the far Pacific, but even the Continents of Europe, Africa, and Asia. Millions of our sons, husbands, and brothers have landed through the surf of countless beaches, without benefit of docks, cranes, or any other apparatus formerly considered essential to landing and supplying an invading army. Americans have set a new pattern for war on a grand scale, and Americans would be foolish indeed not to acknowledge that the same feats can be performed by other nations in a future war that will see America standing forth, physically untouched by war's havoc, rich beyond the imagination of war-stricken lands, and a tempting prey to aggressors eyeing the richest war prize in world history. . . .

Universal military training of all young Americans as they reach maturity will provide such preparedness in the form of trained citizen reserves, in numbers so formidable that no aggressor will dare to attack. Unless America is so prepared, the future organization for world peace will degenerate into another debating society, as did the League of Nations, the World Court, and all well-meant efforts of the past to preserve peace among men. America will again be living in a fool's paradise, the awakening from which may cost millions of young American lives and billions of dollars. . . .

The United States Government is taking a leading part in the organization of the future world order—international understanding, upon which a peace of long duration can be founded. The same government is also asking for the enactment of a peacetime program of universal military training. The American Legion supports those efforts. There is nothing inconsistent in these two steps; indeed, one is a part of the other. There is nothing in universal military training that can be considered contrary to any international agreement, existing or proposed, or contrary to any law of God. . . .

American citizens generally and parents, particularly, should support the immediate passage of a universal military training program wholeheartedly for many reasons, including the following:

First. In the event of a future war, it would afford protection to the youth itself.

It is our sad experience that the flower of our youth, as untrained civilians, cannot be sent against adequately trained troops without American youth paying a terrible price in lives. Parents must give serious thought to this phase of a universal military training program. In the past two wars we have had time to prepare while our allies held the enemy in check. Should there be a future war this nation will not have time to prepare. World War II experience with one new weapon—robot bombs—would indicate that. Our geographic location is a protection no longer. Future war lords will realize the United States has saved the world on two occasions and in their planning will try to strike at this nation first.

Second. It strengthens our national defense by providing a trained reserve and would assist materially in our peace aims.

Universal military training would strengthen our national security and our peace aims by displaying to any future war-minded dictator, with designs upon this great nation, that we are not a soft and unprepared people. A strong, prepared United States would do much to discourage the war ambitions of future leaders.

Third. It is the most economic and democratic form of national defense.

The alternative to universal military training and its resultant citizen reserve is a large, costly regular army. Such an army is not consistent with American ideals and thought. Universal military training is the democratic way because it provides an opportunity for each and every youth in this nation to take a great part in assuring national security.

Fourth. Universal military training would provide the trainee with a larger return than the youth would give to his nation.

The benefits to a youth under a universal military training program would include—

(a) Ability to protect himself in an emergency;
(b) Self-reliance;
(c) Promptness;
(d) The ability to accept and give leadership;
(e) Physical fitness;
(f) Respect for authority; and
(g) A keen sense of responsibility to community, state, and nation.

Universal military training will produce a large group of citizens informed in the use of arms for the defense and security of the nation. It will be a force which with the minimum of retraining or refresher courses could be placed in the field to meet an enemy should the need arise.

Such a reserve of trained manpower is vital to a nation which is the richest and most prosperous of all nations and which is certain to be the envy of other nations.

But there are other reasons for a system of training that will affect every citizen. They are reasons more personal, for universal military training will call for sacrifices from a people that are not accustomed to such sacrifices. If every mother is to give her son over to the government for training, if every son is to leave home to obtain that training, they will desire something more evident than national security. Therefore, it is necessary that universal military training will fill other needs as well as national security.

Through a well-planned system of universal military training we can reasonably expect, in addition to national security, an advancement in public and individual health and physical stamina; we can expect a citizenry better prepared in self-discipline; we can look forward to a citizenry more ready to accept the duties of citizenship; we can know there will be better acceptance of the rights of others and less prejudice in race, creed, and social position.

There are other ways by which we can gain many of these advantages but the burning question must be, "Will they be gained by other means?" History of our past national life indicates that they would not be.

For health among our people we must start even before the child is born and carry on through its entire life. But we are a people far from perfect and we are prone to wait until the fault becomes almost a tragedy before remedial steps are taken.

Health examinations in our schools have disclosed infirmities and no steps taken to correct them. Examinations alone will not bring desired changes. Remedial work must be done and this is often neglected. There are few school systems that provide health examinations. Many do not desire to provide them.

Fifth. Legislation providing universal military training must be enacted at once.

There are many who say we should wait until after the war before asking Congress to take action on this proposed legislation. Also, they say we should wait until the members of our armed forces return, so that they may express themselves on this subject. If there is any dissatisfaction among members of our armed forces in connection with preparedness measures, it is because of their realization they are having to pay a heavy price today for unpreparedness. Through actual polls taken of members of our armed forces it has been found that 68 per cent of our fighting men in the European theater are for peacetime universal military training; 69 per cent are for it in the Southwest Pacific theater, 65 per cent in the Central Pacific, and 69 per cent in the American training camps. Approximately 11 per cent stated they had no opinion and 20 per cent voted against the proposal.

It was most interesting to me that the *Washington Times-Herald* of May 23, 1945, carried an article by Frederick C. Othman concerning Technical Sergeant Yake Lindsey, whom all of you gentlemen saw decorated with the Congressional Medal of Honor by President Truman in the House of Representatives.

Sergeant Lindsey was asked if he had any advice for inductees now going overseas. His reply was, "I'd advise them to take advantage of any training they can get before they go overseas. That's the trouble with a lot of our replacements. Not enough training."

UNIVERSAL MILITARY TRAINING PROGRAM [5]

Through the War Department there has been cabled to me your request that I submit to your committee my general views on the universal military training program after the war. In view of the time element, my comments must necessarily be brief and confined almost exclusively to policy as opposed to any specific plan.

[5] Letter from General Dwight D. Eisenhower, Supreme Commander, Allied Expeditionary Force, read before the House Select Committee on Postwar Military Policy, June 15, 1945. *Hearings.* p. 487-8.

There are certain truths which I feel must be widely and definitely understood before any logical approach to this problem is possible. Some that seem most important to me are:

(a) In spite of all technological advances, numbers (great strength in all arms, land, sea, and air) are vitally important in war, and America's approved military system must aim at the rapid development, after the beginning of any serious war, of the country's maximum potentialities in leadership, manpower, equipment, technique, and industrial capacity.

(b) Fairness to the country and to the individual's chances of survival in war demand that each able-bodied citizen receive in time of peace a thorough grounding in technique, discipline, and understanding of the citizen's obligations in time of emergency.

(c) Integration of the means for waging war is vitally essential. There is no such thing as separate land, sea, and air war. We have proved over and over again in Africa and Europe that, through real integration, forces of the several arms and services multiply rather than merely add their separate tactical effects. Organization and training procedure must be such as to provide the necessary specialization in techniques in the army, the navy, and the air forces, all of which must be coequal in the organizational scheme, but must also be such as to facilitate integration.

(d) Efficiency must be attained with maximum economy. This means:

(1) Expensive duplication must be ruthlessly eliminated.

(2) The great forces necessary in war must be produced through a citizen training system in time of peace; that is, with minimum-sized professional nucleus and maximum capacity for training the national manpower. Individuals under training must recognize that the period involved is one of education and training. Pay must be nominal. There must be no attempt to compete with industry in the matter of wages. The training is an obligation to the state and to the individual himself.

Additional comments under lettered subparagraph below apply to similarly lettered paragraphs above.

(a) There would no longer seem to be any reason for arguing the need for numbers in war. In a serious war the quicker the maximum potential can be converted into tactical power the surer the victory and the less the cost. The whole purpose of military preparation—and this is in consonance with every commendable effort to devise a workable organization for world peace—is to develop this maximum, properly balanced and fully efficient, at the earliest possible moment.

(b) The contrasting character of the performance of only partially trained troops on early battlefields of Tunisia and that of thoroughly trained ones on their first entry into the battlefields of Italy and France affords ample proof of the value of effective training prior to entry into battle. This difference is measured both in tactical effectiveness and in loss of life. Training consists of several parts, included in which are:

Technical training.

Physical hardening.

Psychological and moral training.

To realize the purpose of speediest possible development of maximum power, after an emergency, obviously much of this training must be done in peace. Physical hardening will always have to be repeated after the war starts, but takes the least time.

Technical training takes more time, but with individuals graduated from a full course of training before the emergency starts, units with competent leaders will quickly qualify for service.

Psychological indoctrination and moral training requires the longest time—but fortunately it is never completely forgotten. This type of training is of incalculable importance—through it is obtained battlefield discipline, esprit, an understanding of the basic justice of the fight the country is waging, and a proper perspective of the contributions the individual is making to success. An informed, understanding soldier is a good soldier and units composed of such men are effective battle organizations. There is no possibility of overemphasizing the value of intelligent training of this kind.

(c) Integration of the means for waging war is a psychological problem as well as one of mere organization. The national mass, civilians, and the uniformed services, must have a common understanding of the ideals and reasons for which the United States will fight a war, and the training in this regard must be intelligent and incessant. This is the first step toward integration, and one, but only one, of the important reasons for universal service in time of peace. In the fighting services themselves there must be integration of direction and decision that is achieved first in higher organization. I believe there are several methods by which this might be accomplished, but the one vital factor is that there must be one decisive voice at the top who can give his entire time to problems of war direction. This same policy must apply in every major theater of war. Mere integration of war direction, however, is not sufficient. Particularly for the individuals of the professional forces, who must in any event furnish the greater part of the higher tactical and strategical direction of war, there must exist a unification in thought, purpose, and training that must begin in the earliest periods of their service. Every possibility must be exploited to produce mutual understanding, common devotion to a single purpose, and individual and collective friendliness among the whole mass.

(*d*) Always remembering that speed in full mobilization after the war starts is the surest way of minimizing cost, it is obvious that as much as possible of this task must be accomplished in peace. But any attempt to carry out this task through maintenance of large professional forces or of looking upon the individual's training period as anything else but a period of necessary education, would build up the cost so as to be insupportable. The whole concept of organization should be one involving the "citizen forces" idea.

REPORT ON POSTWAR MILITARY POLICY [6]

In the light of these hearings and of the deliberations by its members on this subject, the committee deems the following propositions to be true:

[6] Report submitted July 5, 1945 by Representative Clifton A. Woodrum of Virginia, from the Select Committee on Postwar Military Policy. *Army and Navy Register.* p. 7. July 14, 1945.

1. The eminent position of the United States in the family of nations is supported by her balanced elements of greatness, one of which is commensurate military power.

2. The future security of the United States, as a sovereign nation, depends upon the continuing willingness and ability of our people to protect, by force if necessary, the principles and ideals which inspired the formation of the World Security Organization.

3. Because the success of the World Security Organization will depend upon the continuing efforts and abilities of the member nations to discharge the obligations jointly and mutually undertaken in the United Nations Charter, a retrogression by the United States to her previous state of military unpreparedness would defeat the objects and purposes of peace-loving peoples throughout the world.

4. The retention by the United States of a degree of military power, in being or in reserve, adequate to her needs depends upon several component factors, an indispensable one of which is an alert and trained citizenry capable of prompt mobilization to meet and deal with any national or international emergency.

5. It is traditional in the United States that in time of peace our regular or standing armed forces are reduced to a minimum; that in time of emergency our able-bodied citizens of military age join with the regular forces in bearing arms in the preservation of the national security. This tradition should be maintained and preserved.

6. Future military and naval operations, whether they are to be employed in the defense of the nation against aggression or in the implementation by force of the decisions of the World Security Organization, cannot be conducted effectively by raw recruits or by partially trained men. In view of the technological advances in methods of warfare and of the intricacy of the weapons now in use and to be used, those who will be subject to military service in the future will require thorough training in order to be able to serve their country well and with a reasonable chance of survival.

7. There is no sound or safe basis for assuming that, before a future aggressor strikes, the United States will be given warn-

ing and an adequate interval to train her men and build up her military readiness. Yet the safeguarding of world security, if not the survival of the nation, may well depend on prompt and successful participation by the United States in large-scale military and naval operations.

8. It is not feasible to rest the future security of the United States upon a large standing armed force; its cost would be prohibitive, the necessary men to fill its ranks could not be hired in time of peace, and it would be repugnant to the American people.

A trained citizenry is only one of several elements necessary to a respectable military posture for our nation in the postwar period. A program of continuing scientific research and development, recommended by this committee on May 2, 1945, is likewise a vital element. A state of convertibility of our vast industrial machine to military production should be preserved. We must have a highly trained regular armed force, minimum in size but with modern mobile strength on the ground, on the sea, and in the air. Yet without minimizing the importance of any of these elements, this committee is convinced that the plan for giving adequate military training to all citizens is perhaps the most vital element of all.

Such a plan is in accordance with our best traditions. Such a plan will not change or regiment the character of our citizens or militarize our people. In the present war, long periods of intensive military training have in no degree altered or impaired the free spirit of the American citizen in uniform. Our national freedom has been indissolubly linked with the valiant performance of our citizen-soldier. Upon his swift readiness to serve in the cause of world peace the nation's future welfare rests. But the time when the citizen could overnight spring to arms, and fight, and win, is gone. Nor can he depend on another training interval bought with the blood and substance of allies conveniently placed in the aggressors' path. He deserves a right to prepare himself to serve, when and if future need should come, with all the skill in modern methods of warfare that timely and intensive training can provide.

For these and for other reasons your committee, therefore, recommends that the Congress adopt, as a matter of broad policy, a system of universal military training for the critical years ahead. While the committee has limited its consideration to questions of broad policy and has refrained from particular consideration of the ways and means in which such a policy would be put into effect, nevertheless, there are certain convictions which the members of the committee share, derived from the testimony of various groups, which are submitted to the Congress in the hope that they will be of assistance to the Committee on Military Affairs and to the Members of Congress in their consideration of specific legislation on the subject.

Your committee recommends that, in any system of universal military training provided by law, full consideration should be given to these features:

1. It should be designed primarily to train men for military service under conditions of modern warfare.

2. It should conform in its details with the requirements shown by experience in this war and by future technological developments, to be necessary to prepare men to serve in the armed forces effectively.

3. It should be universal and democratic, applicable to rich and poor alike, and with a minimum of exemptions or exceptions.

4. It should be fitted into the existing structure of the military and naval establishments as provided for in the National Defense Act of 1920 and other existing legislation or into that structure as hereafter modified by this Congress.

5. It should be made to conform with and preserve the position now held by the National Guard, Reserve Corps, Enlisted Reserves, Naval Reserves, and Naval Militia.

6. It should provide for training of men in youth in such a manner as to cause least interference with their normal education and careers.

7. It should provide for training only and should not require any character of military service. Service would be required only in the event Congress should in the future order conscription to meet a national emergency.

In this connection, the committee would like to emphasize the distinction between "peacetime conscription," a term so frequently used by opponents of this proposal, and "universal military training," the proposal under consideration. In order that there may be no doubt as to what is in the minds of the armed services, the committee herewith quotes verbatim from the statement filed with the committee by Major General William F.

Tompkins, of the General Staff of the War Department, on that subject:

> From a planning standpoint the War Department wants to make it crystal clear to this committee that it does not recommend or desire that trainees be inducted into the army for military service. They should be inducted into training organizations for training purposes only. When the year of training is complete, it is recommended that graduate trainees become members of the Enlisted Reserve Corps of the Army for a period of 5 years, but during that time they are not to be subject to any further compulsory training or service except in the event of a national emergency declared by the Congress.

Your committee further recommends that the Congress give the subject of this report prompt and thorough consideration, with a view to determining what course of action should be followed in this particular. It is manifest that those who are charged with the responsibility of planning the composition of the nation's military and naval establishments will be severely handicapped unless and until the Congress, by appropriate enactment, defines the future policy and thus lays the predicate for an orderly transition from the wartime to the peacetime military organizations. Moreover, your committee is convinced that timely adoption of the principle will provide assurance to the United Nations that this nation expects to retain the necessary military strength to stand behind and make to work the idealism which has inspired the Dumbarton Oaks and the World Security Conferences.

POSTWAR MILITARY POLICY [7]

The problem of the maintenance of the future peace of the world directly involves the problem of the postwar military policy of the United States. The decision regarding the military policy of the United States is directly related to the democratic processes of the government, really meaning the reactions of the people to the services the individual citizen might be required to render the government.

[7] Statement of General George C. Marshall, Chief of Staff, United States Army, before the House Select Committee on Postwar Military Policy, June 16, 1945. *Hearings.* p. 567-71.

Another factor is heavily though indirectly involved and that is consideration of the taxes to be imposed on the citizen for the maintenance of the military policy, to which must be added the very positive reaction of the citizen regarding the taxes to which he must submit to meet the huge existing war debt.

Any fixed legal demand on the citizen for services to the community, the state, or the Federal Government, is quite naturally questioned by the majority and is usually bitterly opposed by at least an articulate minority.

The question of universal military training involves all of the foregoing factors, and the great difficulty as I see it, in reaching a correct decision, will be to avoid details and to get clearly focused in our minds what are the real necessities of the situation, and what will be the best method for meeting them, having in mind our traditions, our national characteristics and the military experience of this government during its short life of 156 years among the nations of the world.

I think it would be best for me to state in the briefest possible form my own personal conclusions in the matter, which are as follows:

A decision regarding the general military policy of this government is a matter of urgent necessity at this time.

A large standing army is not an acceptable solution for three reasons: Its cost would be prohibitive; the necessary men to fill its ranks could not be hired in time of peace; and it would be repugnant to the American people. Therefore some other solution must be found.

To support our determination to maintain the peace, the world must recognize our military powers as realistic and not as a remote potential.

Whatever military system we plan we must have a thorough understanding of the practicability of obtaining the annual appropriations necessary.

I know of no system other than universal military training that will meet the requirements I have just outlined, together with an effective program for industrial mobilization and continuous scientific research.

Until the settlement of the terms of the peace it will be impossible to determine the strength of the postwar military forces to be maintained on an active status. We shall not know until then just what our military obligations or requirements are to be. But it is clear to me that whatever the terms of peace, the fundamental basis of our defense must be universal military training. No other practical solution has been offered.

The acceptance at the present time of a general policy recognizing the necessity for universal military training would in my opinion have a far-reaching effect in obtaining a satisfactory international agreement for the terms of the peace. It would certainly be in keeping with the tragic lessons of our history. It would be a supremely democratic procedure, and would not involve the individual in military service except by further act of Congress and approval of the President. It would be far more economical than any other method for maintaining military power. If we are to have an effective and economical transition from our vast war establishment to our peace establishment, we must now decide on the fundamental basis on which we are to proceed. . . .

It appears to me that those who object to compulsory military training have offered no practical solution for obtaining what is in all our minds today, and that is some guaranty for the future peace of the world.

Whether or not army training methods would have an unfortunate influence on the individual can be determined I think from the experience of this war. I assert that we have produced a democratic army, one composed of self-respecting soldiers whose spirit has not been crushed and who have shown splendid evidences of high morale. I submit that the army has demonstrated that it can efficiently and expeditiously instruct men and that it does this without detriment to the mind and character of the individual, rather the contrary. I firmly believe that universal training would be a stimulant to education rather than a deterrent. It would be a perfect demonstration of democracy, with rich and poor alike, side by side, rendering a common service.

CHAIRMAN WOODRUM: General, we appreciate very much that statement, and, if you do not object, I would like to ask you to elaborate just a little on one very significant statement . . . to the effect that, "The acceptance at the present time of a general policy recognizing the necessity for universal military training would in my opinion have a far-reaching effect in obtaining a satisfactory international agreement for the terms of the peace."

Now, any number of individuals and organizations appearing before this committee have insisted that any action now, and even any discussion now of military preparedness in the postwar period, would indicate our lack of faith and confidence in the efforts made to build a world organization for peace; that it would be an overt act in the minds of other nations of the earth, and that it probably would lead us into difficulties.

Now, the committee of course knows that, above most other American citizens, you not only have had such a rich experience in your high capacity as Chief of Staff, but have been present at any number of these international conferences and have had an opportunity to contact personally the leaders of other nations.

I wish that you would elaborate just a little on that statement and tell us what you think of the logic of such form of reasoning.

GENERAL MARSHALL: Mr. Woodrum, I realize that from a certain point of view I am stepping a little out of my purely military status as Chief of Staff. However, as you have just said, during the past three years it has been given to me to have many opportunities for dealing with—not only meeting, but directly dealing with—a great many of the senior officials of the various governments of the Allies.

My own reaction to the statement that you make of those who fear that some such action by this country would defeat, rather than assist us, in obtaining the character of peace that we would want—my own reaction is exactly the opposite to that.

In many conversations I have had with officials, leading officials of other countries, I find always the fear that we will withdraw into our shell and at the same time endeavor, as they put it, to inflict on the world an idealistic policy without, on our own part, showing any basis for maintaining or backing up such policy of idealism.

It seems to me very clear that if the United States takes a leading part, as I presume it will, in at least proposing stipulations and terms for the final peace, we must either depend completely on a new, and I might well say, unheard-of idealism among European nations or we must be prepared to back up what we put into the terms of the peace.

I am convinced, in my own mind, that it would have a most beneficial effect for the other Allied nations to see that we mean most seriously to endorse our proposals of the terms of peace to our best ability.

I am in no doubt whatever, in the matter. I do not believe at all that it would harm us, and I think, to the contrary, it would greatly assist us. That, I might say, I find to be the opinion of practically everyone that I have discussed this with in the State Department. Certainly it is the unanimity of opinion of my associates who have been with me in most of these conferences. I am not confining myself to just those particular meetings in which the Chiefs of Staff participated; I have in mind many other meetings with groups through all Latin America, as well as in Europe.

I suppose this particular aspect of the problem has been referred to at these hearings many times, but nations, I think, as shown by history and certainly as evidenced to me in this tragic past three years, are very realistic; exceedingly, uncompromisingly realistic. And when it comes to their own interests, and when it comes to the part that we may play in connection with their own interests, they are decidedly skeptical of the purely idealistic point of view.

We have, I think, one asset—a tremendous asset—and that is, throughout the world no one charges us with wanting anything of anybody else's. That is a rather poorly expressed thought, but I am sure you understand my meaning.

They think that we are wholly unselfish in those respects. They also feel, I am quite certain, that we are very determined about our ideas and conceptions when we participate in an international conference. Yet they are somewhat fearful of the commitments that we may insist on their becoming a party to, unless it is shown that we, ourselves, are determined to live up to those commitments with more than lip service. In international matters, our ability to live up to these commitments is gaged frankly by our power to do so.

But as to our use, possible use or misuse of military power, whatever it might be in the future, I don't think anyone is at all fearful; no one is fearful of our misuse of it. That is perhaps the greatest asset we possess in such negotiations.

The weakness in our position is the international fear that we will insist on too idealistic a solution and at the same time decline to maintain the power to back up what we may demand of others in an agreement.

CHAIRMAN WOODRUM: General, if I may follow this with one other question: We assume that our national policy, as well as our high hopes and fervent prayers, support the establishment of a world organization that will minimize and, if possible, prevent future wars; if we may assume that, in addition thereto—or rather to implement that policy—it is going to be necessary for us to have a very much larger military establishment in the postwar period than we have had in the past, then as I understand your statement, we are confronted with the alternatives of either a larger standing professional army or this means of raising the reserve.

Now, would you say just a word on that.

GENERAL MARSHALL: I don't think that is quite an accurate statement of my point of view, Mr. Chairman, for this reason: I regard a large standing army as an impossibility, frankly, both from the standpoint of obtaining the personnel in time of peace, and—of course this is your side of it—because of the repugnance of our people toward a large standing force. I don't think you could raise a large standing army in time of peace, nor do I think you could possibly afford it, unless you go far deeper into our financial resources than the American people would permit. That leaves us with just one course for the rapid creation of a trained dependable organization, universal military training.

I will repeat that, perhaps in better English: I think a large standing army is not of the question. Even though you were to recommend it here, I think you would find it would be an impracticable proposition. I think I can speak with some authority on the matter of obtaining men for such an army, because I have been on that end of it most of my life. You cannot obtain many men in time of peace, except maybe in the midst of a tragic depression, and even then you do not get exactly what you want.

So, the problem boils down to some system that is within our financial possibilities and still is an acceptable procedure. Other than a large standing army, I know of no other system except one based fundamentally on universal military training. In other words, if you do not have that, you cannot, in my opinion, expect to maintain before the world a respectable military posture, and you must go ahead on the basis that we went before; that is, on the hope, the slender hope, that we will again be given time, and a long time, to organize an army.

As you know, I went through all the long agony of the creation of the present armies and the losses that we suffered during that period of delay. I remember the close calls that we had, which might well have been tragic in their consequence to this country.

I hesitate to emphasize the thought that we will not again be given that opportunity because it has been said often, but I think you have to face frankly two things: Either universal military training or the hope—that is all you can possibly have—the hope that you will have better than a year for preparation. Of course, if you decide to repeat the policies of the past and rest our security on a hope, it means that your lack of readiness would, in my opinion, encourage the very thing you wish so earnestly to avoid.

I might add one further comment: From the viewpoint of the Japanese rather than the Germans, I have come to the conclusion—that they were seriously misled, and to that extent encouraged into this war, by hearing so much of the views or statements of our young men in college that "they were not going to fight," and that "they would not participate in any other war even in defense of their country."

To the Japanese, hungering for the riches of China and Malasia, that was almost an invitation to war, and they accepted it.

FOR MILITARY TRAINING [8]

In consideration of the debate about the desirability for universal military training, too little attention, it seems to me, is given to the essential fairness of the proposal. Whatever the temporary inconvenience or minor sacrifice in the individual case or the necessity for readjustments upon us collectively, it is far more just that some responsibility for the maintenance of free institutions should be laid successively upon each generation for a brief time than that periodically every few decades the tragedy of war should be imposed for half decades or more upon generations contemporaneous with the respective emergencies.

I do not assume that permanent immunity from war can be made completely certain whatever we do. On the basis, however, of some continuing contacts with sentiment abroad through the years since World War I, I am fully persuaded that a well-devised and intelligently established system of universal military training would be in very large degree insurance against the frequency of war and might be more. I cannot think of any proposition that I should not consider imperative that decreased in slightest degree the hazard of war or even increased the span of time between one war and another.

I want a system of universal military training established in the United States because I believe it would make wars less likely. . . .

It has been estimated by military authorities that Nazism could have been stopped at the time of the invasion of the Rhineland at a cost of a few hundred casualties at the most, and at the boundaries of Austria at a cost of a few thousand, had organization and will existed among peace-loving nations to have undertaken resistance then. I once asked a distinguished American in the government whether any resistance on those occasions had been considered. "With what?" he replied. "Neither the United States nor England had trained men, matériel or convictions in those years."

[8] By Ernest M. Hopkins, President, Dartmouth College. *Dartmouth Alumni Magazine.* 37 no.9:15. June 1945. Reprinted from the *New York Times.* p. 8E, May 6, 1945.

It isn't reassuring to reflect what would be our situation at the present time if any one of numberless things hadn't occurred, particularly England's dogged and exhausting defense while we slowly came to understanding of what the war was all about; or Russia's entry into the war and her valor in it while we slowly got under way. If we in opulence, inertia and self-righteousness withhold from preparedness for a possible World War III, we will invite it. And when it strikes with robot bombs, rocket guns and all that developing scientific research can afford an aggressor in years to come, its resemblance to Pearl Harbor will be analogous to that of a modern B-29 air attack as compared with a movie representation of an Indian attack on a frontier settlement.

But some one says, "Possibly so, but what does that prove about universal military training?" "Everything," in my belief. The circumstances of modern life demand elimination of any time lag as a factor in preparedness. The measure of our defense will be the extent not only of our provision for war but also of our readiness for it for long time to come, except for agreement more binding than anything now in sight.

Public sentiment in Europe as I saw it in the two decades following World War I offered many warnings of on-rushing tragedy. Increasing year by year subsequent to our refusal to enter the League of Nations the insistent belief cumulatively developed among the peoples of the Continent that the United States not only would not take any responsibility to support the peace-loving nations of the world but that on the contrary we were so confident of our immunity from attack that we believed we could safely accept the hazard of doing nothing to defend ourselves against possible aggression. In 1934-35 this was particularly so not only among the Germans and the Italians but also among the French. German university men, students and graduates, stated frankly that the Reich was about ready to take over supremacy in Europe and Italian Fascist officers boasted of what they were going to do in making the Mediterranean Sea their own exclusive lake. Again and again I asked whether there was no concern at all among them about public sentiment in England and America. With no single exception that I can remember was the question answered with anything except amused tolerance among those most friendly or derisive comments among others as to the lack of public spirit and of virility in the soft and effete democracies.

In Rome a Fascist officer in Mussolini's personal guard told me of voluminous reports of Fascist agents in the United States that the churches were all so anti-militaristic that we would not be able to undertake any preparation for war unless we were attacked, when it would have come too late for us to accomplish anything. At Taormina young German officers, some educated in this country and others in England, assured me that their Secret Service reports showed that schools and colleges in these countries, were almost completely dominated by pacifist sentiment, whether in faculties or student bodies. All cited the Oxford Oath against war as representative of the sentiment of youth in both countries. It was futile to explain to them the casual irresponsibility with which in democracies our student bodies were prone to issue dogmatic statements on questions such as this. It would have been a greater waste of time and breath to have told them where these self-same boys would be found when they should eventually come to realistic understanding of the truth.

The most revealing experience of all to me as to what our attitude was doing to jeopardize our own safety eventually as well as to invite disaster to the rest of the world came in France early in 1935. In conversation with the spokesman of a brilliant group of young physicians, himself a distinguished veteran of World War I and neither rightist nor leftist in sympathies but inclined to lean toward the Popular Front, he said nevertheless that common sentiment held that France had been deserted and betrayed since Versailles by both England and America, that she was defenseless against Germany, and that many believed there was no hope for her except in an alliance with Russia or Germany. Personally he was inclined to think Germany the safer choice. He read me letters to the same effect from other veterans of World War I written to him in great concern as to the trend of public thought. Many of the letters bespoke not only distrust of but antagonism towards the United States and England. "The United States," he said, "if in the League could with England have assured peace in Europe and given France safety. We were led to rely on that. As it is, our only hope of security is not to offend Germany." Then sadly came the conclusion of the whole affair as far as he and his friends were concerned. "Public sentiment being what it is, if some one on a white horse were to ride through the gates of Paris tomorrow, the world would be astonished at the following that would turn out to accept leadership from him." He begged me to make these facts clear to my friends at home.

Again I seem to hear the comment, "But what does all this have to do with universal military training?" Again I answer, "Everything." Any disposition in America towards preparedness would have given Germany and Italy pause and France reassurance. I would at this point, listening to the arguments of those who oppose universal military training, freely grant, as I have stated before, that wars may still be a possibility after a postwar organization for the maintenance of peace is set up. Words will not necessarily preclude war. An organization in which the great powers sit together in continuous session to smooth out differences and to try to maintain peace will be a long step towards eliminating some of the hazards that lead to war. As such it is imperative but it can never in itself be a complete barrier. All available additional insurance against war must be taken out likewise and such insurance could be a population which had been wholly conditioned in body, mind and spirit to the idea that it could have just as much freedom as it was willing to defend, and no more. No such conditioning has been existent for years in the American home, church or school. This, it may be assumed, has something to do with the fact that we have had to fight two wars in less than three decades. There is Scriptural basis for the argument that under certain conditions lives can be saved only by willingness to lose them; somewhat in analogy, frequently ideals can be saved only by willingness to forego them. This is the answer to be made, it seems to me, to those who argue that because San Francisco is designed to lead the mind of the world toward peace, we should forego any organization internally that would make force available to us to protect ourselves against war if it should threaten.

Regarding the arguments of those who say that universal military training will jeopardize the efforts toward setting up a peace organization, let us not ignore the fact that the idealists have had their day—that the League of Nations, the Disarmament Conference, and other such movements were all patterned on the premise that the world had reached a sufficient stage of civilization so that in the future wars would be outlawed. Subsequent events have proved how false that assumption was. Therefore, until such time as the *whole* world has been educated to the belief and is ready to accept the ideal of enduring peace, it is going to be the responsibility of the peace-loving nations to maintain the peace even by utilization of amply equipped force, if necessary.

People ask me as a college officer if universal training would not disorganize college procedures. The answer of course is "yes." However, the problems of reorganizing life in the college, the home or the community do not interest me in slightest degree beside the possibility that a system of universal military training might save our youth from suffering and dying in war a quarter of a century from now. Neither does the plaint that a year of public service of this sort will do violence to scientific research or industrial development or labor organization or budding artistic genius. None of these impulses are as easily blighted as such complaints would imply to be the fact.

The proposal for universal military training is a proposition purely and simply to enhance the military security of our people. Its alternative is a huge standing army for years to come. Protection in one way or another must be given against the necessity of becoming involved in wars engendered by those who may in the future believe, as has been believed twice in our time, that our unpreparedness made it safe to violate every principle in which we believe. Moreover, the proposal to my mind is valueless except as it envisages military training exclusively. Valuable by-products doubtless would accrue to the individual and to society from establishment of the proposition, but military security for the American people in the enhanced possibility of escaping future wars must be the one all-inclusive purpose of such a proj ect. Any considerable attention to any other purpose than meeting military necessity would render the plan wasteful and futile.

Finally, for those who fear the effect of the proposal upon the spirit of democracy, the plan seems to me to embody the very essence of democracy in imposing alike upon all equal responsibility for the maintenance of the democratic state and the freedoms they derive from this. It is possible of course to summon up a host of hypothetical assumptions that this, that or the other thing might work out badly. Any project new in a given circumstance is subject to such attack. Rationalization in regard to untried conditions can always evoke a multitude of reasons why they should not be undertaken. There unquestionably would be some inconvenience and some disappointments involved in the readjustments of such a plan. I grant it. But my eye turns to the pages of fine print in the *Times* by my chair,—the headings are "Dead," "Wounded," "Missing." After this I am not interested in the inconveniences to be met by institutions or individuals. I do not care how great the problems of readjustments may be in the fields of learning, labor or management. I am not even concerned over possible changes in our form of government if freedom be safeguarded or whether our taxes be greater or less. The only thing that seems to me of the slightest consequence in the world is that boys like these shall not again have to walk this Gethsemane,—that these pages of fine print shall never again have to be published. A nation-wide preparedness to such extent as universal military training would provide might make such possibilities into probabilities. I pray it may be tried.

UNIVERSAL MILITARY TRAINING [9]

The security of the nation is a continuous matter. Universal military training, involving as it does a fundamental change in the principles underlying mobilization of the nation's forces in time of wars, is deserving of the most careful advance planning.

A system of universal military training should become operative upon the termination of selective service in the present

[9] By Captain Myron W. Curzon, United States Army. *Cavalry Journal*. p. 69-71. July-August 1945.

emergency. If this is not done, there will be large numbers of men of military age, subject to call in time of emergency, who will not have had the opportunity for receiving this training, and hence will not be ready for immediate military employment. Nothing [less] fair nor less democratic can be imagined than to rest the future security of America on the same heroic men and women who are sacrificing so much to win victory in this war. Millions of these citizens have already been under arms and absent from their normal civilian pursuits, many of them overseas, for three or four years. Surely, our country will not take the ungrateful position that, because some of these veterans may be technically in a reserve status for some years after the war, they and they alone should compose our military reserves in future years.

Unless the program is in effect at the termination of selective service, the army will lose the current "going concern value" of its vast physical organization and establishment. The cost to the nation will be almost prohibitive, if all this value is to be junked; camps, aircraft, and equipment are to be allowed to deteriorate, only to have to be reestablished and built up again in part several years thereafter.

Our adoption of the program now would not be without significance in world affairs. We must encourage all nations to believe that we take seriously our responsibility in the plans which are being sponsored for a peaceful world. Collective security agreements will progress exactly as far as the extent to which the United States participates in such agreements. It would strengthen our hand at the peace table through showing to all allies—strong and weak—that we are a united nation; that we are determined at once to be militarily strong and to remain true to our democratic traditions, a combination which the real friends of democracy everywhere would welcome in the world's foremost exponent of the democratic way of life. . . .

Our training efforts in this war have been directed toward two different but related goals—unit training and replacement training. Unit training, designed to produce units capable of being committed to combat, requires that the soldier first be basically trained and made proficient as an individual, and then that he be trained as a member of a team.

Replacement training, on the other hand, is designed to produce a basically trained individual soldier, proficient in the use of his weapons and trained in elementary squad and platoon tactics to the extent necessary for him to fit into the highly trained veteran team. The replacement who joins a unit made up of experienced soldiers depends upon their skill and guidance for his final training on the job. Graduates of a universal military training program will be the men who, in the event of war, will constitute new units.

The contemplated program for universal military training parallels the present program for large unit training. It will produce divisions, air forces groups, and other large units in the shortest time upon mobilization. It will develop leaders and commanders trained in handling men, weapons and supplies. It will provide a reserve of specialists and technicians trained to fill key positions in units.

The program is far more than a mere schedule of hours, days, weeks and months. It is a carefully integrated 52 weeks of progressive training. All young men would pursue the same course in basic soldiery. This is a foundation of but a few weeks. With this as a start, the young man would be assigned to learn technical subjects which will fit him as one of the hundreds of specialists required in modern armed forces. Curricula and methods of instruction will be modified as changes in training procedure may be indicated as a result of research.

At the conclusion of his training as an individual specialist, he applies this training as a member of a small team, continues it as a member of a large team, and in the last weeks, applies it in large-scale maneuvers. The 52 weeks are divided into five well-defined phases, in each of which training is progressively applied to the end that at the conclusion of the course, the training will stick with the trainee for a long enough time to enable him to rejoin the armed forces upon a declaration of a national emergency by the Congress with a minimum of refresher training, and [he] can take his place on the same kind of team for which he was trained.

When it is considered that the young men to be trained will be preparing to participate in complex warfare against trained adversaries, there should be no disposition to reduce the training period below the minimum essential to do it effectively. In one year, we can train them with sufficient thoroughness to insure that, even though the emergency should arise some years after the completion of their training, the essential knowledge and skills acquired in training will be retained. Less than one year of training would necessitate shortcuts and omissions that would dangerously decrease the value of the trainees as soldiers and would correspondingly increase the hazard of combat to themselves.

The training should be conducted continuously for twelve months. Interruptions will impair the effectiveness of the military instruction on which the fate of our nation may some day depend. If piecemeal military instruction is completed with approximately the same thoroughness, it will require additional time. At the beginning of each period of training, time would be lost in examining, classifying, and reconditioning the trainees. Instruction partially assimilated and insufficiently practiced would require repetition.

From the standpoint of military training, then, and of the taxpayer, who deserves full value for his money, the weakness of a series of short snatches of training is apparent.

Basic military training cannot be effectively conducted in the classrooms and on the campuses of our schools and colleges. The soldier must learn to live and do his work in the field. The large and unrestricted areas of varied terrain necessary to effective basic training cannot be provided in the vicinity of our colleges. The numerous firing ranges, with their extensive danger zones, as well as many other necessary training aids, are not suited to the college environment. It would not be possible to assemble and maintain at any college the wide variety of weapons and equipment required in the combined training that has become absolutely essential to effective preparation for modern war.

It is entirely practicable to conduct effective officer training in the colleges and universities provided that the candidates are basically trained soldiers when they arrive. With universal military training completed prior to the enrollment of students in college, we shall be able for the first time to raise the Reserve Officers Training Corps courses to a real collegiate level. The graduates of the Reserve Officers Training Corps will then constitute a more competent group of junior leaders than ever have been available to the reserve components of our army.

It is obvious from the foregoing that if the program is to provide a reservoir of men adequately trained for the protection of the country, the training should be for one year, should be continuous, and should be conducted in army camps and training centers. . . .

The cost of universal military training and of other provisions necessary to the security of the country must be borne. This cost will constitute insurance against, or will reduce the cost of future wars. This is greatly to be preferred to the dangerous policy of the past, by which we have risked our nation and have incurred, during a few years of war, great costs because all considerations automatically become secondary to that of winning the final victory.

THE FIRST REQUIREMENT OF A CITIZEN ARMY [10]

Universal service, including military training of all suitable young men between the ages of 19 and 22, would be approved probably, by the majority of our people at this time. So far, so good. General Palmer says, however [in the *Saturday Evening Post* for December 23, 1944], that the army of the future would be composed of a "relatively small regular army," reinforced when necessary from a "great citizen army reserve composed of trained citizen officers and soldiers." He states many times in his article that highly trained professional officers would be necessary in sufficient numbers to leaven the whole when it became necessary to expand the army to moderate or great proportions. It is not explained just how these highly trained professional officers would be obtained in sufficient numbers. What number would be considered sufficient?

[10] By Brigadier General Hamilton S. Hawkins, United States Army. *Cavalry Journal.* 54:38-40. January-February 1945.

A man cannot become a highly trained professional officer simply by going for a few years through the course at a military school. The school is the A B C of his training. After graduation in such a school he needs experience in handling troops. He needs experience in training and leading small units, then larger units, and then great units. Staff officers also need both schooling and practice. The training of a professional officer never ends during his entire active service. He must keep abreast of the changes wrought by new weapons, new inventions and new ideas. And experience through all the grades of rank is desirable if not always possible.

It would be impossible for the regular officer to obtain this training and this experience unless he has many opportunities to serve with troops and in staff work. There must be enough troops in the regular army to afford the necessary training and experience for a "sufficient number of professional officers." If a great proportion of the professional officers spend most of their time in supervising the basic training of groups of the citizen army reserves, they will never become highly trained officers. They need training in leadership of well trained regular units up as high, certainly, as the regiment. They need to particpate in many tactical exercises for all these units.

The regular units themselves need to be trained, and to be fully officered and fully manned in order to give regular officers the necessary experience. Otherwise, when regular officers are training the citizen reserves it will be the blind leading the blind.

The size of the regular army must, therefore, be predicated upon the number of troops necessary in the regular army to give this experience-training to a sufficient number of professional officers. First of all, however, an estimate must be made of the number of professional officers needed.

Now, if universal service is established, a great number of regular officers of lower grades—trained in the regular army, not merely in schools—will be necessary to supervise the elementary training of the citizen officers and soldiers. Therefore, many more professional officers will be needed than merely those required to officer fully all the units in the regular army. These regular units must be fully officered at all times. They must not be left to do the best they can with insufficient officers and men in the units. The units must be kept at war strength. Otherwise, the training of officers and noncommissioned officers in the army will not only be insufficient, but absolutely wrong or false in many respects.

During the years after World War I, and up to World War II, the regular officers were dispersed among the Organized Reserves, the R.O.T.C., and the National Guard, to such an extent that the regular units in the army were pitifully under-officered. The policy was to let them "get along" with far too few officers to carry out properly a tactical exercise of the simplest character. Of course, the army did not have the necessary number of men either. Both were necessary. The result was that many officers got no troop training for periods of ten and fifteen successive years at a time.

If this plan of a citizen army and universal training is to be a success, these problems must be solved or the people will be deceived as to the competence of the professional officer and the correctness of the training he is giving to the citizen soldiers and officers.

Training citizen soldiers in basic courses for the individual will not require the highest order of professional ability and knowledge. But leading those soldiers in collective training and battle is another matter. The professional officer must know far more than how to train recruits individually.

The training of the officers of the citizen army, who are not professional officers, presents still another problem. Our system for training reserve officers during the twenty-odd years after 1918 did not work out too well. The best part of it was found in the R.O.T.C. which provided for military training of young men in colleges and schools. But these schools did not always go about it with enthusiasm. The time devoted to it was much too small, and the number of students so trained was very limited. Military training in all high schools, academies and colleges should be compulsory for all students. The graduates of colleges who have qualified for commissions as officers in the reserve army must also be required to devote several years of their lives to the basic training of the citizen soldiers in local units.

If this is not done, too many regular officers will be required for citizen training, and this will interfere too much with their own training in the regular army. As stated before, such was the case in the twenty-year period after World War I, even though the number of reserve officers and soldiers receiving training was many times less than is contemplated in the universal service idea.

Furthermore, the training of students in schools for qualification as reserve officers is not enough. These young men will need the additional training and experience that will be afforded by their assignment to duty as officers of the local units of citizen soldiers. Thus it appears that drastic changes in the training of our citizen officers must be adopted if the universal service plan is put into effect.

It becomes more apparent, therefore, that the universal service idea does not mean that we shall be able to "get along," with a small regular army. It may be true that, as General Palmer says, a *relatively* small regular army may be sufficient. But, as compared with our ideas of the past, the regular army must be very large. A sufficient number of "highly trained professional officers" is not to be obtained by our methods of the last quarter of a century.

One of General Palmer's ideas is that the citizen army plan, based on universal service, will enable us to put a trained army in the field in much less time than ever before. No doubt this is true—but even a comparatively small expeditionary force would require valuable time to organize and be made ready. A sufficiently large regular army from which such a force could be drawn instantly is necessary if such a force is not to be "too little and too late."

Any force of any size, needed in the field at once, must be a trained force. Then while that force is carrying out its mission in the field, a sufficient number of the local units of the citizen army can be concentrated and organized into predetermined large units commanded and staffed mostly by officers drawn from the Regular Army, the National Guard, and the most experienced officers of the Reserve Officer's Corps. With the soldiers already fairly trained, the large units can be made ready for the field in about one-sixth the time it has heretofore taken to activate and train a large army. This, of course, could be done only if equipment earmarked for the contemplated units has been kept up to date in various conveniently located store houses.

Now, the principal difference between this Citizen Army Plan and the Expansible Regular Army Plan is that, in the former plan, there would be universal service and predetermined units into which the citizen soldiers would be placed; and in the latter plan, there would be no universal service and, therefore, no large citizen corps of trained officers and soldiers to call upon for immediate service.

In both plans, a regular army larger than we have ever had before is necessary.

And so, by all means, let us have universal service. By all means, let us have General Marshall's citizen army as advocated by General Palmer—if the plan includes a regular army large enough to produce highly trained professional officers in such numbers as may be determined necessary by a careful study of the subject.

Certainly, the futile system used for twenty-odd years after 1918 should not be perpetuated nor duplicated. In that system a number of officers were trained fairly well for staff duty, but very few regular officers had enough service with troops. Even when they were assigned to troop duty they found the ranks so depleted of soldiers that they could not, in most instances, begin to gain the experience and practice in troop leadership that they sorely needed. To fit an officer for combat leadership, he should have for some years experience in command of small combat units. He should not skip over this training. It is most important if he expects ever to be a competent leader of large combat units. In the past, many officers have attained high rank and have been assigned to command large units—from a regiment up to an army—without having had any really sufficient training in command of a platoon, a company or battalion of combat troops. The results have not been fortunate.

An officer who took the courses in a Special Service School, the so-called Command and General Staff School, and the War

College was deemed a trained officer, whether he had had long experience with troops or not. Most of them had not had such experience.

Universal service without a proper system for training professional officers is only a half measure. It is not necessary to have a standing army large enough to fight a serious war by itself. But it is necessary to have an army large enough to train professional officers with full strength units. To have a standing army which is not adequate for that purpose is to waste at least half of the money that supports it.

A SOLDIER'S SLANT ON COMPULSORY TRAINING [11]

Some nine or ten years ago I was a member of a not unduly disreputable group of young men who, standing in massed solemnity on a college campus, loudly took the Oxford Pledge. By doing so, we committed ourselves with rather heady optimism to nonparticipation in any war. We were not mere conscientious objectors. We were conscious and vociferous objectors. We were so aggressively isolationist that it is embarrassing to recall.

At the time we thus adolescently divorced ourselves from the course of history, Hitler had been in power for a couple of years. Many of us, however, hadn't the slightest notion of the personal implications of his ascendancy. The Japs, at that same time, were not exactly holding hands with the Chinese, but the Orient was considerably beyond our limited perspective. We were the boys who couldn't see the trees *or* the forest. Perhaps our high-priced education failed to give us the full value we had bargained for, but it doesn't much matter now whether we or our teachers were principally to blame for our foolishness. The fact that we were able to feel the way we did does matter.

I am thinking right now, for instance, of four young men, including myself, who took that aloof pledge. Three of us, after college, became journalists, and the fourth a lawyer. To-

[11] By E. J. Kahn, Jr., Warrant Officer. *Saturday Evening Post.* 217:27, 94. May 19, 1945.

day two of us are in the Army, one in the Navy and one in the
Coast Guard. We have all seen combat service, except for one
whose present eyesight is comparable in its deficiency to our
collective shortsightedness a decade ago. We all see things a
little more clearly now.

We, and others like us at college with pacifistic leanings,
had a number of understandable motives for our feelings. We
were young and considered ourselves intellectuals, and it is
traditional for young intellectuals to be radical. All self-
respecting radicals were then pacifistic. We were teetering on
the brink of military age; and military service, especially during
peace, is most abhorrent as a theoretical concept to those most
apt to perform it. We were impressionable readers, and much
of the best literature being published was antiwar literature.
We took a dim view of the students who had enrolled in reserve officers' training courses. They were, to a large extent,
boys who had done so simply because R.O.T.C. was an easy subject on the elective curriculum in which to get a passing grade
with minimum effort, thus freeing the energy of those involved
for relentless social pursuit. The people and publications advocating strong national defense were, in the main, those we
did not much respect, because their stand on so many other
questions seemed to us undemocratic, bigoted or just plain
wrong. Many older men whose opinions we admired kept
telling us solemnly over and over again not to make suckers of
ourselves. I guess we didn't end up as suckers, but we sure
came awful close.

We were not of voting age, and could consequently have
no actual influence, of course, on short or long range national
policy. But we were an articulate segment of a large group of
citizens swayed so exclusively by self-interest that they refused
to think ahead at all. This war and our paradoxical attitude
before it have taught us one vivid lesson: that it is extremely
risky to leave the security of a modern nation at peace up to
those who live in it. A nation must inherit its security from
the generation that has seen that security jeopardized. It will be
no more possible to convince a young man in 1965 that the prevention of war is a personal concern of his—assuming that he is

at peace by then—by describing to him the historical nature of war, than it is possible today to convince his mother of the toughness of the life of an infantryman in the front lines by showing her a few hundred feet of newsreel film that neither smells, runs with bright red blood, deafens her hearing nor rattles her in her seat. That is why I, who not so long ago regarded universal military training as a reactionary absurdity, think that it is essential for us to put such a program into effect right now, before we start to forget again.

It will be argued, I suppose, that those of us now in service who favor universal training are motivated by the comforting realization that we shall not be susceptible to it. That may be true to a certain extent, but if so, what of it? My generation has been much more intimately and tragically enmeshed in the practical application of national defense than was the generation before us or than will be, undoubtedly, the generation after us. Anyhow, it is not selfishness that makes us feel the way we do; it is experience. As a matter of fact, most of us would unhesitatingly and unreservedly back any forthcoming program that included us. We have learned the hard way that it is worth a pound of prevention to avert an ounce of war.

Selfishness, when you come right down to it, is one of the principal stumbling blocks in the way of national acceptance of a universal military training program. There are still simply too many Americans who do not wish to be inconvenienced. They are easy to recognize. They are the people who have the arrogant impertinence to complain about such trivial trials as meat shortages and gas rationing and high taxes and low profits and other citizens who annoy them by proposing that they put themselves out by investing their savings in War Bonds. They are the people who worship with fanatical intensity at the dusty and outmoded shrine labeled "status quo." And in the quiet of the postwar world their indignant protests against a training system that affects their personal liberties will resound as intrusively as the whine of a searching shell. They will be recognizable then in many different forms. There will be the mothers who twitch at the thought of losing their sons, even temporarily, to a military system which can hardly be simultaneously both efficient and maternal. There will be the sons who will self-ishly demur at trading mother's cooking for the quartermaster general's.

Apparently, our military leaders who know about such things have decided that one year is an adequate length of time in which to prepare young men for emergency service. Inevitably, the cry will go up that it is cruel and unjust to take one of the best years of a young man's life away from him. I say that's bunk. I have just had something over three and a half of my presumably better years taken away—and it will not surprise me to be in the service for three and a half years more—and I do not feel that my future, such as it may be, has been sabotaged by this interlude. I think that I shall be fortunate if I have any future and that I am lucky to be alive now, and that there are too many Americans who are insufficiently grateful for their own similar good fortune.

What is a twelve months' hiatus going to do to the lives of our young men of tomorrow? In the first place, they will lose no opportunities for education, employment or advancement. Since military service will, I hope, be truly universal, everybody will lose a year, and the relative score will accordingly be equal. Some statistician could probably prove with not too much trouble that a year in the army would so raise national health standards that the national male life span would be increased by an average of a year, thus losing no time for anybody. Young men physically disqualified for actual military training could spend a year on some less active but comparably patriotic duty. Men physically disqualified even for limited regimented training would probably be so handicapped anyhow in a strenuously competitive society that the jump of a year they would get wouldn't do them much good. Men intellectually lagging could be given enough accelerated schooling before their year's training began to be able to take whatever standard course might be prescribed, and to make them more generally useful citizens.

There are many things that universal military training can teach our youth, and they are not all closely related to the field stripping of a Browning automatic rifle. Here are a few of them:

1. Each war in modern history has been more monstrous than its predecessor; each characterized by new devices as ingenious as they are destructive; each, also, more complicated and difficult to wage. Men prepared to fight in the future will have to be infinitely more proficient than our soldiers today—and today even a single infantry regiment is equipped with nearly twenty different weapons. Americans with technical and mechanical skills will not only be better soldiers; they will be better qualified as citizens to take a vigorous role in a society increasingly dominated by scientific advance.

2. It is high time we become more actively conscious of our responsibilities as citizens. Citizenship training too infrequently goes beyond the automatic recital of the pledge of allegiance and an occasional mumbled rendition of the first stanza of "The Star-Spangled Banner." A soldier is a citizen subordinating his own interests to those of his country. Not enough of us have wholly grasped the idea that it might ultimately be to our advantage to do something for our country. It would be a good thing if more people did that more often.

3. Like it or not, we are going to have to participate intensively in the affairs of the world. The United States as a nation has occasionally been accused of isolationist tendencies, but actually today we are in less danger of being isolationist in our relations with other countries than in our relations with ourselves. There are too few farm boys who understand city boys, and vice versa. There are too few Northerners who understand Southerners, and vice versa. There are too few Protestants who understand Jews, and vice versa. For many young men, army life is an astonishing and enlightening revelation of how little people outside of their immediate circle comprehend that circle. Any soldier who has been through a barracks bull session on geographical origins—and no one has missed it—knows how loyally proud every soldier is of his own community, and how uninformed and disdainful he is likely to be of all others. The army can do a great deal toward breaking down this lamentable provincialism. Military service affords many men their first and only chance to travel to and see other parts of their country, an opportunity that cannot help raising

our national standards of tolerance. It is astounding how well you can come to know and understand other men when you are all rubbing your feet together after a hike.

4. Men serving in the army will come to learn what the army is. This is important. Whether or not you are fond of the regular army, the fact remains that many of our best regimental and battalion commanders today—the officers in command of the doughboys who are building the future that others are discussing—are regulars. They got kicked around plenty in peacetime, and people like me were responsible. I never knew a regular in my life until I was inducted, and all my life I had ignorantly and prejudicially been ill disposed toward the standing army. Well, the standing army stood, and it pulled the rest of us together when we had to be yanked to our feet in a hurry. There are a lot of incompetents in the army, to be sure, but there are a lot in other fields, too, and in the other fields you don't have to establish a beachhead under fire.

The cry will soon go up that there will be no real need for compulsory training, because the peace terms and the postwar international setup will be insurance enough for us. Obviously, we all hope so. But when you build a bridge, you allow a margin of safety. You tack up a warning sign stating that no truck of more than ten tons in weight may cross it, but you are still fairly sure that an eleven-ton truck could squeak by without shattering the span. If you are guarding a grade crossing, you find it expedient to lower the gates a minute or two before the fast express roars through, instead of waiting till it is on top of you. Just so, we might as well have a margin of safety in guarding against another war. Perhaps we shall never be attacked—it seems reasonable to assume that we shall not be doing much attacking ourselves—and the money we shall spend on training our young men will be wasted. Yes, and people who live long and happy lives could also be said to have wasted the money they have faithfully paid out in annual insurance premiums. No one is going to attack us the more impetuously because we are better prepared to act instantly and capably in our defense.

If we do adopt a strong universal military training program, the chances are that a couple of decades from now our young men will howl in anguished protest. Let them howl. They will howl because they will not know how much worse war is than the maneuvers that seem to them so dismal. It is when they become grimly silent that we can start getting nervous. Their complaints of outraged civil liberties will be the voice of the peace of their time, and the more they gripe the farther their country will be from having to make mortal use of the special skill it compelled them to acquire. Parents and teachers are always doing things for the good of their children without necessarily consulting the recipients of this forced generosity in advance. Now is a good time for us to do our children and their children a favor by setting up the sturdy machinery by which they can in future days help to maintain the peace we want to bequeath to them in more than passing trust.

PERIOD OF TRAINING [12]

Two questions appear to be causing considerable concern and are frequently raised:

The first question is: "If you can now train a replacement in seventeen weeks, how can you defend your recommendation for a longer pediod of training under universal military training?"

In the first place, the impression that a replacement enters battle after only seventeen weeks of training is false. That is merely the time he spends at a replacement training center. He receives additional instruction at depots in the United States, during his voyage overseas, and in the replacement depots of the theater. The most of our replacements are receiving a minimum of six months' intensive training prior to entering combat. But the basic thought of the question remains unanswered —"Why will more time be required for training under universal military training than is required for the satisfactory training of a replacement?"

The replacement is always of necessity a partially trained soldier since the manpower and training facilities of no nation on earth are adequate to provide fully trained soldiers as re-

[12] *Army and Navy Register*. p. 26. January 20, 1945.

placements. The replacement joins a trained unit. He is initially assigned to the easiest and most simple duties on the team. He is flanked by men who know the game thoroughly. He follows their lead and is guided by their advice. He performs acceptably well and he learns quickly in combat, as there the incentives to learn are great. Within an incredibly short time the new man becomes a veteran, capable of carrying his full share of the battle and of coaching the replacements who have followed him into the unit. By replacing a relatively few casualties promptly each night, we are able to maintain the fighting efficiency of our divisions through months of grilling combat. If however, an organization suffers considerable losses before it is possible to replace them, the organization must be withdrawn from combat for retraining. As hard pressed for troops as she is today, Germany has been forced to withdraw a number of her veteran divisions from the Western Front to be retrained in the rear areas. She was forced to this action because she knew from experience that the number of replacements required would render those divisions useless in battle. All experiences of war support the premise that a unit, when even predominantly replacement, is unbattleworthy. No army would willingly commit to combat a unit with only replacement level training. The graduates of a universal military training program must be better than partially trained soldiers, qualified only to be replacements. They must be fully trained soldiers, as they will constitute the personnel of the organization of our reserve army; consequently, an acceptable replacement training program cannot be an adequate program for universal military training.

The second question is: "Why must universal military training be conducted during a continuous period rather than being distributed through the summer months of several years?" This question arises from fears that the interruption of one year between the completion of high school and the commencement of university work will impair the readiness of the young men to undertake the higher educational courses. If it will, then four interruptions of nine months each will surely destroy the effectiveness of the military instruction. Any interrupted military instruction would certainly be less efficient and would require additional time for its completion. At the beginning of each period of training time would be lost in examining, classifying, and reconditioning the trainees. Instruction partially assimilated but not sufficiently practiced to insure its retention during previous periods would require repetition. Interrupted universal military training would constitute a devastating interference with the normal lives of our young men. Having entered college or university, many boys are unable to complete their educations without the financial assistance they provide themselves by working during vacation months. Many college and university students are enrolled in courses of instruction in which practical work during normal vacation months is absolutely essential to efficient training. The boys who must curtail their education for financial reasons would find it difficult to obtain any acceptable place in the business world so long as they were required to resume their military training for ten or twelve weeks each year. These examples of interference are sufficient to indicate how unwise it would be to require interrupted training under a universal military training system.

MORAL AND SPIRITUAL EFFECTS OF MILITARY TRAINING [13]

If I thought for a moment that a year of military training would destroy the morals of our men, I would oppose it with all my heart. As a parent and as a clergyman, I could not do otherwise. But this is not my conviction. On the contrary, as a chaplain with twenty-six years of experience working with our armed forces in peace and in war, at home and abroad, I am thoroughly convinced that, far from being a menace to the moral and spiritual life of America, the proposed program of universal military training could serve to support and extend the efforts of the home, the church, and the community to enrich the character of our youth.

[13] Statement of Chaplain Brigadier General Luther Miller, Acting Chief of Chaplains, War Department, before the House Select Committee on Postwar Military Policy, June 15, 1945. *Hearings.* p. 493-5.

I think I have earned the right to say that I know the American soldier. I have lived with him in camps. I have served with him in combat. I have shared his work and his play; his joys and his sorrows; no one who has not been a chaplain can know how intimate is the association between a chaplain and his men. To us, they open their hearts. It is our high privilege to be in a real sense their closest friends. Out of the sacred intimacy of this experience extending over the years, I have come not only to know and to love these men but to admire and respect them, as well. For this reason, I resent deeply the common and ill-considered imputation that the atmosphere of the army degrades and debauches our youth. I do not refute this libel with words. Rather, I would point to the men now serving in our armed forces who have gone through not one, but many years of training and combat. They are the answer to such a calumny. I emphatically maintain that nowhere in our national life will you find a group of men whose character is less open to question than the soldiers with whom it is my privilege to serve. Granted that there are moral weaklings among them. Granted that some are vulgar and some vicious. This minority will find its counterpart on every college campus and in every civilian community, for the problem of juvenile delinquency is not localized in army camps. But of the vast majority, I can say that if character means integrity, generosity, humility, courage and self-sacrifice, it would be difficult to equal and impossible to excel the moral and spiritual excellency of your boys and mine, who are now serving their country under circumstances far more trying than those to which trainees under the proposed program of universal military training would be subjected. The fire of war has tested the character of these men as nothing else could. They have not been found wanting.

Having said this, I hasten to add that it is not by mere chance that the morals of these men have been safeguarded and their characters strengthened. The results are due in no small measure to the policy and program of our army and navy which have always considered of primary importance the moral and spiritual welfare of the men committed to their care. It is extremely doubtful if our boys would have come through as clean and fine as they have if every effort had not been made to guard and guide them on their way. The efforts of the army and navy to this end are deserving of the highest praise and commendation. These efforts reflect the high character of the men entrusted with the training of our boys. I might pause here to enlarge on that point since the type of officers in our services is of supreme importance in considering the effects of the training upon the trainees. It has been my privilege through the years to serve as pastor to many of those who are now directing the army in positions of authority and command and in whose hands will be the supervision of the program you are considering. In such a program, the training itself would be conducted by young officers carefully chosen from our reserves; college men, chiefly, who come from and return to civilian life, selected not simply for their military knowledge, but also for their capacity to work with men. From my experience, I can state emphatically that there are in the American Army no Prussianized militarists, hard-boiled and indifferent to the higher values of life. On the contrary, I have found the vast majority of them to be democratically minded Americans faithful to the highest standards of Christian gentlemen. Their whole-hearted support of the army's religious program reflects their personal convictions. What they seek for their men, they accept for themselves. As they have earned the gratitude of our nation for their professional excellency which has led us from the brink of disaster to the verge of victory in this war, so also they have merited the respect of our people for their personal character reflected in their lives and their leadership.

The program for the protection of our servicemen which they have sponsored and which will be continued and enlarged, should universal military training be adopted, is too complex to deal with in detail. Briefly, it is based on the realization that the character building of youth, whether at home, at school, or in military training, is accomplished best by a threefold emphasis upon work, recreation, and worship.

One of the principle causes of juvenile delinquency is idleness. The busy boy is the best boy, and in the training program, he will find plenty to keep him occupied. The work and study will be of a nature to inculcate habits of discipline, order, cooperation, and initiative which will come as valuable by-products of military training.

The leisure time of the trainee is also decisive in his moral growth. Well aware of this, the army and navy have developed an elaborate organization to serve this need. In few civilian communities or colleges could one find a more comprehensive program. It might well serve as a model for communities seeking to solve the problem of juvenile delinquency through provisions for the worthy use of leisure time. Much of the soldier's recreation will be found on the post itself. Here are the movies, with their thousands in attendance every night. Here are the athletic fields, tennis courts, swimming pools, gymnasiums with expert trainers and directors for the men. Here are the service clubs with their libraries, auditoriums, art classes, game rooms, and so on. You will find on the post none of the malodorous roadhouses, juke joints, or pool halls which contribute so largely to the problems of youth in civilian life. Instead there is provided a healthy, wholesome environment for recreation and entertainment at their best.

Naturally the soldier sometimes leaves the post and seeks diversion in nearby communities just as he would if he were in college. Here he meets the same temptations which exist in his home town, but without the restraining influence of home and family, as is also true of the college student. But unlike our universities, the army seeks to provide protection to its men when they are off duty. Every effort is made to clean up communities adjacent to army camps. Much more could be done with the cooperation of these communities which is sometimes tragically lacking. Much more will be done in days of peace since it must be remembered that the present problems in communities close to camps are problems common to all of wartime America and are unfortunately just as prevalent around war industries as army establishments. The important point is that the army does what it can to control these conditions and protect the men in uniform.

In considering the moral and spiritual environment of our youth in training, however, the most important consideration must be the positive influence for good which surrounds them through the chaplain. As never before in our history and as in no other military force in the world, our government has provided for our men in service the finest of religious advantages. It is no exaggeration to say that our boys in the army and navy come into more vital contact with the ministry of religion than they ever did or could at home, and this is in no sense a criticism of the civilian church. It is simply a statement of fact and is due to the circumstances of military life which permit the chaplain to come into more intimate association with his men than would be possible in his peacetime pastorate.

EMERGENCY TRAINING FOR PHILOSOPHY [14]

Other nations have had compulsory military training, but we know practically nothing about it. From now on we are going to have this equation as part of the chemistry of our national compound.

The equation is not necessarily bad, any more than evil could be charged up to the Boy Scout movement because technically it has certain military disciplines, uniforms, some precision of training and patriotic gestures. The Boy Scout movement has been of incalculable good to a horde of young Americans, and the compulsory training of the army is now about to do similar good for our older young men. If only because it takes up a lot of slack.

American youth of today has not been trained at home. The majority of young persons today are without discipline, and without experiencing discipline the hope for individual success in life becomes remote. To be fit to give an order one must first have taken orders. American youth has desired fondly to have other things hop in obedience to it, without having experienced any snappy toeing of the mark itself.

Tyranny is the natural result when a person is placed in a position of authority who had not grown up on the disciplines imposed downward from that position. Beyond question of doubt today's average young person needs discipline, and with-

[14] By Manly P. Hall, Philosopher, Author and Lecturer; Founder, Philosophical Research Society Inc. Los Angeles. *Horizon.* 1:1-5. August 1941.

out a shadow of a doubt only a few have been getting it. Where it has been administered, it has most often been evolved in parental anger, or whim, directed by personal motive geared to an adult perspective. It is instinctive and intuitive with the young to detect and reject the directional guidance that is grounded in prejudice or thoughtlessless or ignorance, or is self-serving of adult convenience and whim. The priceless ingredient that gives effectiveness to any order or direction is the base of intelligent recognition that a good result grows out of impartially beneficial motive. Personal discipline administered from personal motive can never challenge the supremacy of impersonal discipline of impersonal motive.

Most problems of this life are problems of adjustment. There is nothing particularly revolting or unfortunate in the prospect of a year or so of military training for a young man. The past decade has been difficult for parents in their selection of the way to accomplish transition between school graduation and an intelligent entry into the world of economics. Only very recently, and due almost wholly to defense emergency, has industry been in any position to absorb our school graduates, find a place for trained workers, or theoretically trained workers, and in the waiting period and by the tens of thousands our youngsters have had education extended artificially in enrollments for one specialized school course after another, in order to keep them busy, keep them off the streets. Youth, subject to the racking pains of that inferiority which is seemingly inescapable through adolescence, welcomed the escape out of reality offered in extension of the years of its formal education. And youth was coming dangerously near to acceptance of protracted education as an established right—because the elder generation had blundered things into an economic chaos that provided no place for youth, left no openings for newcomers readied to accept the responsibilities of self-supporting manhood. All that now has been fixed. Youth has been given both place and purpose under a system of conscription that knows no preferentials, that starts all young man off equal. On a serious note and in proper regulated restraint, life has begun in a positive orientation for our youth.

An outstanding virtue of compulsory service is its principle of equality for all. Its huge impersonality—which in certain quarters makes it particularly obnoxious—is sure to provide the most beneficial experience imaginable to those who consider themselves "different."

Consider the effect on the mother who dotes on her only son. She worries that he will not have the proper diet; she feels that lack of cultural environment will unstabilize him, is sure that the officers will not understand him—if any one in the world should have military training, that young man should have. By walking out of his present environment he is escaping a conditioning which in later life would be sure to cause him endless trouble. These indispensible children who bolster up home life for the older generation become incredible sufferers in the tragedies of life that await us all. Breaking abruptly with home life and family ties is the clearly indicated preventative for a large percentage of the world's neuroses and psychological abnormalities such as insanity.

Within our families and in the social order itself we have been busily developing a collection of supersensitive human beings who are just too sensitive to exist here. Fondly believed by those who dote on them to be of very advanced type, belonging perhaps to the Sixth Root Race or the Eighth Root Race, something little less than a cherubim, the net of the matter is they are just plain spoiled children. From constant coddling they have been prevented from developing strength, and weakness is interpreted as sensitivity. When an individual cannot stand the shock of life he is sensitive, but sensitivity is not in reality weakness, it is a matter of acuteness of function. Humanity's fineness is not destroyed by roughing it; there is no genuine refinement at all in human nature that cannot withstand a pushing around. The pseudo refinements can generally be accredited to malnutrition or something of that order.

The stresses and difficulties of living in today's world makes it imperative that our youth have strength to face problems of appalling complexity; no one ever found strength by keeping away from experience. There is nothing to be gained by trying to protect young people from life. A better notion would

be perhaps to try to protect life from young people. How to
fit the individual to live is the real problem, and to this end
we can observe how nature does it. Throughout the animal
kingdom and in all the world of the primitive, the young are
set upon their own resources as soon as possible. It is always
nature's way to create strength by demanding resourcefulness.
It is part of the nobler concept of the human family that it
has no right to neglect its young, that every possible advantage
should be given to the generations that follow after, so that
future men may be wiser and nobler and better than we are.
It is quite possible so to distort this concept that we protect
these generations out of survival. In no way can compulsory
military training be considered a neglect of the young; it com-
bines the experience of exposure to a wide cross-section of
humankind, and the disciplines set up to protect an existing
social order.

Subjected to what we are pleased to call a regimented service, the youngsters most vitally affected are the metaphysically
minded. Prejudices set up an inner conflict, and so do so-called
conscientious beliefs and natural segregative instincts. Practically all who lean toward the metaphysical are self-constituted
recluses. They are generally of the opinion that the world
does not understand them, seldom that they do not understand
the world. They consider themselves students; what they do
not consider is, it progresses the student none whatever to go
on year after year living vicariously. . . . The universal long-
ing of human beings is sometime to be absolutely peaceful. In
such peace they would expire of boredom; conflict is absolutely
necessary to human existence.

When the mystically minded individual is picked up and
yanked into the army the prospect he faces is horrible. All
of material life is unbearable; his thinking has so far pro-
gressed that it is no longer possible for him to associate on
terms of equality with the unenlightened; now his daily contacts are to be set among people not one of whom believes
in metaphysics! In high states of agitation, not a few mothers
have come to me with this problem; and strangely enough, not
one has even asked me if I thought it likely the end of things
would be in her son getting shot. The perturbation and con-

cern is over the contaminating influence of worldliness upon the sensitivity of a metaphysical personality.

The metaphysician who is starting out in life so sensitive that he will be contaminated by army life is almost bound to get contaminated somewhere else along the line. . . . It is to his great intellectual benefit to come face to face with a world that does not believe in metaphysics. With a distressingly large number of metaphysicians the unbeliever is some quaint individual who does not believe as he does. There is himself, and the subnormal. Out of which is produced a definite type of orthodoxy that is as hide-bound and intolerant as any that have graced and disgraced orthodoxy in religion for ages. None can be more certain of the infallibility of their premises than two conflicting schools of metaphysical enthusiasts; they will extend even to persecution of each other in amazing expression of their realization of the brotherhood of man.

Anything that tends to break this up is good. Close and continued contact with those who have no metaphysical philosophy whatever is even better than good, it is perfect. To be pulled out of a completely smug viewpoint, to be brought definitely face to face with the realities that make up the life of the rest of the world, is an important experience, and one that will never hurt anyone engaged in the process of building character, which is an eternal process.

Because metaphysicians who have reached a point beyond mature life lose contact with the younger generation, the metaphysically minded who are coming up are not shown the need of working with ideals by confronting life itself. Any average person today finds out at fifty that he needs to be a philosopher; he regrets that he did not know this at twenty-five. But he has had to experience facing life, he has had to find that life itself is unendurable without philosophy. It might be thought that philosophy can be taught, and it is; but those whose philosophy is the result of being taught are a sorry lot. The successful ones are those who experience.

Philosophy is a doctrine of building character, not of nourishing weakness. Strength of character comes from contact with life and not from running away. Religion has for centuries sought to bring man to a state of peace by teaching him formulas for running away from life, on the assumption that by embracing religion he becomes acceptable in the light of the Lord. The difference between that viewpoint and philosophy is practicality. Philosophy's place for working is right here, in this world, offering a most indispensible tool for intelligent living. Philosophy conceives its duty as helping people in community existence, in individual life, in business associations, and in every branch of daily affairs, in the aim to live as normally, intelligently and constructively as possible. It cannot be applied by the individual who is overshadowed, spoiled, and untrained. . . .

Plato and Pythagoras and Buddha taught that obedience is the beginning of wisdom. The first thing to learn to do in this world is to obey, which is the last thing anyone wants to do— surely the last thing our younger generation had in mind, if at all. It is obedience, willing and instantaneous to authority, that is the basis for training individuals for philosophy. Philosophy is obedience from beginning to end; its adherent first obeys his teachers, then obeys Law, and finally obeys the Universal Law. Philosophy is gained out of obedience to required training and discipline.

So, a year or two or even more under a top sergeant is not at all a bad start for our young people; it will concentrate for them more discipline and training than most of them would otherwise experience in their normal life. Out of world confusion and conflict has arisen the imperative need for obedience, and it will result in a new human and racial strength. Never can we be truly wise until we have brought strength to wisdom. We are on the way to acquiring it through obedience which in turn will build up the philosophical faculties of man.

PROGRAM OF UNIVERSAL MILITARY TRAINING [15]

I have been astonished at the shopworn catchwords and objections which have been advanced before your committee against

[15] From statement of Henry L. Stimson, Secretary of War, before the House Select Committee on Postwar Military Policy, June 15, 1945. *Congressional Record.* 91: (daily) A3290-1. June 25, 1945.

this program of universal training. They are old acquaintances, often called on in past years to take the place of research and careful thinking. They have certainly shown ignorance of the history of the system which they oppose. Universal training for national defense did not have its birth in militarism or autocracy. It has almost everywhere followed the banner of freedom and democracy. It has been simultaneous with the growth of interest which the entire people take in the affairs of government. Such training has come equally in a free republic like Switzerland and in a constitutional monarchy like Sweden. It represents the steady growth of an ideal in justice and fair play, namely, that he who has a voice in the selection of his own government is bound in honor to be trained and ready to defend that government.

There can be no more curious contradiction of fact than the fear that universal military training makes nations more likely to go to war. Such training has, on the contrary, been the very means by which the professional soldier—the man who spends his entire life in planning and thinking about war—is reduced to the lowest possible number in the nation. Under the old system of standing armies such professionals constituted the entire army, and their presence in the nation constituted an element whose aims and ambitions were at variance with their fellow citizens. Under the new system their place is taken by men who learn the art of national defense as a part of their normal education, and then after the period of training is over at once become merged in general citizenship of the nation. These men thereafter have no special leaning toward war. Their subsequent occupations, habits, and ambitions lead in the same peaceful direction as those of their fellow citizens. Under the proposed system they can only be called into war service by the Congress in the event of a national emergency. Under the proposed system the only body of professional soldiers left in the nation is a comparatively small professional nucleus in the shape of the regular army. Whether such a nucleus can become a source of militarism in a nation or not depends far more upon the attitude of the nation toward that nucleus than on any other consideration. If they are treated as a privileged and ruling caste, as has been the case in Germany and Japan, the danger may become real; if on the contrary they live constantly under the Anglo-Saxon tradition that military authority is ever subject to the civil as is the case in America, the danger in my opinion is wholly imaginary.

Not only would the unwelcome features of maintaining a large standing army in peacetime be absent under a system of universal military training, but there would accrue to the young trainees many incidental advantages which I shall touch upon. But in mentioning them, these by-products, I do not for an instant lose sight of the primary objective. That primary objective is to fit men to protect the national security . . . .

Finally, I do not overlook the opportunities which such a program holds for matters of the spirit. From long past centuries we have inherited such catchwords as "rude and licentious soldiery." It is high time that such catchwords should be revised and rejected in regard to our present armies. The bringing together of young men in large bodies for patriotic training and discipline offers an unusual opportunity for lessons in decency, in mutual consideration, and in many of the other things which tie us to the spiritual side of human behavior. I know I am not mistaken when I say that this opportunity has been well taken care of by our chaplains and our other leaders in morale and general education in our present army. In my present post I receive thousands and thousands of communications, written and verbal, from the parents of sons who are in the army. I think that perhaps the most frequent comment from these parents has been gratification at the development in consideration, self-respect, morale, and responsible behavior which they have observed in their sons. Furthermore, I think each of us knows within his own intimate knowledge of American soldiers in our last two wars how deep and real have been the religious convictions of our men in arms, how their service has stirred within them springs of faith that in their civil life they scarcely knew, and how much solace they have drawn from their religious belief. Instead of a peril or a handicap to religious growth, the gathering together from the four corners of our nation of our youth during the training year will present an unparelleled opportunity to our churches of every denomination to sow the seeds of religious faith in good ground. . . .

If the United States is to adopt universal military training in peacetime, the basic framework should by all means be enacted now. The European phase of the war is over. We are in the midst of redeployment, and partial demobilization is already underway. The transition from a war economy to a peace economy should be gradual and carefully planned.

We hold accumulated today an immense investment in equipment of all kinds, both arms and implements of war, camp installations and training grounds, and the millions of trained men now under arms. This investment has today what is known in industry as a going-concern value. Disband and junk this organization and that value is completely lost. To reestablish once more such an organization would involve our country in a cost comparable with that incurred in preparing for this war.

There is also another aspect, often overlooked, of our present military readiness which cannot be so adequately appraised in dollars and cents. I mean the time and effort that had to go into building up our existing training organizations. Key elements of these organizations would be invaluable to us in setting up a postwar training program. If we are not able to plan for the future now upon definite assumptions as to what will be authorized in the future, the going-concern value of these organizations also will be lost.

Our determination should be made now as to which parts of the physical equipment will be disposed of and which parts are capable to use in a postwar training program. Until we know what kind of program we shall have, we cannot make intelligent plans for disposal and dismantling of the various parts of the colossal machinery of war. These are some of the material reasons for now making decision on this fundamental national policy.

But I am also persuaded by another and different reason. My experience tells me that it is very real. We Americans are not warlike. We take up the sword only when we must, and after we have laid aside that sword we try to forget the atrocious necessities that forced us into conflict. After World War I we did forget—but had a rude awakening. As peace unfolds after this even more terrible struggle, we shall want again to forget. But I tell you that we owe it to the next generation, and those who will follow them, that we shall this time make decision while the lesson of experience is fresh upon us. . . .

If the nation is to retain its status as a world power, with a dignity and strength commensurate with that status, an orderly transition from our wartime military establishment to the peacetime military establishment is essential. Such an orderly transition can be made only if we are to know in the near future something of the character of the peacetime establishment that will be authorized by the Congress.

In determining the character of such an establishment, you, whose duty it is to plan the nation's future military policy, will be thinking how already in this century we have twice been forced to plunge our youth into the cauldron of world war. In the future we may again be forced to send our young men into combat against armies of sudden aggression. We have no right to gamble on the hope that our country for the third time will have even the little breathing space she has had in these two wars for hasty preparation. We have fully experimented with unpreparedness as a means for avoiding war. It has not prevented war and it has led us into staggering costs and sacrificed lives. As one who has personally come very close to these experiences of two world wars, I beg you to cease listening to the false prophets of "no preparation." If, as history shows, wars recur, we owe it to our young men to provide a system of military training in peacetime. Then they will be ready to fight a good fight, and in that fight will have a decent chance to survive.

EXCERPTS

Mr. [Robert A.] Taft said his own son had received fourteen months of training before being sent overseas, adding that the final few months had taught him most of the "know how" to minimize the dangers of battle.—*Commercial and Financial Chronicle. Mr.* 1, '45. p. 966.

I am clear in my own mind that, as an essential factor in the maintenance of peace in the future, we must have universal military training after this war, and I shall send a special message to the Congress on this subject.

An enduring peace cannot be achieved without a strong America—strong in the social and economic sense as well as in the military sense.—*President Franklin D. Roosevelt. Message to Congress, Ja. 6, 1945.*

The essence of the plan they have in view [at San Francisco] is that force shall be used, when necessary, to prevent aggression. To illustrate the point concretely: force shall be used if it is needed, five years from now or ten years from now, to prevent Japan, having secretly rearmed, from embarking again upon a conquest of Manchuria. When this happened before, in 1931, the nations of the western world stood aside, partly because they were not ready to use force, but even more fundamentally because they had no force in existence which was capable of offering effective opposition to the Japanese armies.—*Editorial. New York Times. Je. 5, '45. p. 18.*

I wish every boy in the country could have this year of training at the end of his high school course, or at the age he would have reached had he gone to high school. I wish all our young men could meet at least for that one year on terms of absolute democracy. I should like to see the young conservative bunking in with the young radical. Whatever became of their theories later, they would know each other as human beings. I should like the boys from one section of the country to do their year of service in another section. I should expect that those who after this year of service went on to college study would go with a maturity of mind which is not at present noticeable in freshmen or sophomores.—*John Erskine, Author, Teacher, Musician. From Foreword of his pamphlet Universal Training for National Defense. Mr. '40. p. 4.*

At [President Roosevelt's] press conference held on August 18, 1944, he stated that a study was being given to the matter of the youth of the country giving what he characterized simply as a year of service to their government. This he said would apply to young men in the 17-21 age bracket. The President emphasized that the program could not be described as compulsory military service, although he thought there would be some military training. Along with this year in which the men would get some military training, they would get vocational training. He pointed out that the government now had many training camps to accommodate several million men. Vocational training, said the President, might be something to equip the trainees for government work, making it easier to pass civil service examinations.—Editorial. *Army and Navy Register*. Ja. 13, 1945. *p*. 8.

Moscow's announcement of the biggest peacetime military training schedule ever ordered in the Soviet Union, with thousands of 15- and 16-year-old boys called up for Red Army training, lays an emphasis on national defense, an emphasis which should not be lost sight of in the United States. Not because this country need expect or fear war with the Soviet Union—there is every reason to believe that the two nations can and will live at peace—but because of the wisdom of universal military training.

Twice within a quarter century the United States was caught without adequate military forces when attacked. It can happen again. . . .

Russian Lieutenant General N. N. Pronin, chief of the training administration of the Commissariat for Defense, announcing the call for Russian youth, said, "General military training in the present period should be conducted on an even higher level than in the days of war. The peaceful period into which our country has entered should not lessen our attention to the problems of defense." He stressed, too, the value to the youth of the nation of military training, for physical hardening, for the inculcation of decisiveness, endurance, stubbornness, and initiative.— *Gould Lincoln. Congressional Record. Je. 1, '45. p. A2840. Reprint from the Washington Evening Star.*

After the fight for conscription during wartime had been won, and after the [World War I] itself had been won, leaders kept up a fight for compulsory military training as a permanent peacetime policy. Conspicuous among them was Gen Leonard Wood, who was a candidate for the Republican Presidential nomination in 1920. But peacetime compulsory military training did not have enough vitality to become an important campaign issue. America would have none of it.

During the quarter century since that time, America has learned some things. There is proof. During the present war, there was no material opposition to compulsory military service. America had become reconciled to the obligation of the individual to be drafted in war. The present question is whether we have become reconciled to the obligation to be drafted for military training in anticipation of war.

One thing we should have learned from the suddenness of the attack on Pearl Harbor. As Under Secretary of State Grew put it in the hearing this week, "Latent power is not enough." Our power should be trained and ready for instant action. At Pearl Harbor, within less than two hours, some hundred Japanese planes put out of commission over a fourth of America's naval strength. In future wars, if, they come, attack will be equally sudden and more devastating; probably there will be several simultaneous attacks at different points.

The lessons of 25 years ago and since point plainly toward a present program for America. It would be a double program and would be the opposite of what we did after the First World War. The program would be to unite in the international organization for preventing war, to hope it will work, and to strive to make it work. At the same time, by permanent universal military training, and by other means, be prepared for war in case the peace organization should fail to work.—*Mark Sullivan, Columnist. New York Herald Tribune. Je. 6, '45. Copyright 1945, New York Tribune, Inc.*

In the first place, such proposals should receive the fullest possible discussion. It would be most unfortunate if a plan were "put across" by a pressure group without adequate discussion in the light of the fullest possible information. . . .

In the second place, we must not be unduly influenced by the unquestioned fact that the requirement of universal national service would constitute a radical change in our national policy. Hitherto in peacetime, we have had only a small standing army and moderate-sized navy, a national guard, and a corps of reserve officers. We have recruited, trained, and equipped a large army and navy only after the emergency was upon us. This system worked not too badly in the past. But technology has made the world very different from what it was a hundred, or even twenty-five, years ago. Moreover, in the last two world wars we escaped disaster because our allies held off the aggressors while we got ready. It is not likely that this lesson will be lost on would-be aggressors of the future; if there is another world war we probably shall be attacked first. Hence the burden of proof should be on those who insist that a change is not needed rather than on those who believe that it is.

A third consideration that deserves attention has to do with social responsibility on the part of our citizenry. Probably most persons would agree that one of the besetting sins of Americans, young and old, is irresponsibility. The Nazis have demonstrated that compulsory national service can be a powerful instrument in developing in young citizens a genuine social concern. Certainly we do not want to nazify our youth. But if it can be shown that universal national service can, by means consistent with democratic ideals, contribute substantially to the development on the part of our young people of a genuine concern for the welfare of the country and the advancement of free institutions, that will constitute a weighty argument in favor of requiring it.—*R. H. Eckelberry, Editor, Educational Research Bulletin. N. 15, '44. p. 218-19.*

Those of us who have served in either world war, or both, know that training saves lives. One morning, during the course of the Meuse-Argonne battle, the writer, then a first lieutenant in command of a company of light tanks, slipped into a shell hole under heavy machine-gun fire. There was a private already in the hole about to reload his Springfield rifle. He took a clip of five cartridges from his bandolier and proceeded to take a single cartridge from the clip and insert it in the chamber of the rifle. The whole clip was meant to be placed in the receiver designed to take it, and the cartridges injected into the chamber by the action of the rifle bolt. Obviously, this private was untrained. Yet here he was in the front line, a few yards from the enemy. In reply to a quick question, he said he had been drafted just one month before to the day! Before he could be stopped, he had his elbows on the rim of the shell hole preparing to shoot his rifle. Instantaneously, there was a short burst of machine-gun fire and the boy fell back dead, shot through the neck. He never had a chance. When troops engaged in battle need replacements, they must have them from any source available.

Now a still more tragic example from World War II. In mid-December, there was a quiet sector on the Belgian front. Just the place for a division newly arrived in France to undergo its baptism of fire and gain some battle experience. Therefore, the Golden Lion Division, the 106th, full of fight and rarin' to go, took over the sector. Five days later the German counter-offensive struck and in another two days, two entire regiments with their supporting artillery and armor were completely wiped out. Only a handful of men—fewer than 300—came back from the two regiments. Subsequently the Secretary of War announced that the 106th Division had suffered 8,663 casualties.

There is no substitute for training, no short cut to preparedness. Don't let us fool ourselves into thinking that if another emergency should arise, we can create an army over night. That way lies madness and national suicide.—*Col. John W. Castles, Vice President, Citizens Committee for Military Training of Young Men, Inc. Independent Woman. Ap. '45. p. 99, 112.*

To summarize, Dumbarton Oaks is a means by which it is hoped we shall attempt by active steps, backed by force if necessary, to keep the peace in a world where lasting peace has never yet been achieved. Americans might not all agree that universal military training—applicable democratically to all young men alike—is the preferable way to build up this reserve strength, but at least it has its points. It seems to fit the idea of our role in a Dumbarton Oaks plan better than a large standing army would.

We do not control or seek to direct world affairs. That would be contrary to the principle that other peace-loving peoples have their rightful part in shaping them. We do want to influence world affairs in what we believe to be peaceful directions, with due regard for the rights and views of others. Thus our first care will be to avoid wars by all honorable means. But in this attempt to outlaw war, we shall never gamble with our national security. . . .

The inevitable conclusion that any future aggressor could not miss is that the United States should be attacked and defeated *first*. Failure to do this has twice cost the aggressor his war. We know—and we may be sure that he will know, too—that distance has been a saving factor for us in the two World Wars. We also know, as does he, that modern implements of transport and warfare no longer make distance the barrier that it was, even in the early days of this war. Unless we blind ourselves to reality, we will realize that distance will be an even less formidable obstacle in the future development of planes, rockets and ships. So, the question of which nation an aggressor would attack first deserves a lot of consideration by all of us who love our country and want to hold on to it.

If such an attack should come—and it could come from anywhere on the globe—and if our situation is then similar to our state of unpreparedness in 1940 when France fell, what would be our prospect of a successful defense? What would be our course, despite all that we might do as a member of a world peace organization?—*John J. McCloy, Assistant Secretary of War. Collier's. Je. 9, '45. p. 27.*

In designating universal military training as a measure of economy your Committee wishes to emphasize that, to the extent that such training provides insurance against the outbreak of a third world war, its cost would be repaid manyfold. The cost to the United States of the present war may amount to $300,000,000,000. The cost of training some 1,000,000 young men over a period of one year your Committee estimates roughly at $1,000,000,000, plus probably 1 per cent more for refresher training, which is optional under the Committee's proposal.

The figure used by your Committee was adopted after examining various estimates of *current* cost components and after consultation with members of the armed services. It is naturally impossible at this time to estimate with accuracy and in detail the cost of maintaining the military establishment over *future* years. Such elements as future prices of food, clothing, and munitions are obviously unpredictable. So also are rates of pay, allowances and dependency benefits for the trainees, which can be determined only by the Congress.

Based on information from the armed services, your Committee estimates that approximately 1,200,000 young men would be available for training each year, but that due to rejections about 1,000,000 of these actually would be accepted for training. Assuming the use of the present available facilities, the annual cost of training each accepted young man is estimated at a little over $1,000.

Under a system of universal military training the defense reserve of the United States could be enlarged annually by an increment of some 1,000,000 trained men at a cost which would be less than would be required to maintain in peacetime the larger standing regular military establishment needed in the absence of such a reserve. For example, over a period of five years, *five* men could be trained and maintained for what it would cost to train and maintain *one* man in a regular standing military establishment for that same number of years.

It is the belief of your Committee that, in addition to all other considerations, it would prove more economical to maintain a comparatively small regular military establishment, reinforced by reservists resulting from a system of universal military training, than it would be to maintain the much larger military establishment required, in the absence of military training, to provide an equal degree of national protection.—*Chamber of Commerce of the United States. Universal Military Training in Peacetime. Referendum no.* 85. *O.* 8, '44. *p.* 5.

The citizen army is a better bulwark against fascism and militarism than just "no conscription." A citizen-reservist army helps to keep military affairs in the right political perspective. Military service becomes the part-time civic duty of the citizen instead of the full-time job of a special group. The broader the class of reservists is, and it would include the thirty-year-old alumni as well as the active twenty-year-olds, the less chance there is of building up a powerful clique of full-time professionals. All who are or have been reservists will be much more alert, as *civilians,* to the way military affairs are handled. With the public circulating through the army, that institution is bound to be more democratic in outlook and more sensitive to civilian opinion than a strictly professional army could ever be.

Moreover, militarism is better served by professionals than by reservists. The citizen who chooses to be a reservist rather than a full-time soldier has obviously decided to make his place in the civilian world and is not likely to seek glory through war. On the contrary, he will be extremely desirous that there shall be no next war. Eagerness for a "good fight" is more likely to develop among full-time regulars who spend all their time preparing for one. Those who oppose conscription claim that the period of training will make militarists of our youth. But there is no reason to assume that a short period in the army will influence their attitude more than the years of civilian life before and after their term of service. The absence of a military tradition among the people of this country is further assurance that conscription will not necessarily bring such a change. The existence of a professional army creates the illusion among civilians that perhaps they will not be called upon to serve if war comes and so lessens their interest in preventing war. If war does come again, the civilian must be conscripted into the army anyway, and the country, not the enemy, pays the price of last-minute extemporization.

The citizen army also has the advantages of flexibility and youth. As reservists grow old, they automatically become inactive; the professional army cannot rid itself as easily of its over-aged regulars. And since the size of the citizen army can be more quickly adjusted by extending or shortening the periods of training or of active reserves, it will be easier to keep the citizen army large enough to enforce the peace and yet small enough to keep ourselves peaceful.

The superiority of the citizen-army pattern over the professional is so pronounced that it must be established even if the price is conscription. The method of recruiting is not going to determine whether or not we become militaristic. The political and social atmosphere in which it is conducted, especially the attitude of the civilian and the soldier toward each other, will be the controlling force. We have had conscription for more than four years, and no one can say that it has fostered militarism or fascism among us. If those conditions did not develop in war time, there is no reason to assume that they will in peace time, when civilian controls over military affairs can be more extensive.
—*Irving Lipkowitz, Economist, Department of Justice. Nation.*
Mr. 3, '45. p. 246.

Regular officers need a great deal of experience in commanding and gaining the confidence of a cross-section of the population, including, as it does, brainy and well-educated young men. They must have opportunity for the display of initiative and ability in the face of responsibilities similar to those suddenly thrust upon them by war. Our army must not be allowed to relapse into the outrageous prewar system of promotion by seniority and a record clean of errors because free from initiative. The regulars must be subject to informed criticism and to the competitive standards of civil life and they cannot afford to be less educated in the scientific foundations of modern warfare than are the men they command.

Civilians, on their part, must be acquainted with our military establishment if the ultimate civilian control of the military appropriate to a democracy is to be intelligent and wise. This is not a responsibility to be evaded merely because it is inconvenient.

Ignorance of military matters not only leads to delay in mobilizing our fighting power, which might be fatal in some future emergency when we might not have Britain to stand off an enemy while we prepare, but, what has rarely been pointed out, it stands in the way of the most effective use of our great scientific and engineering strength. In the future, far more even than in the present, scientists and military men, in order to become effective partners, must be familiar with what is possible in the realm of each. Despite the far better collaboration during the war the general ignorance of scientists concerning military operations and the scarcity of men competent to carry on needed operational research has permitted not only faulty weapon design but more serious loss in their use. Many illustrations of this could be given.

I am not advocating military training consisting largely of close order drill or even of the methods of warfare now in use. Those who object to it because they assume that the army authorities will look backward instead of forward are citing the very danger against which civilian participation can furnish the greatest and perhaps the only safeguard. Brass hats cannot well be worn in civilian company.—*Joel H. Hildebrand, Chemist; Dean College of Letters and Science, University of California, Berkeley; liaison for Office of Scientific Research and Development, London. New York Times. Jl. 1, '45. p. 8E.*

My feeling with regard to all of the delegates at San Francisco with whom I talked was they came there determined to make this thing succeed, determined to do their part of it, that is, to turn out a charter which would be a reasonable basis for security.

They also came there with the very real realization that the writing of the charter was only the first step in a long series of steps, the first step on a very arduous road and that the success depended not only on them but on people who would come after them in the third and fourth and fifth generations who had to find the means to prevent this world and civilization from being torn part by weapons man has made.

One of the means of doing so, one of the means that every civilized nation has found necessary is to keep power, weapons, ability to protect the peace in the hands of those who are law-abiding members of the community and to deprive those who might disturb that peace of the means to do so.

We do not let criminals or we do not let anybody, any irresponsible citizen, run around Washington with a machine gun. You have to take the same attitude toward other possible disturbers of the peace in the world community.

I think the people came out there with that feeling. There is no serious divergence on that point between the British and America and there was no serious divergence on that point between the American delegation and the Soviet delegation.

They all came there with the same purpose of mind. The Russians came there with suspicions of us and the Americans with suspicions against the Soviets, but in building up confidence between the Western World and Russia lies much of the hope of future success and we will not gain the confidence of the Russians by laying aside our weapons and going back to sleep.

That is what they are afraid we will do. They say, "All right, you have licked the Germans and you are going to lick the Japs, and then you are going back to your peaceful ways, just like you did before, and in twenty years we are going to have these people to deal with alone."—*Statement of Major George Fielding Eliot, Commentator, Columbia Broadcasting Co., before the House Select Committee on Postwar Military Policy. Hearings. Je. 4, '45. p. 33.*

Our five major foreign wars have been, the Revolution, the War of 1812, the Mexican War, World War No. 1, and World War No. 2. During the Revolution the Colonies used a total of 395,858 men, at one time or another, against a British force of 62,196 men. It required seven years and the assistance of the French to secure our independence from a nation whose people had so little heart in conquering their own kinsfolk that their government had to complete their forces with hired alien troops.

In the War of 1812 we used a total of 527,654 men passing through our forces to face a force of 81,502 British. During four years we lost every battle fought on land, except one, and many of them under disgraceful circumstances. Only at sea did we distinguish ourselves and there we fought with trained men.

In spite of the large number of men we used during the Revolution and the War of 1812 we were never able to keep more than small poorly trained forces in the field at any one time due to lack of a sound military policy.

The Mexican War was not against a military power and we were the aggressor.

In World War No. 1 our civilian soldiers did not rush out and sweep the enemy before them. . . . When drawn into that war we were unable to fight at all, even with a token force. It was more than a year before we could place even a small force in battle and some 18 months before we could mount an offensive. During all that time we were sheltered by the armies of our allies. When we did finally go into battle it was to take over a portion of a line the major part of which was still manned by our allied troops. . . .

World War No. 2 is a repetition of World War No. 1. Pearl Harbor found us unprepared and if the Japanese had not been attempting to conquer China and take British and Dutch colonies in the Far East, all at the same time, they could have taken Hawaii and invaded our Pacific Coast. We were unable to do any serious fighting for more than a year and again prepared for war under the protection of allied armies. . . .

To anyone familiar with military matters it is obvious that the greater the use of mechanical equipment the greater the number of men that will be used. The reason is simple; war entails a maximum effort on the part of the nations engaged. Mass-production methods have permitted the equipment and supply of much larger bodies of troops than ever before and armies promptly increased to the largest size made possible by the new production facilities.

When mass production permitted the construction of large numbers of cannon and the production of huge quantities of ammunition the amount of artillery on the battlefield and the quantity of artillery fire leaped to unheard-of heights because neither side could afford to let the other outmatch it. But this did not decrease the need for infantry.

The mechanization of the battlefield itself, particularly in transportation and communications, still further increases the number of troops who can be supplied and controlled and therefore forces the use of still larger numbers of men, not less as stated.—*Col. Lewis Sanders, United States Army. Congressional Record. My.* 10, '45. *p.* A2368.

A system of training so organized would have obvious advantages. In a general way each training camp would become an educational center. More specifically, the annual inventory of our educational shortcomings would point out for our school system the task to which it should address itself. Undoubtedly, the result would be that year by year the schools would send to training camps generations better prepared; by keeping the election of the courses in the training camps entirely free we should be able to assist each student to make progress from the point at which his education had left off, and the gradual rise of standards in the courses in this year of training would be the barometer of the intellectual progress of the nation. The year of training would also show which parts of the country were providing adequate facilities for education, and means could be taken by the national government to improve the elementary schools in those districts. It is not unlikely that as a result of this national training and of the statistics which it would make available the nation would soon be persuaded, as it should have been persuaded long ago, to establish in the Federal Government a strong department of education, and that department would collaborate with the army in training for citizenship.

But the most direct advantage would be for the large majority of our young men who at present receive no high school training at all, nor even much elementary education. To insure for them a reasonable start in life would be worth any cost and any effort. In no other way than by national training, undertaken as a national expense, can this vast body of each generation be sought out in the small town, on the farm, in the overcrowded city, and can be taught the things essential to each individual case. To care for this neglected majority would be really to train our nation.

Perhaps the by-product of such a system of training as is here outlined would be the bringing of the army into a sane relation with society. Through the fear of militarism which possesses the modern world it has become our custom to support the army and to admire military science only in moments of extreme need. As a result, the soldier in wartime receives an adulation perhaps exaggerated and in peacetimes he is neglected, feared, certainly put to no good use. At this moment, when our army thinks of returning, it is interesting to consider that every man in it hopes to go back to some constructive work for his country, except the professional soldier. He can look forward only to inactivity until the spasmodic need of him arises again. Perhaps society is wise in fearing the army which has nothing to do; it has been stupid, however, in finding no use for the army in time of peace. If we could add to the military functions of our army the constructive kind of national defense, we should be providing a noble and honored career for the man on whom in extreme moments the life of the nation depends; we should be bringing the soldier into constant relation with the social needs of the country he serves, and we should be teaching every youth within our borders that large conception of citizenship expressed for the Anglo-Saxon race by John Milton, "I call a complete and general education that which fits a man to perform justly, skillfully, and magnanimously all offices, both private and public, of peace and war."—*John Erskine, Author, Teacher, Musician; Chairman of Army Educational Committee, American Expeditionary Forces, 1918-1919. From his pamphlet Universal Training for National Defense. Mr. '40. p. 15.*

I believe the 4Fs should be included, for the American people will not like a compulsory service that exempts 20 per cent of the boys and permits them to get a job or go to college, so they will appear to be a year ahead of their friends who return from the training camps. Nor will they like a plan that bars boys who are eager to accept all the benefits and responsibilities of training, but who are disqualified because of punctured eardrums or flat feet.

Unless a boy is mentally or physically incapacitated for any sort of training, and cannot be rehabilitated, he should serve his year along with his friends. There will be a place for him. In the old days, military training consisted entirely of drilling and shooting. Today there are thousands of jobs in the armed services that can be handled by men whose physical ratings are below par. . . .

In mechanized warfare there is a place for almost every profession and trade. The boys may learn to be mechanics, chemists, chefs, photographers, electricians, printers, marine engineers, draftsmen, tailors, carpenters, storekeepers, physicists, medical assistants, weather forecasters, aviators, radio operators, musicians, stenographers, chauffeurs, mathematicians—the list is endless. Those who are interested in a military career will have an opportunity for appointment to Annapolis or West Point, for from these boys will come our future officers. Intensive research by the army and the navy will continue, and from these boys eventually will be selected the scientists who will carry on this work. It is absurd to say that a year of military training will take a year out of a boy's education. It will add a year—a most valuable year.

Many fathers and mothers are deeply concerned as to whether a year in service will destroy much of the moral influence of parents and of the church. This concern must be met by a definite policy, that will strengthen, not weaken, the moral fiber of every boy. The churches, rightly, will want much to say about the way the boys are handled, and their assistance should be encouraged. The selection of the right kind of chaplains should be as much their responsibility as it is the army's and the navy's.

There will be many reasonable applications for exemption, and these must be given the most careful consideration. The problem of conscientious objectors, for instance, must be resolved. Thousands of boys will be the sole support of their parents, 8,500 of the 18-year-olds will be married and many will have babies. These boys should not be exempt, but Congress should provide allotments for needy dependents. As is the practice now, instead of exempting intelligent illiterates they will be taught to read and write.

In normal times, 488,000 of these boys will be in school and 486,000 will have jobs. There will be 367,000 living on farms, some in school, but a majority of them helping on the farms.

There should be no exemptions because certain boys are "necessary" workers, but I believe all should be given a choice as to when they will begin their training—perhaps any time between the ages of 17½ and 21—so they can adjust their education, their work, and their personal affairs.

While individual employers will be inconvenienced when boys leave for training, the 18-year-olds are such a small percentage of the labor force that their induction will have a minor effect upon the labor market. But perhaps Congress will recommend that, if they wish, the boys shall return to their old jobs at the end of their training.—*Harry L. Hopkins, Special Adviser to President Roosevelt. American Magazine. Mr. '45. p. 101-2.*

NEGATIVE DISCUSSION

POSTWAR COMPULSORY MILITARY TRAINING [1]

Amid the storm and stress of war and its concomitant emotions, citizens of the United States are being urged to adopt postwar compulsory military training. We should approve of it now, it is said, because, after the war, Americans may become apathetic, even hostile, towards such a measure of military preparedness, out of keeping with their tradition. The Gurney-Wadsworth bill (S. 701; H.R. 1806, February 11, 1943), recently under consideration by the Military Affairs Committee of the houses of Congress, proposed one year of naval or military service at age 18, or within three years following, and enrollment as a reserve for four years, such training to begin six months after the war, or earlier if Congress so decides. The May bill (H.R. 3947, January 11, 1944) would have required military or naval service of "every able-bodied male citizen" and all male resident aliens at age 17, or at completion of high school, whichever comes first, and reserve enrollment for eight years with refresher periods of training, the same to be operative as soon as the present Selective Service Act ends. A similar bill (H.R. 515, January 3, 1945) is now before the 79th Congress.

Another measure is being prepared by the House Committee on Post War Military Policy (authorized, March 28, 1944, by H.R. 465), charged with assembling "information, plans, and suggestions" relative to military requirements of the United States after the war. Fourteen of the twenty-three members of the Committee, which is under the chairmanship of C. A. Woodrum, are from the committees on military and naval affairs. What the Committee's proposals will be is uncertain, but they will probably reflect the wishes of army and navy

[1] By Thomas Woody, University of Pennsylvania, Philadelphia. *Social Studies.* 36:191-6. May 1945.

leaders who have long favored and planned for universal conscription.

What reasons are brought forward to support the proposed legislation? Prevention of war and preparation for it, improvement of health, perfection of citizenship, its bearing on our economy in a number of ways, and its democratic character are generally set down to the credit of military training in peacetime. Are these claims valid?

Back of the proposals for universal training is the *idée fixe* that military preparedness prevents war, and lack of it leads to them. Representative May's formula declares: ". . . the experiences of the present conclusively establish that the lack of such a system results in unnecessary wars, the needless sacrifice of human life, the dissipation of the national wealth, and useless disruption of the social and economic fabric of the nation, and causes international discord and interracial misunderstandings." The Citizens' Committee for Universal Military Training argues to the same effect: ". . . international agreements, unsupported by established military policy, have invariably failed." The "military defenses" of the United States have always been set up "too late to prevent war." "We wanted peace in 1917 and again in 1939," says another advocate, "but each time we were unprepared and so we had war."

The *Philadelphia Record* wants compulsory training as "an insurance policy for peace." President Seymour of Yale declares that, if we had had compulsory military training, as Washington and Knox once wished, "we should not have had to undergo the holocaust of the past five years. By means of such a system the Swiss democracy has maintained her freedom in peace." Thirty-one per cent of those polled by the National Opinion Research Center believe that wars would be less likely if we and other nations required universal military training.

Does the history of national compulsory military training lend any weight to such claims? France established the pattern of compulsory service (1793, 1798); Prussia followed suit (1806), and the German Empire pursued the conscriptive training policy after 1871. In neither case has universal training for war prevented its advent. A vast conscript army gave Napoleon power for his drive to conquer Europe, but when other nations adopted the same method, the brief initial advantage to the innovator was neutralized. Even the prodigious preparations of France, both by training forces and by building the Maginot Line, neither secured her from attack nor made her strong in resistance.

The Soviet Union's extensive, peacetime military training did not preserve her against attack. Her sturdy resistance of invasion, and ultimate success in driving invaders out owes much, perhaps more, to her internal unity, mass resistance, singleness of purpose and leadership, economy of means, elimination of private profit, territorial factors, and the like. If these great powers that had compulsory training, and yet were attacked in spite of it, had required a year or two more of it, would that have preserved them from war? Would England have been spared, if she had instituted universal military training after World War I? If the United States had adopted such a program in 1919, would it have kept her out of this war? Would it have speeded her entry into it? As for smaller states, did compulsory training save Belgium, the Netherlands, Poland, Italy, Finland, Norway, Czechoslovakia? If they had had more training, would that have prevented war's advent? Europe's sad history for 150 years suggests that those who want to institute compulsory military service in the United States should find a sounder argument than that such a program will prevent wars, or that it will win them.

Far from preventing our engagement in a third world war, the immediate adoption of postwar military conscription by the United States might be an important factor in bringing it to pass. When the war ends, we shall have 12,000,000 or more trained men. Add to these a million and a quarter each year, and keep up armaments in proportion (for no one thinks trained men would suffice without up-to-the-minute equipment), and what nation would not have good reason to fear our strength? Instead of proving our intention to back up commitments that may be made in respect to a United Nations' organization for security, universal peacetime conscription might be viewed as a danger to such a system—an evidence that we wished to be strong enough to repudiate any proposed settlement of disputes not to our liking.

With or without a United Nations' security system, what effect might one expect our immediate adoption of peacetime conscription to have on our "Good Neighbors" to the South; and on Canada which even in wartime has striven to avoid conscription for overseas service? Latin Americans have not forgotten the "Colossus of the North," despite the era of "good neighborliness." Perhaps Argentina keeps old memories green. What might they not fairly fear if the Colossus, heretofore unpretentious in respect to military might, were to put on her whole armour? If rich and powerful Germany and France, with the greatest compulsory training system on the continent of Europe, have for a century and a half been the matrix of world war, from which their smaller neighbors were unable to isolate themselves, what may reasonably be expected if the richest nation in the Western world embarks on a program of universal preparation for war?

A choice is to be made. We should make no mistake; universal military training is preparation for war, not peace. It is proposed as a measure of defense. Against whom? Germany's military power is to be totally destroyed, and Japan is to be reduced to the status of 1896. So our leaders have assured us; and we have given them unstinted backing in men and materials to fulfill their promises. Prostrate Germany and Japan cannot be the dangers against which we need to prepare by peacetime conscriptive service. The only great armed nations remaining are Great Britain, the Soviet Union, and China—our allies who have vowed with us to establish collective security. Adoption of universal conscriptive training now would appear to be an admission of defeat of collective security before we have risked anything in its behalf. Such a program makes more sense as a foundation for national isolationism and expanding imperialism than it does for international cooperation. Congressman John M. Costello defends it frankly as our "big stick," which "we can present to the world . . . to preserve law and order." The world's peoples may well tremble, if each policeman decides how big a club he will carry.

A second argument for universal military training is that it will improve the nation's health. The Director of Selective Service reported, February 25, 1944, that over half of those registered failed to pass physical and mental tests. About four million have been classed 4F for various causes, approximately one sixth of them for remediable defects. Obviously there is room for improvement. There is reason to doubt, however, whether compulsory military training is the best way to secure it. Such a program would take "able-bodied" youth about 18, test them thoroughly, fix their teeth, and remedy other deficiencies, as far as possible, feed and clothe them well, and give them plenty of exercise. Doubtless the group thus cared for would be ruddier, more rugged, slimmer, and straighter at the end of a year. But does any physician or physical training expert think that 18 or 19 is the optimum moment for initiation of a health regimen; or that, once properly conditioned, individuals will continue in good trim, even with occasional refresher courses? Obviously, many weaknesses, such as will be discovered at 18, should have been found and remedied long before 18. A large fraction of the rejections could have been prevented by early remedial measures. A year's regimentation of health, diet, and exercise cannot undo the effects of bad environment and habits of all the preceding years.

If we want a nation with good health (we need it, and should want it, whether for peace or for war), we shall clearly have to begin at a tenderer age than 18, taking care that children be properly fed and housed, be provided with ample facilities for recreation and physical training during the school years, and have medical attention whenever needed. I say children, not boys only. A nation cannot go far on one leg. For both boys and girls these facilities to promote health and physical fitness should be provided by the expansion of appropriate, civilian, community services, aided where necessary by state and federal subsidies.

Compulsory peacetime military training is also recommended, by many advocates, as a discipline for life and for democracy. It will teach us self-denial, they say, inculcate the ideas of democracy, impress a sense of our obligations to government, teach respect for authority and obedience to superiors, and will promote good relations generally between all citizens, if we are compelled to live and work together for a year under martial discipline. A Spartan training has often been admired by those who never lived under it. All of these are phases of citizenship training. That education for citizenship has long been one of the purposes of our general system of education, is well known; but military training, it is asserted, will add something not learned in schools and colleges. It should be noted, of course, that the legislation now being debated in Congress does not specify all these goals. The bills are designed simply to provide military training. The peripheral values of such prescriptive service are read into it by some who are inclined to find a panacea in one bottle. Take it; it's good for whatever ails you! It is quite probable that if the proposal of compulsory service becomes law, its passage will owe much to pressure groups that anticipate results quite apart from military competence in defense of the United States.

That certain by-products will derive from compulsory military training of all male youth is accepted by those who oppose conscription, as well as by those who urge its adoption. The character traits developed in the army are looked upon with skepticism by many. Others are emphatically sure they do not want them. "Soldiering" is not a concept that arose from civil circles. Learning the "great army game," however useful in the army, is of dubious value in competitive life outside of it. Opponents object to the system also, precisely because the concomitants of universal military training are not serviceable to democracy but to totalitarianism of one form or another. A democracy may introduce, but it cannot long survive the militarism which universal conscriptive training nourishes and ultimately perfects.

A year of instant obedience to commands and indoctrination with ideas of government, at the hands of officers whose education is not primarily or broadly political and certainly not necessarily democratic, may well develop attitudes that are inimical to self-government. Sound knowledge of social, economic and political affairs, an open mind towards opinions of others, critical judgment, and independence of thinking and acting are indispensable to democracy. Individual thinking is the best antidote against mass thinking. Reason is the first and last defense against authoritarianism. Competent, independent thinking is not easily developed, even in institutions that are designed to promote it. Armies have never favored its encouragement. As Frederick the Great said: "If my soldiers would really think, not one would remain in the ranks." Mr. Bedinger, librarian at West Point, once declared that army training there sought to break "any attempt at self-expression" and "to destroy every trace of independent thinking."

Subservience to superiors and readiness for commands are valuable, indeed indispensable, to armed forces and to authoritarian governments. The discipline required in a democracy is self-discipline, however, not that of drill sergeants. By what logic should democratic, "peace-loving" Americans fight a half-trillion-dollar war to break Nazism and Fascism, and then impose on their own sons the most conspicuous feature of the dictatorships of Germany and Italy? If there are really so many democratic values in universal military service, we have gone to a strange school and have paid a high tuition fee to discover them. That we did not need to go so far, or to such teachers, for a militaristic interpretation of democracy, is shown by the United States War Department's *Training Manual, No. 2000-25*, used for some years after 1928, which described democracy as "communistic" towards property, leading to "mobocracy" and other undesirable features of government.

We shall choose. If the choice is universal military training, let it be made with our eyes open. Militarism can grow—in the United States as it has elsewhere. It has strong roots; only fertilizing and cultivation are needed to make it flourish. Men and money are its nourishment; training is its culture. We are apt to be deluded by an old, established notion, to the effect that certain peoples (Germans and Japanese) are innately warlike, born sons of Mars, far beyond all others. Such, too, were the early Romans, according to popular belief. Polybius, Cicero, Livy, Josephus, and others, however, though recognizing they were generally good material, stressed the excellence, thoroughness and strictness of their training that made them warlike and won wars. The ancient Romans, so competent modern scholars tell us, were once as peaceful as any other peasant farmers. Step by step, from small wars to greater ones, by hard training and diligent study of warfare, they gained a name for military prowess, such as the ancient world had never seen. Rome's army ultimately ruled the state, made and unmade emperors.

In line with this thinking (some nations warlike, others peace-loving) it is alleged by the advocates of universal military training, that such a system would be democratic, because the American people are so, and that it could not foster militarism here, though it has elsewhere. Our hearts are pure; they can't be changed by training! Such a view rests on an unsound, static interpretation of the nature of institutions. Institutions grow. A hundred years ago military training in schools was a distinct rarity in the United States. The Civil War saw it pushed forward rapidly. World War I, which was to "end all wars," almost brought us to the adoption of a universal, peacetime military training program in 1920. World War II has seemingly sold most citizens the system we fought two wars to destroy. Fortunately, the dead have no ears.

Postwar military training is also urged for economic reasons. A billion dollars a year ($1,000 a head for 1,000,000 trainees), it is said, will be a most significant economy for it must be compared with the cost of waging war. Take out this $1,000,-000,000 insurance premium and avoid war. Unhappily, the insurance salesman's arguments fall flat, since all the great nations for over a hundred years have been buying expensive policies and paying for wars besides.

The argument of economy has several other phases: it concerns the use of present camps, other military establishments and trained personnel; it is proposed as a relief for postwar unemployment; and it will also be a boon as vocational preparation. In respect to the last, it is said, army training today is highly specialized, and a year of it will give trade training for jobs in later life, such as vocational schools cannot supply. Granting that some youths would certainly acquire new skills, it is doubtful, nevertheless, whether trade training gained in the army, whose primary goal would be mastery of military matters, would prove really adequate for the peacetime employments of more than a few. The year's interruption of normal life at 18 would certainly postpone for many the choice of occupation, or profession, and preparation therefor. However consequential or inconsequential such interruption and delay might prove to be, it seems most probable that youths can be prepared best for peacetime employments by vocational institutions, which have long been serving this purpose—and which can be modified to meet new demands whenever they arise. Military camps for vocational training seem, indeed, to be the longer road home, and not by any means the less expensive.

The President spoke hopefully of the camps and war plants that have cost us millions. Many others have stressed the economy of using rather than destroying them. Everyone knows well what they cost. Moreover, we shall have ready at hand a vast number of officers already in service, who could take charge of training and never have to doff their uniforms. Of course, if we were to decide that we wish to militarize the nation, it would be economical to proceed at once to utilize both material facilities and men. But this would be penny-wise, pound-foolish economy. Everybody knows that expenses for a universal military training program would keep mounting. The first billion dollars or so does not tell the tale. In brief, economy is not the real issue. What is to be decided is not whether we should save a few millions by putting all male youth into army camps that stand ready to receive them, but whether we want the social and political consequences which throughout history have flowed from universal militarization.

Universal conscript training for a year has been proffered as a remedy for unemployment. When 12,000,000 service men and other millions of men and women now engaged in our prodigiously expanded war plants return to the peacetime employment market, the competition for jobs will be acute. To these must be added the million and more of young people who normally want a job as the 'teen age draws to a close. A million and a quarter of young men, taken from the market about 18, would relieve the pressure of competition. And if one were to demobilize the men now in service very slowly, since, as General Hershey once said: "We can keep people in the army about as cheaply as we could create an agency for them when they are out," the pressure could be reduced still more.

Such a pill for unemployment would probably gag many. Even if swallowed, it could not do much good. Anyway, if we wish to relieve unemployment by keeping every male youth a year longer at school, the whole problem of desirable variations of that schooling should be examined at once, rather than stretch 1,250,000 on a Procrustean bed, never designed for education. Here again, obviously, we should keep our eyes on the ball. Military training is really designed for military, not economic, ends. To delude ourselves that it will solve unemployment problems is the grossest error.

Unemployment is a major malady of modern industrial society, as now constituted. If we want to cure it, let's stay at home and study it, rather than go visiting Mars. We had the illness long before the war. Neither the nursing care of apple vendors nor the pills of Dr. New Deal did more than dull the pain. Only the peacetime draft before the war, full mobilization of armed forces after Pearl Harbor, and turning industrial plants to making the sinews of war, at last absorbed the unemployed. When the war ends, the illness promises to flare up immediately, and with complications previously unknown. Postwar conscription of a million young men each year would, at the very best, be a slight palliative.

Democracy must discover the true roots of this economic paralysis and grub them out, if it is to endure. Pruning some of the tangled branches by induction into the army is of no avail. If it drains some temporarily from the labor market, it prepares them for a renewed destructive process—which it cannot prevent and may encourage—the ultimate consequence of which is still greater poverty and unemployment. Hitler promised to eliminate unemployment. He did so by this self-same means, putting men into military service and setting industry to the production of the materials of war. We, too, can keep youth and adults from begging on the street by putting them at this "busy work," but who can show that the remedy is not worse than the disease? What does it profit men to work so hard, and in the end clip the coupons of impoverishment? Aristotle observed truly that man labors that he may have leisure, and through leisure the good life, happiness. Employments that promise no leisure, but ever-increasing burdens of labor and of debt, lead not to the good life but to slavery.

In defense of the present proposals it is sometimes asserted that compulsory training is in harmony with American tradition. The argument of "harmony," however, is obviously weak. Washington and Knox did recommend a compulsory system, to be sure, but it was turned down by Congress, and the principle has been shunned consistently by the American people. The most conspicuous "harmony" discernible is that which exists between the principles of totalitarianism and universal, compulsory military service. Without total conscriptive service Hitler and Mussolini would have been powerless to throw the world into chaos.

It is argued, furthermore, that conscription is the embodiment of liberal democratic principles, even though American citizens have been loath to accept the practice. Principle and practice may be out of harmony, certainly. Let us examine the principle, without regard to past or present modes of practice. Democratic liberalism rests on a number of important concepts; without them it loses that which sets it off from other political systems. Freedom of religion, of thought, of speech, of assembly, and of publication lie at its very foundation. Considered from the standpoint of numbers, democracy is inclusive of all, regardless of race and sex. This mass aspect of democracy is often uppermost in present-day thought and utterance; and it is very important, certainly; for, not long ago, Negroes and women were not recognized as politically competent. But, it must not be forgotten, the principle of numerical inclusiveness cannot be permitted to obscure, or negate, those principles pertaining to freedom of the mind. Certain great totalitarian states are democratic, in so far as numerical inclusiveness is concerned. But no one thinks they are democracies in any general sense, just because of a counting of noses. If one were to add to their mass character the principles of freedom of religion, speech, assembly, publication and so on, they would cease to seem a threat to democratic liberalism in the western world.

Since democracy is dependent on these liberties, if the element of inclusiveness as to numbers and the voice of the majority be carried to the extreme point of denying them, the result is tyranny, not democracy. Certain limitations on freedom are inimical to human beings, regardless of whether they are imposed by one, the few, or the many. Herbert Spencer put the matter precisely: "If men use their liberty in such a way as to surrender their liberty, are they thereafter any the less slaves? If people by a *plebiscite* elect a man despot over them, do they remain free because the despotism was of their own making?" Mill noted, long ago, the tendency of modern states "to stretch unduly the power of society over the individual, both by the force of opinion and even by that of legislation." The evil, he thought, was not only likely to decline but would grow to more formidable proportions.

The disposition, whether on the part of one or of the majority, to impose judgment on others is so strong in human nature that it is scarcely restrained by anything save lack of power. This "tyranny of the majority," whether exercised in formal or informal fashion, may issue "wrong mandates instead of right," may interfere "in things with which it ought not to meddle," and may even enslave "the soul itself." Against this, Mill declared, protection is needed. "There is a limit to the legitimate interference of collective opinion with individual independence; and to find that limit, and maintain it against encroachment, is as indispensable to a good condition of human affairs, as protection against political despotism."

Mill thought this general proposition not likely to be contested in his day, but he understood clearly that on the "practical question, where to place the limit," little or nothing had been done. If he were alive today, he would see that throughout a large part of the world even the general principle is denied. National systems of education in many lands have now to an extraordinary degree established that "despotism over the mind, leading by natural tendency to one over the body," which he deplored. In the rigor and completeness of its dominion over the mind and body of man, there is no phase of present-day education that quite equals universal, compulsory military service and training. Herein it comes at last, in many instances, to the enslavement "of the soul itself." In this form, its meaning can be read in the discriminations and punishments meted out to religious or philosophical objectors to military principles and practices. Apart from this, once in the military forces, authorities are in agreement as to the bearing of training on freedom of thinking.

A "receptive mood" and "immediate obedience" are the results sought at West Point, says R. C. Richardson. "Unconditional blind obedience" was one of the chief supports of the German army. Army discipline, said Major General J. F. O'Ryan, must be so perfect that it produces "an obedience so prompt and unquestioned that the act is performed subconsciously." Spencer, speaking of the despotism of compulsory military training on the continent of Europe, remarked: "The sphere of individual will is such only as is allowed by the will of the superior. Breaches of subordination are, according to their gravity, dealt with by deprivation of leave, extra drill, imprisonment, flogging, and, in the last resort, shooting."

In the last analysis the right judgment concerning universal, compulsory military training must be in harmony with sound, democratic principles, and in the light of what it promises respecting human liberty and justice. The advancement of civilization is measured in terms of the growth of liberty of mind. Anything that will operate more and more to restrict it, is a step downward. Military despotism over the masses, accomplished by the universal principle, led to the establishment of despotism over the schools in Napoleon's day. "It was impossible," said Taine, "for the essentially military character of Napoleon not to be marked in his work" in education. "The University, in fact, was organized like a regiment." All initiative and inventiveness were abolished. De Lanneau declared: "I am nothing but a sergeant-major of languid and mangled classes . . . to the tap of a drum and under military colors." The sharp restriction of the freedom of schools in Germany, under the Kaiser and under Hitler, and in Italy under Fascism, was contingent upon the absolute power of the state—a power resting on military force.

So it was with certain military despotisms of antiquity. It seems wishful thinking, indeed, to fancy that it will not become so in those that some are intent on building for tomorrow. Those who deal with returning veterans have often expressed regret that so many of the men seem no longer able to think for themselves; they expect to be told what to do. One may regret this result of army discipline, but no one can complain of it. Men do not gather grapes from thorns, or figs from thistles. A nation that regiments its young men of every generation in such habits of instant compliance with orders, is doing the best it can to make them the ready servants of another's will.

COMPULSORY MILITARY TRAINING? [2]

May I summarize my position at the start? Postwar world conditions may require that America break her long tradition and adopt universal compulsory military training for young men. But the case for it has not been established as yet. I, therefore, favor delay in order that the decision may be made on the basis of realities after we know what sort of a peace we are to have, and not in the basis of emotional preconceptions inflamed by the war. Let us keep on an even keel, in this matter as well as in others, until we can calmly assess the pros and cons. If universal training does become necessary, let us remember that it will be equally necessary to regiment our industrial life for total war. If we must prepare on such a scale, it will not be sufficient merely to train our young men in the art of war. I believe, therefore, that the decision should not be so hurried as the advocates of universal training propose. Finally, I believe that the so-called educational advantages of military training are easily exaggerated. If we are to have it, let it be military training as the army wants it. It is not fair to the army or to ourselves to ask it to compensate for the failures of the church, the home, and the school. If it turns out that we need universal military training, let it be

[2] By Harold W. Dodds, President, Princeton University. *Educational Record.* 26:17-26. January 1945.

military training and not some compromise compound of training for war and vague gestures towards education and social service.

Throughout, let us remember that the proposal is for *universal compulsory* training. Each of these adjectives, and particularly the adjective compulsory, introduces new elements into public service in a democracy in peacetime, elements that will have wide and unpredictable repercussions on our democratic attitudes. If I were either a Communist or a National Socialist, I should heartily approve the most extensive, all-embracing compulsory service legislation that would have any chance of adoption. It would be a precedent much to my liking. When all the implications are considered, such a measure would represent a long step toward the realization of a planned society. It would call for corresponding industrial controls, which would have grave effects upon our system of private enterprise, which I for one, being neither a Communist nor a Socialist, cherish greatly.

In all probability we shall require a considerable military force for a number of years merely to dispose of the aftermath of the present war. In that case there is no alternative to a continuance of the drafting of young men as long as may be necessary for the purpose.

The proposal for universal training is not being put forward to complete the business of this war but to prepare for the next. It is none too early to begin to think about the next war. But the place to begin is with the plans for the peace. Let us dispose of them first.

To adopt universal training today would confirm the dangerous spirit of cynicism toward all proposals to expand the scope of collective security and reign of law among nations. It would carry America to the peace conference with notice to the rest of the world that, while the Atlantic Charter was useful as a morale builder at the beginning of the war, it is not to be taken as a serious objective for the peace conference. Secretary Stimson says that we need universal service to impress other nations that we can fight. But would not the real effect at this time be to impress other nations that we place no hope in the possibility of international institutions which would tend to make world wars unnecessary? I think it would. Certainly it would confirm the sense of defeatism in respect to what we are fighting for, which Mr. Churchill expressed when he stated that the ideological aspects of the war are not so significant now as they once were. Now that it is clear that America will escape invasion —and probably even bombs—in this war, and because we are not yet fully conscious of the casualty lists yet to come, I sense on the part of the American public a most unfortunate complacency toward the next war.

Yet when one contemplates what would be the scale of another world war and the aftermath of social and economic costs, the urgency of preventing it overwhelms all other considerations. Nevertheless we are being asked to adopt compulsory universal training before we know the nature of the peace; what our international commitments will be; what areas of the world, if any, we shall be called upon to police; what we shall be called on to supply in the way of the international force contemplated by Dumbarton Oaks; or how heavily the other nations will go in for huge military establishments. To me this just doesn't make sense.

It is important that we be realistic about force in international relations. Of course force will continue as a large element in international relations so far as anyone now can foresee. But this does not exclude the evolutionary development of the reign of law among states to mitigate and direct force on an increasing scale over the years to come. It would be unfortunate indeed if the United States takes action today that would prejudge the peace or the possibility of the establishment after the war of certain practical and promising international agencies of collaboration, if only as the first concrete steps. For if such steps are not begun promptly we shall have to await another world war for an equal opportunity.

The nation must keep its head in the matter of force versus law. It must think clearly for a soft head can do as much harm as a hard heart. If we are to be even reasonably secure in the predictable future and if our influence is to count for collective security and the reign of law, we must be willing and able to fight. If we are to have an influence for international law and order, as I think we can and should, we must maintain those conditions which will make our influence count. Unfortunately this will involve force. As a nation we face, therefore, the necessity of a difficult psychological balance between a readiness to maintain the degree of force required to make us influential in the world of international relations on the one hand, and on the other a persistent zeal for the expanding reign of law among nations to replace that self-same force. If we plump for force alone we are doomed. If we ignore force we are equally doomed. It is easy to go all out for force; it is likewise easy to go all out for disarmament. The grave danger is that we shall as individuals fall into one or the other of these traps in our thinking about military training.

But the fact that we must be willing and able to fight by no means establishes the case for universal training in peacetime. The degree to which we should arm ourselves is related to what other nations do. To adopt it now before the terms of the peace are known would prejudice the establishment of the first elementary conditions of world order.

We do not yet have enough facts on which to base a judgment regarding the need for universal training. At this writing the army and navy have as yet withheld some important knowledge from us. General Marshall states that a large professional army is out of place in a democracy. How large a standing army does he mean? What is being planned as a standing army for the postwar period? Is it to be an army of 500,000 men, or 1,000,000 men, or 1,800,000 men? There have been military opinions favoring each of the two extremes. If the army heads consider a large standing army necessary, is the disruption of the lives of millions of young men by supplementary training justifiable in peacetime, in view of the speed with which the techniques of war seem to change these days? And why is a sizable standing army more out of place in a democracy than universal peacetime conscription? If this war brings no agencies of international collaboration in which we can place substantial hope of security, the regimentation of young men for war will be but one phase of national regimentation at all levels. In that case, will not the totalitarians really have won the war?

It is said that we need universal conscription because the volunteer system has always failed to give us even the small peacetime armies authorized by Congress. Has the volunteer system ever been really tried? Has the government ever sought to make a volunteer tour of army duty attractive, either in pay or in experience which a man could capitalize afterwards? The answer, I think, must be no.

Furthermore, on the strictly military side we need to know more of the experience in other countries. For example, did universal training strengthen France or weaken her by contributing to a false sense of security, which has come to be called the Maginot Line psychology? Nothing could be worse for us, as we enter an era in which the techniques of war will change so rapidly, perhaps to the degree of altering them fundamentally, than to assume that universal service is a substitute for national will. Certainly to be a prepared nation, we must be alert to the importance of science and technology; not just a nation whose young men have all had basic military training.

We are always prone to view the next war in the pattern of the last. Spectacular mobilization of armies may not signify as much as before. Scientific and engineering research may replace them as our chief line of defense.

There is another phase of national preparedness that is often overlooked; namely, ways and means of keeping aggressor nations weak and thus reducing the relative need for large forces on the part of peace-loving nations. For several generations the studied, deliberate philosophy of national aggression has been restricted to two parts of the world. Victory will give us an opportunity to remove these points as military threats. Obviously it will require wisdom to devise the best plan and persistent determination to enforce it. At this stage, to talk about peace-loving nations adopting peacetime conscription only muddies our thinking as to how to demilitarize Germany and Japan and keep them so. In my opinion a soft peace, or one that fails to restrain the Axis nations as military potentials, may well compel us to go over to total military preparedness. This is one reason why I regret the rise of any issue now that may divert us from attention to the nature of the peace.

Up to this point I have been urging as a citizen those considerations that call for delay in deciding the question of universal training.

I now come to the issues on which educators have a special right and duty to speak as their minds and experience dictate. I refer to the so-called educational advantages of universal military training. Here it is necessary to clarify our thoughts, for to use a vulgar phrase, you can't work both sides of the street for military training.

My thesis as to educational advantages is perfectly simple. To repeat, if the army is to make up for the shortcomings of the home, the church, and the school, it will not be able to give us the trained manpower it says we need. It can't do all these things and train for combat too. In Chapter I, Volume I, of *Platoon Training,* a textbook for officers, occur these words, "Success in battle is the ultimate object of all military training." No truer word was ever said on the subject. When the objective departs from this principle it becomes neither military training to meet our requirements of military power (whatever they may be) nor education for civilian responsibilities.

Take the question of discipline first. Every old man knows that the younger generation is poorly disciplined. It has always been so. I confess myself to enough gray hairs to think that many young people need discipline which they are not getting, but which in earlier days they received automatically when family conditions and economic conditions rested on a more domestic economy. While formal education is no substitute for home influences, modern pedagogy must accept its share of blame for any lack of civilian discipline in a generation, which, by the way, seems to be doing all right as soldiers.

Discipline for peacetime responsibilties and discipline for military responsibilities are two different things. Success in battle calls for its own peculiar form of discipline. It comprises the physical, mental, and emotional equipment of a soldier. I am willing to accept the word of the army that it takes one year to accomplish this, that it cannot be done properly in three summer sessions. And even a year leaves little time for frills. It would of course embrace such technical training as might be

useful to a soldier, but at a high cost of time and money compared to much more that could be done under civilian auspices.

Can a thoughtful educator argue with confidence that for
most people this peculiar attainment, military discipline, is trans-
ferable to the ordinary demands of civilian life? I think not.
Military discipline is imposed from above. It very properly consists in willingness to obey orders with the threat of punishment
for disobedience always present to control the conduct of the
individual. Civilian discipline must be self-discipline functioning from within. We all know young men who seem to have
been helped and matured by military training during the past
three or four years. What we do not yet know is how much of
this development will be carried over into civilian life afterwards. The history of past wars suggests that the brutalizing
experience of war does not carry over. Returned soldiers are
not killers. Nor does history indicate that the common soldiers
have been helped by their military training for civilian life afterwards in any significant proportion. One of the great worries
of college authorities is how they will deal with the students
returning from military service who will react against their experience with military discipline without having developed corresponding self-discipline for a peacetime way of life. How we
can get such students back into the stream of civilian responsibility will be a problem.

The advocates of universal military training have made much
of the improvement of our national health. They tell us of the
large proportion of young men who have been rejected on physical grounds.

While in many cases such rejection does not prove that the
individual cannot look forward to a long and healthy life, there
can be no doubt that the health of our youth is a matter of grave
national concern. However, the pertinent question is: Will a
year of military training materially improve the health of the
nation?

Of course most young men who qualify for military training enjoy good health while in training. Nourishing food,
regular exercise, and regular sleep and living conditions will
improve anyone's health. But, like habits of discipline, health

habits, enforced from above, will not carry over in any degree comparable with what cheaper medical care and an expanded health program in the schools and health centers would accomplish at less cost. President Roosevelt has referred to those boys in the army who didn't know how to brush their teeth. This condition is indeed regrettable, but its causes run deeply into our social life. Not brushing one's teeth is but a superficial symptom of ignorance and underprivilege, and the causes require more attention than the army can give.

Two things need to be remembered if we are to be sensible about health. One is that, if the army is to remain concentrated on national defense (which is the only reason for having an army), it cannot accommodate those young men whose physical defects bar them from being good soldiers. It cannot use those who are most in need of remedial health services. Bad teeth can be rectified and hernias corrected but by and large the army cannot turn itself into a health center, even if the year at its command were sufficient to work basic improvements for young men under par.

The second fact is that many of the conditions which render a man physically unfit occur before the lad is of military age. His ailments may run to earlier illness, malnutrition, underprivileged environment, or mere failure to receive the best remedial medical attention. Some defects are noncorrectable by most complete medical service. Poor eyes, punctured eardrums, and certain heart conditions are examples. Asthma and hay fever cannot be cured by a year in the army. Emotional instability, about which we hear so much, requires different and more prolonged treatment than the army can provide. I suggest, therefore, that universal military training will contribute little to national health. Again I repeat, much broader and more fundamental results can be attained in other ways at less cost.

The final argument which I consider unsubstantial is the proposal for a year of as yet undefined national service for all youth in which military training would be but one element. It is advocated that this plan be extended to young women and no one would be exempt. It would be presumabily a year devoted to training for good citizenship and the inculcation of ideals of public service in all youth. Secretary Knox declared that "responsibility of citizenship under a popular form of government could be taught" through military service; but he didn't say how. Others, feeling some skepticism in respect to the benefits of mere military training, would add various other features on a universal compulsory basis. In a way this is the most dangerous position of all, because it is seductive to some who dislike to face the realities of military training, even if it becomes clearly indicated that we need it in the postwar world.

Let me say at once that I am a firm believer in the value of work-on-the-job as an educational force. The large proportion of our youth who are missing this experience in their late adolescence is appalling. Work experience should be a part of the life of all young people, but it is best performed under conditions of free men and not under those of conscripts. And this goes for national work camps under any guise that rests upon compulsion by the state. It smacks too much of nazism to suit me. If events prove that we must go over to compulsory universal military training in peacetime, let us not try to mitigate the great social and economic costs by self-deception.

All this holds also for those proposals which link the inculcation of zeal for participation in public affairs with compulsory military service. The army officers with whom I have talked have no illusions on this point, although some educators seem to have fallen into the trap. Indeed, from my contacts with army officers I believe they realize that a year of compelled service is more apt to make a boy think that he has sufficiently performed his obligation to the state than to fill him with a sense of duty towards public service. It is this fear that suggests that special inducements will be required to impel young men of the right sort to continue voluntarily their preparations to be officers, after the year of compulsory service.

So far I have said nothing about the adjustment which will be required of higher education if universal training is adopted, because I regard it of less importance to the other questions I have discussed. In most cases it would result in a year's delay in graduation from college, and the average age today, twenty-two years plus, is already high for what the college gives. The consequence will be a reduction in the number of educated men, particularly among the less well to do, whose services the country cannot afford to lose. From this standpoint the effect would be substantial and serious, and I am willing to court the charge of protecting vested interests in education by saying so.

Although I am as yet far from certain that universal military training is in the national interest, of one thing I am sure. If America decides that it is necessary, the colleges and universities will find ways and means to make the appropriate adaptations, and will lend themselves loyally to it. They will faithfully and effectively contribute whatever is asked, accepting, as Americans should, the verdict of the people as to what is required of them.

IS CONSCRIPTION THE WAY TO PEACE? [3]

There is no problem facing the American people which has such tremendous import for the future as the issue of military conscription. No decision has such tremendous potentialities in its influence upon the bodies and minds of our youth. There is no question, the answer to which will have such far-reaching influence upon every institution of society—the home, the church, the school, and the fundamental principles of our democracy. No issue will so seriously influence not only the conferences at the peace table, but the whole course of world developments toward permanent peace or intermittent wars.

There likewise is no problem regarding which it is so difficult to think rationally, to free ourselves of the tense emotionalism of the present, and, in calm judgment, to render a decision. Seldom, if ever, have we had to make a major decision at a time when it was so impossible to chart the course of future developments and to foresee the results of our action.

Facing an unknown future, our emotions torn by the inescapable human losses of war, we are being driven by the aggressiveness of the military to make decisions that, even though they may be rescinded later, will have an irreparable influence upon negoti-

[3] By Francis J. Brown, Consultant, American Council on Education; Director of Study of Higher Education conducted by the House of Representatives Committee on Education. *California Journal of Secondary Education.* 20:130-5. March 1945.

ations at the peace table. It is unfortunate that we are forced to make a decision now. It is even more unfortunate that many are willing to make it now, prompted by the intenseness of our emotions rather than by the deliberations of our minds.

The deep conviction in the minds of all of us is that we must take whatever steps are necessary to do all in our power to prevent a repetition of the cataclysmic losses of war and that we must assure security for America. Recognizing these two facts, many give eager and instantaneous acquiescence to the question, "Should we have military training?" But this is not the issue. The issue is, shall there be conscription of all 18-year-old males for one continuous year of military training in military establishments, exclusively under military control?

What are the issues involved? Let us raise them by posing four questions:

1. What is the purpose of conscription?
2. Must it be universal?
3. Is there an equivalent to conscription?
4. What will be the effect of conscription upon negotiations at the armistice table and upon the future peace of the world?

There is no clean-cut answer even to the first question, "What is the purpose of conscription?" At one time conscription is justified as being of value to the individual; at another, as a means of assuring security to the nation. The two are not necessarily in opposition, but if the purpose of conscription is even secondarily to make up the deficiencies of education in terms of health, discipline, and literacy, then there is a definite admission that security alone is not sufficient justification for so drastic a departure from all that we have valued in terms of freedom for the individual.

No one asserts that education has done a perfect job, but is it necessary to give one year of military training to a million youths in order that a few may have dental work or be given the benefit of a stringent physical examination and physical outdoor exercise? If this is the justification for military training, then the army should train only 4F's; and even for these a small fraction of the amount of money required for military training, if given to public health agencies, would prevent, rather than seek only to remedy, such defects. Granting that there is juvenile delinquency, must the 95 per cent be given military training in order that the 5 per cent may have the benefit of discipline?

One may raise the serious question as to whether the external element of military discipline will in any material way build the internal disciplines that are necessary for effective citizenship. Even now, it is clear that the anonymity of the uniform and the artificial segregation of military life break down the social control of the family, the church, and the community.

For every one of these tangent values except the development of physical stamina, which will be lost again within a few months after the cessation of training, one can name equally important deleterious effects of the artificial life inevitable in a military establishment. For every illustration of a young man benefited by military training, one can point out another who has lost fundamental social and moral values not to be easily regained.

If military training is to be justified, it can be justified only on the basis of military security. The burden of proof rests with the military.

Even assuming that it can be demonstrated beyond the shadow of doubt that conscription is necessary for security, must the training be for one full year? World War II has demonstrated clearly that ground is gained only by the slow, bloody advance of infantry. Even granting the technological character of modern warfare, is it not possible to acquire the minimum knowledge, skill, and attitude in half or quarter the year the military is asserting is necessary?

Recognizing that the instruments of war will be in constant change, could we not maintain even greater military security by a period of six, or perhaps only three, months, as in Switzerland, of continuous training, followed by intermittent periods of two to four weeks until the individual is 30 years of age—too old for military service? For those who are to operate tanks, planes, and battleships and for whom longer training is required—actually only a small proportion of the total military force—could not a volunteer system with reasonably high pay and definite training in technical knowledge and skills required provide greater security than a minimum and maximum of one year?

The second question likewise can be raised pointedly, in the light of the experiences of World War II, namely, "Is conscription of *all* youth necessary?"

The record of this war demonstrates clearly that not more than three out of every ten men in uniform ever see combat. For each three men under fire, seven are required to keep the instruments of war at hand, to service planes and tanks and guns, to maintain the unprecedented movement of men and material, and to create and experiment with new instruments of destruction. To a very large degree, these skills are those required for parallel civilian activities. Why should military training be required of all ten, when only three will do more than handle mail, operate trucks, repair engines, or maintain communications?

Again, would not three months of basic military, *only when and if required by war*, be all the military training which will ever be utilized by these seven out of the possible ten? Such selective training would result in enormous economy, and, through assignment of men to military posts as nearly as possible paralleling civilian skills, would assure security equally well as universal conscription, for civilian experience and civilian education would be of even greater value than military training in equipping the seven for essential non-combat service in the armed forces.

The war has demonstrated a second factor, that it is necessary also to keep the wheels of industry turning at maximum speed, to maintain research laboratories, and to assure a minimum of civilian health. To take one year out of the lives of those who will remain civilians is to delay the effectiveness of production of the instruments of war. Certainly, for them there can be no justification for military training.

A possible answer to the third question—namely, "Is there an equivalent training that will assure equal security, yet without the losses to the individual and to the nation inevitably involved in regimentation under the military?"—already has been implied. What is a possible alternative? There is one—a voluntary system of enlistment.

Such a plan may well involve several basic principles: (1) Enlistment should be for a short period, not to exceed one year—possibly for six months—but with opportunity for such continuous reenlistment as the individual and the military shall desire; (2) Military training should include opportunity for instruction, if only in off duty time, in knowledge and skills that will have value for return to civilian life; (3) Careful individual assignment of the individual in terms of his ability and experience; and (4) Pay and opportunity for promotion such as to be a positive incentive for the individual.

An integral part of such a volunteer system should include part-time military training through such programs as the R.O.T.C. and the National Guard. Careful planning will be necessary to evolve a unified volunteer program, but through such planning the basic principles of democracy can be preserved—the right of free choice on the part of the individual in time of peace—and adequate security be provided for the nation.

Some will assert that we have tried a volunteer system in peacetime and that as a result there were but 160,000 men in the army when the Selective Training and Service Act was passed in 1940. The answer lies not in the principle, but rather in the prewar attitude toward the army and navy, and the lack of incentive. Such a program as outlined above has never been tried. Is it not worth the effort rather than now adopting a program of conscription?

To those who assert that a volunteer system is undemocratic, one can reply that the right of free choice is the essence of democracy; that regimentation of mind and body, essential in war and willingly surrendered for the interim, is the exact antithesis of every principle of democracy in times of peace.

The fourth question is the most fundamental of all. There are no facts that can be marshaled to prove one position or the other. One can only raise it as an issue and hope that whatever decision is finally rendered by the people and the Congress will not later be proved wrong. That question is, "What is the best strategy in international diplomacy, to go to the peace table with daggers in our teeth and a loaded gun, or to go with honest and sincere confidence in those with whom we shall negotiate and a belief that it is possible to lay the framework of permanent peace?

Can such a peace be built by having already taken the steps to prepare for World War III? Can we at one and the same time seek to create and participate in a world organization to maintain peace, and openly admit that we know such efforts will fail?

Those who will sit with us about the table will know that our potential enemies cannot be our present enemies, for pray God they shall be so defeated that they cannot rise again short of a quarter-century, and then only if we or our present Allies betray the peace and give them the materials for the reconstruction of their instruments of death. Each of our Allies will know, therefore, that we are anticipating that one of them is an almost certain foe and that all of them are our potential enemies of World War III. Is this an atmosphere in which there can be mutual confidence? If we are the first to take this step through this legislation, shall we not be initiating a race of arms such as the world has never known?

Mark you, we shall not go to the peace table unarmed in any case. We have demonstrated our potential strength. We shall have a reserve force of not less than ten million men, at least five million of whom will have had actual military duty and be young enough to pick up again the hideous weapons of war. Is World War III so imminent that there will not be adequate security for the years in which a world organization for permanent peace can be created?

The most alarming statement which I have heard in all of the discussion of military training was made recently by one whose voice is well known across the nation, "We must be ready to meet all comers, friend or foe." Peace cannot be secured permanently with this attitude of mind and in such an atmosphere. Have we not at last, as we apparently had not on November 11, 1918, destroyed enough cities, sacrificed enough of the accumulated culture of the centuries, mutilated enough bodies, and shed enough blood to sit down now as individuals and as nations, confident that all seek peace, and build a world ruled by cooperation and not by competitive armaments, by reason and not by emotion, by peace and not by the eternal fear of war? . . .

History does not support the statement, often made, that if we had been armed Pearl Harbor would not have been bombed. Pearl Harbor was the result of our failure; in 1921 to participate in a world organization to maintain the peace; in 1931 when no international move was made to resist the Jap invasion of Manchukuo; in 1935 when Hitler's goose-stepping puppets crossed the narrow bridge into the Saar Valley and began the erection of the series of forts that is now the grave of tens of thousands of American youth. The will to peace and an international police force would have prevented Pearl Harbor.

The beginnings of a new world order were charted at Dumbarton Oaks. Shall we even now, before it can be created, turn our backs again upon world organization and resort to individual defense and the mailed fist? Such a policy of military isolation can lead only to economic and political isolation at a time when the world is being drawn ever closer together by trade and commerce for intellectual cooperation and for security. We cannot at one and the same time give lip service to world cooperation and maintain an individualistic attitude of defense willing "to take on all comers, friend or foe." Suspicion and cooperation cannot exist together.

THE CASE AGAINST PEACETIME
CONSCRIPTION [4]

There is being proposed at the present time, *a permanent policy of peacetime conscription* which would make it compulsory for all able-bodied young men to undergo a year of continuous training in the army or navy. Liability for service would begin with the eighteenth year or within four years thereafter. Youth of seventeen years of age who had completed high school could volunteer for induction with the consent of parents or guardians. After completion of training, the trainees would be

---

[4] By Rev. Edward V. Stanford, O.S.A., M.S., LL.D., Augustinian College, Washington, D.C. *National Catholic Educational Association Bulletin.* 41:17-25. February 1945.

enrolled as reservists in the land or naval forces for a period of six years.

This proposal contemplates a radical departure from our traditional policy of the past 160 years. It would have far reaching implications not only on the lives of our youth but upon the whole political and social structure of our nation. It would be folly to rush into the adoption of such a policy without giving careful study and weighty consideration to its purpose, its necessity and its probable effects.

Unfortunately, much of the propaganda and many of the arguments employed in favor of peacetime conscription have clouded the real issue and have made for confused thinking.

In order to get at the heart of the matter, the following considerations need to be stressed:

It is a peacetime, not a wartime measure that is being proposed. Therefore it has nothing to do with fighting the present war. It is not intended to affect the operation of Selective Service. It is not envisioned as a means of shortening the period of service of the men now under arms or who may be called to arms under Selective Service. It is not designed as a method of providing an army of occupation after the defeat of Germany and Japan.

It is possible to be opposed to peacetime conscription on reasonable grounds without being a pacifist, an isolationist or one guilty of short-sightedness as regards national defense.

It is possible to be opposed to peacetime conscription and still believe that a type of universal military training can be secured in peacetime by other than conscription and under other than the exclusive control of the army and navy.

It only beclouds the issue, to link up with peacetime conscription such matters as: Improving physical fitness, developing habits of character and discipline, indoctrinating in the democratic way of life, removing illiteracy, etc.

It does violence to the meaning of words, whether in war or in peace, to call military conscription (the favorite tool of dictators for more than a hundred years) the *more democratic method* of raising armed forces.

The point at issue may be stated simply: Compulsory universal military training in peacetime *is or is not* the advisable way, the necessary way, the American way to meet our future problem of national and international security.

There are those who hold with conviction that peacetime military conscription *is not* the advisable way, the necessary way or the American way to meet our problem of providing either for our national security or for international peace. In this conviction I heartily concur, but at the same time I believe that we shall have to maintain a large army and navy with adequate reserves for many years to come, not only to help safeguard the peace under whatever international organization may be adopted, but also for our own national security. Furthermore, there must be provided an effective means of recruiting a large army and navy with adequate reserves. I have sufficient confidence in American ingenuity to believe that this can be accomplished without resort to the extreme method of peacetime conscription.

In all this talk about the paramount importance of adopting a policy of peacetime conscription, it should be clearly understood that the maintenance of a reserve of manpower sufficiently trained so as to make possible the rapid expansion of the armed forces in time of need, is *only one of the means* of safeguarding our national security. There are other important safeguards that must not be overlooked and should not be considered apart from peacetime conscription.

The forging of a just peace and the building of an international organization to protect it, can make the best and most lasting contribution to national security. It is pertinent to ask whether the adoption at this time of a permanent policy of peacetime conscription might not jeopardize the possibility of such an organization even before it is born.

A well-trained professional army and navy, supplied with the most modern equipment and kept constantly up to date on rapidly changing military techniques is essential. The year-round job of training hundreds of thousands of conscripts would cut into the efficiency of the regular army and navy.

The part played by invention and scientific development in the present war, needs no comment. Therefore, the carrying on of continual research and development in the science of defensive and offensive warfare is an important protection for national security. Peacetime conscription for all our youth will nip in the bud many of our promising candidates for higher studies and research, and by interrupting their development, turn them off into other activities less profitable for the nation.

The present war has been a war of production. Excellent management and skilled craftsmen and mechanics have given our armed forces superiority over all others. It is difficult to see how peacetime conscription would contribute here.

In the interest of national security, it is important to build up adequate stockpiles of strategic raw materials and to establish standby production arrangements with industry for prompt conversion to war needs. Peacetime conscription can render no assistance here.

When the problem of national security is viewed as a whole, it is difficult to follow the War Department claim that peacetime conscription is the *keystone* of their plans to meet any future attacks. The efficient systems of conscription which were in use in France, Belgium and other European countries, did not prevent these countries from going down to defeat before numerically inferior forces.

Making all due allowances for the importance of having a pool of military trained manpower in peacetime, conscription, at the best, is but a doubtful way of attaining this objective. Although military conscription has proved to be very successful in wartime, this is no guarantee that it will be even moderately successful in peacetime. The whole environment and psychology of peacetime differ radically from that of wartime. Peacetime measures, which have the character of permanence, will have a vastly different effect on our social and political structure than the same measures would have when adopted as emergency or temporary expedients in wartime.

Peacetime conscription, as presently proposed, will be more detrimental than helpful to our country. It will be detrimental to the *morale* of our youth; it will be detrimental to the *vocations and careers* of our youth; it will be detrimental to the *re-*

ligion and morals of our youth; it will be detrimental to our *political and social institutions.*

It will be detrimental to the morale of our youth. Because of the gravity of the present war, the savagery of the fighting and the heavy casualties, there is strong motivation for youth to take military training seriously as a life and death matter. Facing the possibility of actual combat, youth of 17 and 18 years and older are more serious and mature than they would be at comparable ages in peacetime. They are more amenable to officers, to chaplains and to restraint in general than they would be in time of peace. In brief, the morale problem will be much greater in peacetime than in wartime while the agencies and measures now in use to keep up morale will tend to be weaker, much less effective or disappear altogether. Our present experience with the morale of large numbers of young men in camps and out of camps is much better than it was in pre-Pearl Harbor days and it is much better than we can expect in peacetime.

It will be detrimental to the vocations and careers of our youth. A young man will be taken away from his family and community at the very time that he is thinking and preparing for a vocation or career in life. Particularly if he is thinking of one of the learned professions and has ambitions and abilities that would enable him to qualify as a doctor, clergyman, scientist, etc., a year in a military camp—with its "soft-pedaling" of initiative, its "don't think, but obey" maxims—could really do things to an impressionable youth which would change for the worse his whole life. Almost any educator can bear witness to the harmful effect, particularly on the superior-type student, of taking him away from his studies for a whole year at this period of his life. The dislocations in the ambitions and careers of our youth under peacetime conscription would bode ill for our country.

It will be detrimental to the religion and morals of our youth. The proposed plan of compulsory military training would remove young men from home and community influences at a time when they need this environment most as a protection against moral and religious laxity. The isolation of large numbers of men in camps, away from the helpful influence of home and community is notorious for bringing about a coarsening of manners, speech and morals. When released periodically from the constraint of camp life, there is great temptation to drinking, carousing and sexual laxity. There is every reason to believe that this problem will be greater in peacetime than in wartime. The young men will all be of the same impressionable age, whereas now the wider distribution of ages helps some. They will all be essentially "buck privates" or "boots." Officer training will be reserved for other programs which are to be superimposed upon the year of military training.

During the present war extraordinary efforts have been made by the government and by civilian agencies to protect the religion and morals of the men in the armed forces. Under the motivation of war intensive efforts have been made which would tend to peter out under a long-term policy of peace. The young men presently in the armed forces have the motivation of a deadly serious war, the help of chaplains and religious services, the various activities of the U.S.O, and of private agencies and individuals, to help, in place of home and community environment, to keep them straight. In general, counteracting forces for good will either disappear or be much weaker in peace than in wartime.

It will be detrimental to our political and social institutions. In our form of government, military cliques, military dictatorships and the military mind have been conspicuously absent. Ultimate policy and decision in military matters, even in wartime, have been kept under civilian control while allowing full place to the judgment and recommendations of professional military leaders. It is important that we keep it so. We have tragic examples in Germany and Japan of what can happen if it be otherwise.

There are those who feel that a permanent policy of universal military training under the complete control of the military would jeopardize this traditional balance. It would also have a disruptive influence on home life, insofar as the government would be stepping into the home and taking therefrom youth during their minority, for at least a year of training apart from all parental influence and authority. It would, in a sense, usurp the functions of our educational system during at least one year of a youth's life. It would tend to weaken the hold of the church upon the young as many chaplains and church leaders can testify.

The developing of better health and discipline for our youth are sometimes urged as benefits to be derived from a program of compulsory military training. It is fallacious to assume that a year of military training can adequately solve these problems and there is no reason whatever to permit the military system to usurp the obligation and function of the home, the school and the community in this regard.

Peacetime conscription is not the democratic and up-to-date method of protecting ourselves against future hostile attacks. Although compulsory military training in peacetime would be a radically new idea in the United States, it is not a new or untried idea in the world at large. It was not designed to meet the problem of modern war and there is no evidence to show that it has met that problem. France, Belgium and other countries of Europe have had compulsory military training for years, but it did not enable them to withstand the "luftwaffe" and the "blitzkrieg." It would seem, rather that it had lulled them into a false feeling of security. Now that we are in the war on all fronts, there is ample evidence that our soldiers have not met better or more intelligent fighting men in Germany, Italy or Japan. Yet these nations have had universal military training for years.

We realize that we are no longer protected by wide expanses of ocean. We can be the prey of the airborne troops, super-bombers, robot engines of destruction and the more fantastic weapons of a future enemy. We are prosecuting the present war with vigor, with imagination and with ingenuity. We should not make the mistake of adopting what well may be an outmoded system to enforce peace and to meet the future threat of ultra-modern war.

We need a sufficiently large and well-trained army and navy, properly equipped. We should have adequate reserves with sufficient training to enable our armed forces to be rapidly expanded in time of need. We want our youth to be physically fit.

We want to preserve and enhance the scientific, inventive, mechanical and productive genius of our people. We want to preserve our spiritual inheritance with maximum freedom for the individual.

Under the hysteria and confusion of war, why rush into a program that goes so contrary to our traditions and may endanger that which has been, up to now, our national strength? Why is there so much need of haste? When the war is over and the pattern of peace is clearer and most of the men and women presently in the armed forces, whose children would be vitally affected by the proposed legislation, have returned, it will be possible to act much more intelligently. In the meantime Selective Service will take care of our needs, not only during the war, but also for sometime afterwards if necessary.

We need more study, discussion and planning to appraise properly our problem and to gauge the probable effects of the measures proposed to meet it. Have we given sufficient consideration to meeting the need for a large army and navy by making voluntary service in the armed forces more attractive as a career, financially and otherwise? Are we sure that a more beneficial type of universal military training cannot be worked out through the schools and colleges, through the National Guard and through summer military camps? A plan, which would utilize all these agencies and assign to each its share in the program, might even require by law the participation of all youth physically able and still avoid most of the dangers that seem inherent in the proposal now before Congress. Such a program might be more difficult and expensive to operate—and it is not the way the totalitarian nations would work it out—but would it not be more in accord with our ideal of maximum liberty for the individual?

SHALL WE CONSCRIPT YOUTH FOR PEACETIME MILITARY TRAINING? [5]

In the first place, peacetime conscription is not necessary in order to insure the occupation of Germany and Japan, or to meet

[5] From a radio address by Dr. V. T. Thayer, Leader of the New York Society for Ethical Culture, July 8th, 1945. 9p. mimeo. New York Society for Ethical Culture.

the obligations we shall assume in the period of transition from war to peace. The present conscription act can be extended to carry us safely through this period. There is no need to confuse what is essential in order to win the war and to insure the inauguration of peace with what shall be our permanent policy in the postwar world.

Secondly, it is important not to identify the so-called educational advantages, often associated with military training, with the cold realities of conscription. Nothing illustrates more pathetically the American's antagonism to war, and all of its trappings, than his tendency to cloak military training with educational virtues. Only thus can we explain the repeated efforts to bait the hook of conscription so as to conceal its true nature.

For example, it was hinted vaguely early in the campaign for peacetime conscription that it might be associated with a national youth program. In response to this suggestion public school superintendents, as indicated on a nation-wide questionnaire, voiced considerable sentiment in favor of combining military training with a program of national service "on useful public projects" and camping experiences "which emphasize such things as health, physical fitness, outdoor living, recreation, work experience, leadership training and individual guidance."

The superintendents who grasped at this straw forgot for a moment that, as good and loyal members of the National Education Association, they were also opposed to all efforts at developing anything that resembles a federal program of education. The most powerful organizations of educators in this country are fearful of education under army auspices and will oppose it just as they fought and succeeded in killing the N.Y.A. and the C.C.C. In this they are supported heartily by the American Legion and the United States Chamber of Commerce as well as those who do not intend that military training shall serve as an excuse for reviving anything analogous to the National Youth Administration. These people wish no boondoggling or "socialistic" experiments in connection with conscription. Likewise our military leaders have stated bluntly, in hearings before Congress, that they do not want to assume responsibility either for a remedial health program or a system of general vocational education. They know their whiskey and they prefer it straight.

To this we should add the plain fact that the courts would hardly uphold the right of Congress, under our Constitution, to conscript young men in peacetime for education or for work upon the public domain or for camping experience as envisaged by the educators. Consequently we must assume that whatever benefits of an educational nature may derive from conscription are those which follow incidentally upon military training; not those we would add to it, if we could.

What are these incidental benefits? Here, too, we can observe a tendency on the part of many to seek consolation through rationalization rather than to face hard facts.

First is the argument of discipline. Thus former Congressman Costello, one-time member of the House Military Affairs Committee, states, "The sound discipline of military training will produce a most salutary result in our youth who, too often, due to broken homes or inadequate parental supervision, lack all sense of discipline. In each young man will be emphasized the respect for authority, attention to duty, obedience to superiors and faithful execution of orders."

Perhaps, but many will question the wisdom of imposing upon all young people measures that can apply only to the few. Not all homes are broken, nor are all parents neglectful of their children. Moreover, in those instances in which children are delinquent because parental affection and guidance are wanting or misplaced, the cure is not of necessity military discipline. For the one immature individual who thrives under military routine with its regimentation and subordination, there are many for whom this experience results in stunted, if not retarded development. On occasion the military camp may bring companionship and affection to the emotionally and socially undernourished individual, and he will respond as we all respond to the realization that we are loved and are needed. But this is a happy accident, not a product native to military training. Indeed, those who look to military training to discipline character, in peacetime, will do well to contrast the low state of morale in the training camps prior to Pearl Harbor with the changes that came immediately thereafter. Life in the camps is by no means restricted to marching under orders or training in unquestioned obedience to one's superiors, which seems to be the ideal of many. It includes as well vacant periods of idleness and boredom, and hours off duty without the disciplinary influence of healthy purpose. Hanson Baldwin, in the March *Harper's*, has remarked of the disciplinary value of conscription, "Without a major revision of the disciplinary and leadership methods of the services (particularly of the army), the desired end—improvement of the national character—probably would not be accomplished." And he quotes a G.I. who states, "In regard to discipline, I am not quite sure what people mean. . . . No one knowing the army can describe the standards of morals and habits formed there as uplifting. Quite the contrary. . . . The discipline our young men need is that provided by a job which they respect, and which, in its requirements of punctuality, interest in work, and skill, and in its demands for visible accomplishment, provides a chance . . . to grow and to acquire positions of higher responsibility. The army, except for a few who are professionally inclined toward an army career, does little to give this real discipline. It does much to destroy it, and is thus an evil to be lived through."

No, military discipline is not identical with the requirements of discipline in civil life. And why should it be? The purpose of military discipline is to simplify action so that men can fight and kill efficiently, unhampered by disturbing inquiry or normal compunction. This discipline is of an order different from the discipline that makes for intimate, wholesome, and satisfying relations between people in family and neighborhood, or the more impersonal associations of business, professional and political life.

We do not need military training in order to prepare young men for civilian life. There is also some reason for believing that modern conditions of warfare render conventional notions of military discipline out of date.

Compare, for example, the German and the American on the Western front. The German was the ideal product of military discipline. The American was not. And, for this reason, the American exercised an initiative and a resourcefulness totally lacking in the German. Harold Denny, writing for the *New York Times* from the Ardennes, pointed out that the American lacks utterly the abject subordination to authority so characteristic of the German. He is an individualist and for this reason, says Denny, he is less likely to be bewildered and discouraged by a new and unexpected situation. Indeed, Denny attributes the American's success to qualities precisely the opposite of those extolled by ardent advocates of military training. It is the American's self-reliance and initiative that enable him to carry on in desperate emergencies—when he has lost all his officers and has to think for himself. This same American, continues Denny, is "critical of his officers and unwilling to respect their rank alone." "In a tight place American soldiers have been known to disregard an incompetent or cowardly officer and take over command for the duration of that particular emergency." This trait makes for lack of discipline, but, to quote Denny again, "it certainly keeps officers up to scratch." On the other hand, the American soldier is wholesouled in "admiration for a man he is willing to consider as good as he is."

The value of compulsory military training as a means for discipline and character development is thus highly questionable.

Will it contribute, as many believe, to a raising of the level of citizenship? For example, the late Secretary Knox wrote that it would help young men "to find a purpose in life, a place in society," and other enthusiasts have added that it would "promote a law-abiding citizenry."

Many sincere and competent students of human nature fear precisely the opposite. For example, the distinguished sociologist, Charles A. Ellwood, holds that military training may render more violent the conflicts between capital and labor and rival racial groups. Thus, he states, "When the whole population has been trained to the use of armed force, they naturally resort to armed force as a political weapon." What will strikes become, he inquires, "if the strikers are trained in military methods?"

Doubtless both of these remarks are overly partisan. Military training, as any experience, affects individuals differently. It is conceivable that the routine and regimentation of the army camp will meet the mental hygiene needs of a small number of insecure and immature individuals. This same discipline together with the cramming, learning by rote and the mastery of specific operations without inquiry into underlying principles, will drive others well-nigh insane. So, too, will men vary in their response to the indoctrination that Secretary Knox evidently identified with instruction in citizenship.

In one respect, conscription can contribute toward democratic understanding. I refer to the mingling in the camp of young men from varied backgrounds and all economic and social groups. In Switzerland, we are told, this experience has exercised a positive democratic influence. At best, however, this is but a rudimentary step in a genuine education for citizenship. To assume that in itself it will produce the qualities essential for responsible citizenship in civilian life is naive indeed.

Nor is there anything in the military camp designed to inculcate the habits and the ideals which constitute the heart of democratic procedure: the conference method and the spirit of compromise, a willingness to talk things over and, in the course of discussion, to search for an understanding of the other fellow's point of view in the hope that imagination and good-will will create solutions that can harmonize warring interests.

The argument that universal military training will raise the health level of our people is also at best an exaggeration. It is true that an annual inventory of rejections with their causes might serve a useful purpose. But to introduce military training for this purpose is both a costly and a complicated method of confirming the fact that the barn is locked after the horse is stolen.

As a matter of fact, the draft would apply only to young men between the ages of 18 and 22. It would not benefit girls nor would it reach back to correct defects in childhood, when serious defects can alone be anticipated. The major causes for rejection from the army and the navy—tuberculosis, heart trouble, mental deficiencies, neurological disorders, crippling injuries—would remain untouched by conscription. Indeed there is danger that reliance upon military training as a means of improving the health of our people would retard health measures at points where they are badly needed. The easy assumption that one year of military training can offset the failure of home and school and community might encourage us to neglect health programs at their most crucial point; namely, in the early years of childhood. It is in these years rather than at 18 and thereafter that the health of our nation is determined. Nourishing food, hygienic conditions in home and community, assured medical care, good housing, and a sound educational and recreational program constitute the conditions for good health.

One of the most amazing achievements of the army and the navy in this war has been the rapid and efficient preparation of large numbers of young men for the highly specialized operations of modern war. So impressed are many with this success that they would make over our schools in the image of army instruction. It is not surprising therefore to encounter the argument that compulsory military training can serve both a military and a vocational function.

This overlooks certain pertinent facts. In the first place the army and navy programs are not weighed down at present by a dual purpose. They center instead upon the skills and techniques required for specific performance as defined by the rapidly changing requirements of war. No time is wasted in developing either the theory or the basic understanding essential for flexible adjustment to change and progress. Research and inquiry, in short the genuinely educational functions, are assigned to specialists. As machines are outmoded or demands on the front change, men are shifted from one operation to another, often at great personal loss in time and training. But this is inevitable, since wars are not won by consulting the interests and needs of the individual.

Vocational education for civilians, on the other hand, is an altogether different problem. Success turns upon securing a general understanding of basic principles that cut through specific operations and are applicable to what we might term families of occupation. The individual is thus prepared to meet new conditions and at best to become the master and not the servant of change.

The notion that valuable vocational training and guidance can be combined with compulsory military training is a dangerous will-o-the wisp. It will not stand inspection as a sound procedure for the mass of individuals affected. It cannot benefit young men who will enter the professions or occupations that call for a different order of skills. Nor can anyone trained for a brief period in the specific operations appropriate to military performance be assured that these will correspond to the most up-to-date methods in business and industry or, for that matter, in war, shortly thereafter. Finally, we should hesitate to delegate training other than military to the military. The American people should deliberate long and prayerfully before they entrust a national system of vocational education to our military establishment, thus taking education away from the localities and the specific characteristics and needs of the civilian vocations.

To associate general vocational education with military training is thus questionable from an educational point of view. It is also a doubtful military expedient since it would require military leaders to combine two quite different functions. To quote Hanson Baldwin again, "A program of vocational and educational training plus military training would be neither fish nor fowl; the military program—which is the fundamental purpose of conscription—would be hopelessly hobbled, nor would there be sufficient time to educate properly. The net result would be boondoggling."

The army realizes this and asks that it be permitted to stick to its last. Moreover many military leaders fear that the training of large masses of men each year will keep experienced officers so busy that they will lack the time and the opportunity to study the tactics and the strategy which alone can keep our military equipment up to date and personnel ever on its toes. And need I mention the very real danger that conscription will foster the growth of powerful groups and establishments with huge investments and active interests in equipment and supply that would operate to retard the innovation and inventiveness and the initiative demanded in modern war? In this connection we cannot afford to ignore the experience of France under conscription. What leads us to believe that we shall withstand better than she the corrosive influences of a military bureaucracy? The development of special interest groups within and without the government who organize to resist change and to perpetuate old methods and defunct equipment? The exercise of influence that wins promotion without respect to ability or fails to weed out incompetents?

It is by no means self-evident that we should have been better prepared to fight this war had we introduced conscription immediately following the First World War. Who knows how badly this would have weighed us down with antiquated equipment and still more antiquated officer personnel? It was rather the depression with its debilitating effects upon American industry and technically equipped manpower that caused our preparedness program to resemble an empty sack in the critical days of 1940 and 1941.

This brings us to the basic issue. Is conscription the wisest and best method to employ as a means for national defense?

I have said that most people either favor or acquiesce in conscription because they can envisage no alternative. They want to meet our international obligations under the World Charter and they do not propose to tempt an aggressor nation in the future to attack us unprepared. And, since our military authorities seemingly agree that this spells conscription, they are ready to accept conscription.

They need to be told that this is not altogether correct! Censorship of thought and of expression are always dangerous. But when censorship is imposed upon men who are professionally and technically equipped to express judgment upon this profoundly important question of conscription—then it may prove to be doubly dangerous. And yet there is evidence that this is precisely the situation today. There are large numbers of able men in our military establishment who believe that conscription is not the wisest policy to follow, from a strictly military point of view. These men are not free to speak their minds. Why? Because the army and the navy have officially decided otherwise. These men should be heard before the American people take final action on conscription.

Many distinguished military authorities regret the official decision of the army and the navy to take advantage of the war in order to force peacetime conscription upon the American people. Liddell Hart in his book, *Why Don't We Learn from History?* argues that conscription does not fit the conditions of modern warfare—its specialized equipment, mobile operations, and fluid situations. General Frederick C. Fuller, writing in the *Encyclopedia Brittanica*, states that "conscription is the military expression of an agricultural democracy and when natives cease to depend on agriculture—it rapidly becomes a burden." "Military power today," he continues, "depends on the numbers of skilled mechanics, not only to manufacture war machines, but to fight them. The advent of the motor-driven battle vehicles has reintroduced armor as an essential in tactical organization." Therefore, he argues, the trend of the future is toward smaller armies "in which quality will replace the quantity theory of the present cannon fodder masses." And, he concludes, that "the theory of conscription has run its course and is today out of date. . . . The fighting armies of the future will be voluntary, highly professional and highly paid; consequently, comparatively small. This is the whole tendency of present-day military evolution."

John Fischer's thoughtful article in the January *Harper's* on "The Future Defense of the U.S.A." does not deal directly with conscription; but it does argue that defense requires not a huge military establishment but a relatively small army, a flow of fighting machinery as against a big reserve of equipment and munitions and, above all, an industrial plant operating at high efficiency and maintaining a generous pool of technically equipped personnel.

The arguments of these authorities who look to the future rather than to the past in order to formulate the conditions of sound national defense suggest the wisdom of going slow in this issue of peacetime conscription. For some years to come we shall have available a reserve of millions of men tempered in the fires of actual warfare. Surely we can safely employ as a substitute for mass conscription a policy designed to keep us up to date in the requirements of modern war.

1. We can subsidize military research so that in the event of war we shall not be fighting with the ideas or the machines of a previous war.

2. We can provide generous scholarships in mathematical and engineering skills so that we shall have available always a reserve of technical experts.

3. We can establish officer training schools with adequate financial and professional inducements so that officer personnel will always be at hand to train a citizen's army.

4. We can maintain through adequate financial inducements a professional army sufficiently large to serve our peacetime purposes and to act as a nucleus in case of war.

5. And, finally, we can take steps as a nation to insure that our industrial plants continue to operate on a level of employment sufficient to provide when necessary both a trained personnel and an essential equipment. John Fischer has said that "from a strictly military standpoint we cannot afford another depression."

Such a policy, supplemented by generous federal subsidies designed to insure the adequate care of children and a fair measure of educational opportunity for all young people, would seem adequate for any emergency we are likely to face in the foreseeable future. It avoids alike the waste and the evils of conscription and it provides us with military resources more than adequate with which to meet our obligations under the Charter of the United Nations to associate our armed forces with the forces of other nations in the maintenance of world peace. In short, it assures an intelligent and adequate preparation for war, if, unhappily, war should come.

I have endeavored to show that conscription is not a healthy measure to employ with our youth. Let us, therefore, be honest with them. If national survival does in fact demand this sacrifice, let us look them squarely in the eye and request it of them, rather than to gloss it over with false educational values.

But I have also shown that conscription may be a doubtful military expedient. Until this issue is clarified, we should hesitate to impose it upon our young people. Certainly we should not act hastily. We have ample time in which to investigate the needs of national security and our responsibilities for the peace. When Japan falls we shall have erased all immediate danger to our national security and we shall have available a huge reserve of trained manpower to use, should the impossible happen and one of our allies turn upon us. And, may I add parenthetically, that all who now engage in the whispering campaign against Russia would do well to go to Russia and observe the task of reconstruction that confronts the Russian people. A little first-hand information on the suffering and the destruction endured by the Russians and the huge problem of rebuilding that faces them might generate a sense of reality and more generous and humane feelings in these misguided individuals.

I repeat, we have time, ample time in which to plan wisely a program for national defense. Congress and the President should take advantage of this interval to establish a commission to study the problem thoroughly. On this commission all shades of military opinion should find representation, and before it, all views should receive a free and full hearing. We need all the light we can get. This is no time for military censorship. We need as well the best thought of other groups—of business, labor, agriculture, education, religion. Only when Americans have sincerely, honestly and thoroughly explored this problem can they wisely and appropriately act.

To do otherwise is to express a cynicism and a moral defeatism in no way supported by present facts. President Truman emphasized in his address before the United Nations Conference in San Francisco that fifty nations "have tested the experience of cooperation in this war and found that it works. Through the pooling of resources, through joint and combined military command . . . we have shown what united strength can do." But he called attention as well to the machinery now set up to insure a united determination to keep the peace. This machinery insures the opportunity of any nation, facing the threat of aggression, to bring its case before a world court of opinion in the Assembly of Nations. Secondly, there is a Security Council pledged to use force, if necessary, in order to curb aggression. Third and probably most important of all, in terms of the future, there is set up an Economic and Social Council designed to anticipate strains between nations. This Council is charged specifically with the task of studying the economic and social causes of war and of recommending remedial action in advance of possible conflict. Machinery thus exists, as President Truman states, "which men and women of good-will can use to help correct the economic and social causes for conflict."

The American people are under a sacred obligation to give this World Charter a fair trial before they resort to peacetime conscription. To do otherwise is to proclaim to the world either that we lack confidence in the Charter or, what is worse, that we intend to disregard it. What else could we mean, since conscription is foreign to our tradition? As a people we have always opposed it except in times of the greatest national danger and we have discarded it immediately when the crisis was past.

I repeat, there is nothing in the evidence at present to warrant the adoption of peacetime conscription. But the times are critical. The United States occupies a position of great responsibility. As our country goes, so may the United Nations, go. Franklin D. Roosevelt stated in his last inaugural address, "We can gain no lasting peace if we approach it with suspicion and distrust—or with fear. We can gain it only if we proceed with the understanding and the confidence and the courage which flow from conviction."

We manifest this confidence and courage when we pledge our loyalty to the Atlantic Charter and its commitment to collaborate in all efforts designed to bring about the abandonment of the use of force and, specifically, to "aid and encourage all practicable measures which will lighten for peace-loving peoples the crushing burden of armaments."

The road thus indicated is not the road of compulsory military training. Such a program is not good for our youth. Nor is it clearly the most effective measure to insure adequate national defense. I thus conclude of peacetime conscription that national defense does not require it, and national honor cannot afford it.

DO WE WANT PERMANENT CONSCRIPTION? [6]

Anybody who opposes the plan of the army and navy for universal military training in peacetime must run the risk of being charged with opposing national security, health, morals and democracy. Universal military training is the new infallible patent medicine which will automatically confer all these benefits upon us; and without universal military training we cannot hope to achieve any of them. The thesis of this article is that uni-

[6] By Robert M. Hutchins, President, University of Chicago. *Collier's.* 115:15, 27. June 9, 1945.

versal military training will not promote national security, health, morals or democracy; that, on the contrary, it will weaken or destroy them; and that, if we want national security, health, morals and democracy, we should keep universal military training out of this country and get rid of it, if possible, in the rest of the world.

In the first place, half the population of this country is female. If military training is necessary to make the young men of the United States healthy, moral and democratic, how can we be so brutal as to ignore similar benefits for our young women? Furthermore, universal military training is scheduled to begin at the age of seventeen or eighteen and to last one year. Can it be supposed that after sixteen or seventeen years of unhealthy, immoral and undemocratic life, young men can be made just the opposite by the armed forces in one year? If we want health, morals and democracy, we shall have to start earlier and do more, and we may at least raise the question whether the army and navy are the best agencies we could select to educate our youth in the habits we want them to have.

Take health. The army and navy are certainly not going to accept young men who are physically unfit. It is not their job to repair the defects which civilian health agencies have not cured. The army and navy are fighting forces, not health resorts. The Surgeon General reported, for the year 1941, that 43 per cent of the million men who had been examined under the Selective Service Act were physically unfit for general military duty and 28 per cent for any military duty. Thus the group which needs the alleged health benefits of universal military training most would not be permitted to take advantage of them.

Nor does military training inevitably improve the health of those trained. It is doubtless true, as the War Department asserts, that the serviceman in this war is healthier than the civilian "because from the point of view of medical science, he is living in a more 'controlled' environment than in civil life, and because he is obliged to go to the doctor and, possibly, the hospital, for even minor ailments." The "control" which the War Department speaks of cannot permanently improve the health of a man who has some day to control himself. Venereal disease, which is a matter of morals as well as of health, has always been a major problem in military forces. That the civilian population is freer from it than the military is indicated by the Surgeon General's report that the regular army venereal rate was depressed in the early months of mobilization and has now risen to its peacetime level.

It is notorious that the incidence of psychiatric disorders has skyrocketed in the army, not only in remote posts abroad or on the battlefields, but in the camps in this country. Many men, it is true, respond favorably to the regular hours, substantial food and outdoor life that go along with military training. Many others are broken by the herding, the impersonality, and the lack of privacy which characterize army life. To say that such men are weaklings and ought to be made to "take it" is to put a premium on roughness and toughness, to elevate the heavyweight prize-fighter into the model for American youth.

What I have said about health is equally true of morals. This is certainly the first time in history that it has ever been seriously argued that barrack-room life is improving to the young. Soldiers probably commit fewer police offenses than civilians. There would be still fewer police offenses if soldiers received no furloughs and civilians were kept in concentration camps. But if we are going to measure morality by statistics, I suggest that some attention be paid to the only figures I have been able to find on the moral effects of military service. The 1923 *Proceedings of the National Conference of Social Work* records that by the latter part of 1922, 600 ex-servicemen had been incarcerated in penal institutions in the state of Wisconsin.

"This," the director of the Wisconsin Psychiatric Institute said, "is an abnormal situation. The incidence of criminality is far above that ordinarily found in the civilian population for the age group concerned."

Whether military training is morally beneficial depends on what we mean by morality. The essence of morality is choice— free, independent choice. Geraniums, infants and idiots are not regarded as moral or immoral; they cannot make choices. Nowhere is a man so far removed from making choices as in the army.

A soldier is not merely prevented from making moral choices; he is prevented even from choosing which pair of shoes he will wear. He is not taught self-discipline; he is taught discipline. He is not trained for the life of choice which is the democratic life for the individual and the community; he is trained to obey orders. The proper object of military training is, and must be, to train men to fight. I think it is generally admitted that German military training achieves this object. It is generally thought, however, that the beneficiaries of German military training are neither very good men nor very good democrats.

The notion that democracy is promoted by universal military training seems to rest on the vague impression that it is good for every kind of boy to associate with every other kind of boy. Perhaps it is. The American public school accomplishes this. This country needs fewer lessons on the desirability of free association among all classes than any other. If additional lessons are needed, they should be learned in some other way than through universal military training. Nobody argues that the present generation of German boys has been made democratic through military association.

Democracy presupposes the participation of the individual in the choices that are made for the group. The soldier has no more part in choices made for his group than he has in choices made for him as an individual. Militarism and democracy have always been opposed in history. They are also opposed in theory. You cannot put together a system which requires blind obedience with one which presupposes independent, individual action. A democracy must have military forces; and in those forces, obedience must prevail and personal aims must be sacrificed. But a democracy which deliberately embraces a military system as training for democracy is digging its own grave.

If universal military training can be justified, it can be justified only by reason of military necessity. Every community will try to preserve itself at all costs, even at the cost of the ultimate good for which the community exists. The financial outlay required for universal military training could not be less than three or four billion dollars a year, a sum equal to and perhaps greater than the cost of the whole educational system. Far greater costs are involved in the departure from the tradition of our country and in the imposition of militarism upon it.

Still, if universal military training is necessary, we must have it. We can go further and say that if we have to have a very large standing army after the war, conscription is the democratic way to get it. Of course, if we have to have a very large standing army after the war we have lost the war. We will have failed in our principal object, which was not merely to repel the assault of the Germans and the Japanese, but to organize a world free from fear. We are hardly free from fear if we are so afraid that we must have, in addition to regular troops, a million boys a year being trained to fight.

Whom are we going to fight, and when? Under the Selective Service Act we have drafted some thirteen million men and can draft every man in the country. Where would the danger come from six months, a year, or two years after this war? Our present enemies will be crushed; our present allies will be impoverished. We are now the strongest, richest military power in the world. No one now believes that the war will cost us as much of our strength as it has cost our major allies or enemies, all of whom went into it weaker, poorer and earlier than we.

John J. McCloy, Assistant Secretary of War, has said that peacetime conscription is not concerned with the next few years, but with wars that may come twenty, thirty or forty years from now. If Mr. McCloy is right, we shall be training men *now* to fight when they are thirty-eight, forty-eight, or fifty-eight years old. They will be obsolescent then, also their training and their weapons.

General Charles de Gaulle, in *The Army of the Future,* published in 1934, argues that under modern conditions of military action and equipment, "the era of picked soldiers and selected crews has arrived." Conscription, he adds, was "a costly conception . . . and an emergency conception," suitable "when armament consisted of a single type of portable weapon and a single kind of gun."

History is on the side of General de Gaulle. There is no evidence that conscription protects countries from sudden attack, as witness France and Poland in this war. There is not even any evidence that conscription helps countries win wars. England, without peacetime conscription, has won every time out in a general war; France, with it, has won seven and lost five.

The proposal for universal military training after the war is, in effect, a proposal to keep the country on a war basis indefinitely. But if the country is to be on a war basis after the war, we should all be on a war basis, and not just the eighteen-year-old boys. Why should we discriminate against the young? Why should not industry be on a war basis, and labor, and the consumer? Why should we not continue the W.P.B., the W.L.B., the O.P.A. and the War Manpower Commission? Why should not the scientific men of universities be kept on a war basis?

The greatest problem of this war has not been the mobilization of millions of soldiers; it has been the mobilization of scientific research and industrial production. It is safe to assume that the greatest problem of the next war will be the same, and that if we must be constantly prepared for war, it is upon science, labor and industry that the burden ought to fall. Reliance upon masses of men with obsolescent training has led to the practice of fighting the last war, thus sending country after country down to defeat when confronted with new military technology.

The argument that our military experts insist upon is that peacetime conscription gives a country a head start in military encounters with other nations. What kind of country is it that wants a head start? Listen to the words of General MacArthur, describing the military program adopted by Congress in 1920. He said: "This system places ultimate reliance for the nation's defense upon a citizen army, the great proportion of which must be organized, trained and equipped after the beginning of any emergency. Thus it deliberately contemplates a delay of several months between any declaration of war and the time large-scale operations could be initiated, a circumstance that gives convincing proof of its nonaggressive intent." The inference is that only an aggressive nation could desire any other system.

The Dumbarton Oaks proposals commit the United States to membership in an international organization devoted to the maintenance of universal peace. Proposal Number Four of the Principles commits the United States to refraining from "the threat or use of force in any manner inconsistent with the purposes of the organization." But peacetime conscription in the United States would be the greatest threat of force ever devised. If it costs us our fellow men's faith in our intentions, it may prove the greatest obstacle to durable peace.

It would seem sensible for us to go to the peace table unarmed, except for the ten or twelve million soldiers we shall have left after the war, and demand the abolition of peacetime conscription everywhere. This is what Woodrow Wilson did in the first Paris draft of the Covenant of the League of Nations; the course of history might have been different if he had stuck to his point. If we now propose to outlaw conscription, we shall be giving the world, in General MacArthur's words, convincing proof of our nonaggressive intent. And what would we have to lose? If our proposal broke down, we should still be the strongest, richest, most heavily armed nation in the world. If there had to be a war at the end of the peace conference, who would be in a better position to fight it than we? If an armament race begins the day the treaty is signed, who will have more of a head start?

But if we cannot make the effort to procure the abolition of conscription everywhere, we can at least save ourselves from the cost, the inefficiency and the danger to our institutions which universal military training would visit upon our country. The proposal to fasten universal military training on the United States is a militaristic proposal to establish here the kind of system from which millions of immigrants fled to this country. It is an antidemocratic proposal; for those who are urging adoption now boldly say that the reason why they are doing so is that after the war the country will be pacifistic and will decline to have anything to do with peacetime conscription.

Those who take this view do not trust democracy. They admit that public opinion now, in the midst of war, cannot examine military issues objectively. Now it is treason to contradict a general. Those who insist upon adopting peacetime conscription at once argue that in addition to being abnormally conditioned in war, democracy is also abnormally conditioned in

peace, and is therefore never reliable. Or they argue that the
normal condition of democracy is hopelessly pacifistic.

"It is a historical fact," said Mr. Stimson, urging peacetime
conscription in 1917, "that in times of peace, our citizens have
habitually paid no attention to even the most self-evident necessities."

Our faith in democracy ought to be stronger than this. I am
glad that churches, educational organizations, farm groups and
trade unions are insisting that a decision on peacetime conscription be postponed until after the war. A step so repugnant to
our tradition should be taken only when it is irresistibly clear to
a calm and informed majority that there is no other way to save
the country.

NATIONAL POWER AND FOREIGN POLICY [7]

If one of [the major signatory] Powers should become an
aggressor, it could not be dealt with save in a war of global
proportions. International police action of the kind contemplated by the Charter would not come into play. In effect, the
security enforcement role of the organization will be limited to
dealing with those minor disturbances with respect to which all
the member Great Powers can agree upon a common policy. . . .

The indicated conclusion is that we would need universal
training only for our own national defense in case we were
threatened by an aggressor of great strength. The number of
possible situations from which such a threat could come is
limited. Conceivably, it would appear: (1) if we allowed our
present enemies to regain impressive military strength, comparable to that of 1939; or (2) if there were some irreparable
disagreement between ourselves and any of our present major
allies. It is difficult to see how a program of universal military
training bears importantly on the first of these alternatives. If
there remains unanimity of policy among the Allies toward the
Axis states, no such danger will arise. If this unanimity disap-

[7] From article by Grayson Kirk, Associate Professor of Government, Columbia
University. *Foreign Affairs.* 23:622-6. July 1945.

pears, then our ability to deal with incipient threats from Germany or Japan will be a matter of political decision. A training program of the sort described would not go far to enable us to take swift action at an early stage of the developing threat. It can be justifiable only on the assumption that we shall once again allow such a threat to develop to the point where it cannot be countered except by a massive military effort. If we keep our wits about us and maintain our willingness to act at a given moment—in other words, if we have intelligent and determined leadership and follow it—we can protect ourselves adequately by a strong navy and air force and an army of moderate size

The remaining possibility is, of course, the implied major premise in the minds of most proponents of universal peacetime training. There is no denying that if we should become locked in a titanic struggle with one of the other great states we would need all our own resources—and perhaps more besides—to win. . . .

The general relationship of military policy to foreign policy deserves more attention than it generally receives. We can perhaps best explore it by attempting to estimate the probable consequences of a decision on our part to adopt a broad postwar policy of universal military training; to retain great numbers of overseas bases; and to maintain a huge navy and air force in conjunction with a much larger professional army than we have possessed hitherto.

The argument can be made that such a course would have a favorable effect on our political relations with our major allies, who would regard our changed policy as an earnest of our determination to carry our full share of responsibility in the international security organization, and to maintain an unremitting vigilance against the resurgence of our present enemies. It can be argued, also, that the new evidence of vigorous strength on our part would contribute to the maintenance of peace generally because never again would it be possible for a predatory state to hope that it could strike quickly, and present us with a *fait accompli* before our latent power could be mobilized. . . .

The problem has its domestic ramifications, too. . . . If the popular reaction were that our officials regarded another global conflict as probable, if not inevitable, it would be a powerful stimulus to American isolationism. It would be all the stronger, too, because it would come at a time when the new organization was weathering the first storms of Allied disagreement over the war settlement and its aftermath.

One must also weigh the possibility that such great military power, including compulsory training, might strengthen regionalism as well as outright isolationism. For some time there have been indications that the erstwhile leaders of American isolationism will now support a policy of hemispheric defense as a means of destroying, or at least vitiating, the power of the central international organization. If the United States couples a great military program with support for an inter-American regional organization with full powers of policy-making and initiative in security matters, Americans can scarcely object in good conscience if the other great states follow the same course in regions where they have special interests. No great argument is needed to show how favorable such a development would be to the fundamental interests of American security. No threat to the United States will originate in this hemisphere; if our security is endangered, the threat will come from across one of our frontier oceans. If we are to be able to check the growth of threats to our security arising in either western Europe or eastern Asia at a time when they can be met with relative ease, we must be prepared to take an active interest in the political affairs of the borderlands across both oceans. This . . . means merely that we must be able to intervene, without encountering the charge of improper meddling, whenever and wherever necessary for the protection of our own interests. Only in a central international organization, in which regional agencies have a minor and subordinate role, could this be possible. And if the tendency of our military policy were to make this less easy, because of its regionalistic implications, then the harm might far surpass the benefit to the nation.

These considerations suggest the conclusion that the fundamentals of our future security are essentially political rather than military. Skillful statesmanship, supported by a reasonably strong force in being and backed by the immense military potential of the United States, gives us the maximum likelihood of future security. For this combination the strongest standing military force alone is not a satisfactory substitute.

COMPULSORY MILITARY TRAINING IN PEACETIME WILL DESTROY GOVERNMENT BY THE PEOPLE [8]

It seems improbable to me that the training of a million and a quarter boys a year would ever be necessary. The vast reserve provided could only be needed for a great overseas expedition like that in which we are now engaged. For such an expedition, it would take several years to organize ships, planes, and munitions, just as it did in this war. We would surely have to have new modern equipment in many fields, and it would take longer to build it than it would to train the men, as we found in this war. It would seem that for sudden attack, or for attack from the air or from attack by rockets the great mass of millions of reserves would be of little value. I should think we rather need an expert army with the most modern weapons. In the event of a sudden attack, our main reliance would have to be a regular army of highly trained and technically trained men, and during such an attack they would not be much aided by 10,000,000 reserves. The argument that we can save in the size of a professional army by having many millions of reserves bears all the earmarks of a propaganda argument instead of one based on common sense.

Having determined that we need an army of a certain size, with certain reserves, we could then decide whether we could get it by voluntary means in the American tradition. Suppose we need a million men in the armed forces. We expect to have at least 50,000,000 people working at civilian jobs in this country. Surely we can make the army sufficiently attractive as an occupation for 2 per cent of these to be willing to volunteer. With good pay, reasonable treatment for men and their families, and

[8] From address by Senator Robert A. Taft of Ohio, delivered at Gettysburg National Cemetary, May 30, 1945. *Congressional Record.* 91: (daily) A2814-16. May 31, 1945.

provision for retraining and retirement when a man is too old to stay in the army, I don't see why army life cannot be made just as attractive as working daily on a machine, mining coal, or engaging in hundreds of other occupations. Many jobs in the army should give highly technical training with interesting knowledge which makes the trainees capable of advancement in other activities in life.

To provide the necessary reserves, it could be made worth the while of many boys to take the necessary training. Many alternative plans have been suggested to a year's conscription. For instance, adequate reserves might be provided by training 200,000 boys in each age group. It should be possible to obtain volunteers in that number for a three months course and basic training during one summer, courses in school and a later three months summer course in the field. The boys could be paid a sum which would assist them in their regular education during the winter. Additional courses could be provided for those who wish to become reserve officers. What I have suggested is only one idea and there may be many others. The army will immediately criticize any plan, because they are determined to have conscription. They want the boys for twelve months consecutively because they want to change their habits of thought, to make them soldiers, if you please, for the rest of their lives. Nothing less will do. We are indeed bankrupt of ideas if we cannot provide a method by which necessary military forces and reserves are provided by an American voluntary system.

The other arguments for conscription seem to me almost too trivial to discuss. It is said it will teach the boys discipline and that they need it. My own opinion is that we need more initiative and original thinking and less discipline rather than more. Our present army is not the most disciplined army in the world, but there isn't any better army for the simple reason that the boys do some thinking for themselves.

It is said the army will improve their health, and that they need it because so many failed to pass the strict health requirements of the army. As a matter of fact, the great bulk of defects were those relating to teeth, eyes, nerves, mental and heart conditions, all of which had arisen long before the age of conscription. There is nothing to show that the army would conscript any of these boys. To improve their health, we must reach them at a much younger age.

The argument that it would improve the morals of our boys has almost been dropped because of its foolishness. If there is one place where morals will not be improved, it is in the vicinity of army camps.

It is true that there are some boys who are benefited by army control, but to improve a few, let us not change the whole character of the American life which I believe has been the cause of success in this war.

It is said that we are going to teach the boys citizenship in the camps. This argument makes clear a real danger in the whole system. By handing boys over for twelve months to the arbitrary and complete domination of the government, we put it in the power of the government to indoctrinate them with the political doctrines then popular with the government. It has all the dangers of federal education and none of its advantages. Attempts along this line have been made with the present army, and a large amount of propaganda sent out to be taught to the soldiers. In wartime it is bad enough; in peacetime, it would be intolerable.

Some have supported this project on the ground that the training is only to be part military and a considerable amount of it is to be character training along other lines. We have already a complete school system in this country. If it isn't adequate and does not give education in citizenship, we can well spend our time and money in trying to improve that system. As a matter of fact, it is already the finest system of education the world has even seen.

Military conscription is essentially totalitarian. It has been established for the most part by totalitarian countries and their dictators led by Napoleon and Bismarck. It has heretofore been established by aggressor countries. It is said it would insure peace by emphasizing the tremendous military potential of this country. Surely we have emphasized that enough in this war. No one can doubt it. On the contrary, if we establish conscription every other nation in the world will feel obliged to do the same. It would set up militarism on a high pedestal throughout the world as the goal of all the world. Militarism has always led to war and not peace. Conscription was no insurance of victory in France, in Germany, or in Italy. The countries with military conscription found that it was only an incident and not the determining factor in defense or in victory.

Military training by conscription means the complete regimentation of the individual at his most formative period for a period of twelve months. If we admit that in peacetime we can deprive a man of all liberty and voice and freedom of action, if we can take him from his family and his home, then we can do the same with labor, we can order the farmer to produce and we can take over any business. If we can draft men, it is difficult to find an argument against drafting capital. Those who enthusiastically orate of returning to free enterprise and at the same time advocate peacetime conscription are blind to the implications of this policy. They are utterly inconsistent in their position. Because of its psychological effect on every citizen, because it is the most extreme form of compulsion, military conscription will be more the test of our whole philosophy than any other policy. Some say it is unconstitutional. It makes very little difference whether it actually violates the terms of the Constitution. It is against the fundamental policy of America and the American nation. If adopted, it will color our whole future. We shall have fought to abolish totalitarianism in the world, only to set it up in the United States.

Government by the people can only exist if the people are individuals who think. It can only exist if the individual is free to rule the state and if he is not ruled by the state. We must be constantly vigilant to keep alive the thinking of freemen, and there is no such threat to that thinking as the course which would impose on the nation compulsory military training.

PEACETIME TRAINING PROPOSAL [9]

The only valid argument for a year's compulsory military training for all American youth is that if another world war

[9] By Dr. John Thom Holdsworth, Dean Emeritus, School of Business Administration, University of Miami. *Commercial and Financial Chronicle.* 160:2824. December 28, 1944.

should come, say, 20 years after we have finished this one, and we become embroiled in it, we should have a very large reserve of young men (and women) all ready to go places the minute the shooting begins.

Hitler's rapid over-running of Western Europe and the near accomplishment of his satanic designs was due to long preparation, to the minutest detail, to the military and "master race" indoctrination of the entire German people and, above all, to the development and utilization of the most modern strategy and machinery of war-making. The peace-loving nations of Europe, not thus prepared, fell one by one before the motorized Nazi juggernaut. In nearly every one of these over-run countries compulsory military service had been required for years. Against the mechanized, swift-moving might of the German war machine they might about as well have tried to defend themselves with their bare hands. If the civilized world fails to lay firm foundations for an enduring peace future wars will be still more mechanized and infinitely more destructive—witness Germany's belated robot bomb.

Admitting the conception that yesterday's wars, and in large part today's wars, depended mainly for their outcome upon the foot soldier armed with gun and grenade, will that be true for tomorrow's wars—if they come? Unless men's capacity for thinking, inventing and planning become atrophied, future wars will surely be more and more scientific, mechanized, robotized and directed by highly trained technicians, and less and less combat manpower will be needed. Why then take millions of our youth from peacetime pursuits and production to spend a year in the arts of destruction? A year taken out of the life of every 18-year-old boy to be trained for "the kind of wars we used to have" is a mighty serious business, a frightful waste of time and good stuff—unless demonstratably necessary.

So, retorts the militarist, you are opposed to regular over-all military training of our youth for the defense of our country and our liberty. Most certainly not! I am protesting, rather, against the assumption that the peace-makers cannot make a peace that will stick; and if this assumption be accepted we shall not make the mistake of looking backward instead of forward, of training our youth to fight yesterday's wars rather than tomorrow's. This is neither isolationism, defeatism, or smug contentness.

Assuming that future wars—if they must come—will be wars of chemicals, incendiaries, destructive gases and germs, and still newer weapons of destruction designed to annihilate whole populations, should not our defense program emphasize training in these new scientific, technical and engineering fields? And, if so, cannot this be done on a voluntary basis through West Point, Annapolis, and air schools, expanded and geographically distributed—and all consolidated under a Department of Defense? Thousands of young men now in the service and others coming up would elect to remain in it if assured of further training, and a career. Even with an assured peace there will be a wide and attractive field of service for the technically trained officer all over the world.

Supplementing these officer training schools, expand and modernize the R.O.T.C. in our colleges, with emphasis upon science, history, modern languages and business administration. Some part of this training might well reach down into our high schools and academies. Not, basically, for any special disciplinary value such training is assumed to have (physical, moral and mental discipline can be as well, if not better, inculcated through other channels—the home, school, church, clubs, etc.) but rather for its value in team work, unity and coordination, tolerance, and the give-and-take of competitive effort. And, for older men and those unable or indisposed to go on to college, technical and professional schools, invigorate and enlarge the home guard, state militia, and other military and semi-military organizations.

Having thus provided for a continuous supply of well-trained, well-educated young men to serve as commissioned and petty officers and a volunteer reserve force of officers and men subject to call for short periods for special training to keep them abreast of changing war procedures, what if another war should come, and suddenly? Whence, then, will come the millions of youth to be quickly trained for the national defense? Answer: from the same sources as yielded the 11 million to fight and, with our allies, to win the present war—enlistment and the draft. If, in spite of the assurances that the coming peace must provide against secret or open preparation for aggression, blind war-makers should march (better to say fly) again, the draft surely will have to be employed as in past wars. The youth being trained in the year the war breaks out would certainly not be adequate in numbers or military proficiency for this emergency. Granted that the preceding classes of trainees would augment the number having "rudimentary training," yet most of these would have to undergo refresher, up-to-the-minute training for the new type of warfare. What real advantage, then, in taking each year millions of our youth from preparatory and productive effort to prepare for a war which, if it comes, will certainly call for more and different over-all training?

The burden of proof rests on the militarists and those who have no confidence in the wisdom and foresight of those international statesmen who will write the coming peace in terms which will make aggression and war-making the most difficult and hazardous of all human ventures; or on those little isolationists who cannot visualize either a Supreme International Council or an International Supreme Court, as projected at Dumbarton Oaks, which would function in the arbitration of international disputes and the administration of justice among nations, great and small, as effectively as our courts and arbitral organizations function here at home; or, again, on those who scoff at the idea of an international patrol or police alert to prevent incipient war preparations or to quell the disturbance before it gains headway; or, finally, on those who have lost faith in the good, old, homely virtues of goodwill, live and let live, honest dealing and friendliness, the Golden Rule, and "the passion for peace" applied to international relationships.

And if the militaristic isolationist can prove his case before the bar of public opinion, if he can persuade the American public that compulsory military training is either necessary or wise, he must still justify the taking of a whole year for such training rather than, say, six months or less, broken into two stretches of three months each.

In any event, we should not be hurried into such a momentous decision. It will be better to wait until the emotionalism of this war has passed, and the probable effectiveness of the peace can be calmly appraised. In making this decision, not delay but precipitateness is dangerous.

UNIVERSAL COMPULSORY MILITARY TRAINING IN PEACETIME [10]

This question represents a national dilemma which is far from simple. Every American citizen wants to assume that the government is honest and sincere in a matter so vital to our national life. The Association of American Colleges is eager to bring to the issue the greatest intelligence of which its membership is capable and to consider the proposal in the spirit of candor and in complete devotion to our national welfare.

The institutions which we represent in this section of the Association are devoted to two important convictions in education, viz., the faith that liberal education is the basis of sound leadership in democracy, and to the proposition that spiritual and moral values are indispensable to a vigorous and abiding civilization. Since the details of the proposed system have not been disclosed our reaction must necessarily be confined to the bill itself, to the general principle upon which the system rests, and to the manner in which it may affect the objectives which our colleges seek to serve. I desire to present against this background four brief considerations.

First: The experience of European nations for the last two hundred years is in sharp disagreement with the premise upon which the May Bill is based. The statement that the experience of World War II "conclusively establishes the fact that the lack of universal military training in the United States has resulted in unnecessary wars" is open to serious question. It is equally erroneous for Congressman May to insist that the lack of such a system has led to the "needless sacrifice of human life, the dissipation of national wealth, the useless disruption of the social and economic fabric of the nation, and has caused international discord and interracial misunderstandings."

[10] By Paul H. Bowman, President, Bridgewater College. *Christian Education*. 28:160-4. March 1945.

This statement which appears in Section 2 of the Bill is without factual support and is lacking in genuine perspective. It forces upon us a degree of mistrust of the efficiency and intelligence with which the question is being approached by members of Congress.

It would be nearer the truth to say that the system of compulsory military training adopted by France in 1793, by Prussia in 1807, by Japan in 1873, and by every important nation in Europe except Great Britain, between 1875 and 1914, had engendered such international fear, suspicion and strife among the nations of Europe that security and peace for either Europe or the rest of the world has become impossible. If universal compulsory military training is a guarantee of peace and order then Europe should have been the most peaceful and the most orderly place on earth during the last half century.

Second: As representatives of liberal education, we can scarcely avoid misgivings with reference to any system of universal training under the direction of military authorities. The system will undoubtedly reflect the "army and navy mentality" in education and neither we nor the country at large are ready to subscribe to the view that the only sound pattern of education is that of the military authorities. One year is a short span in human life. It is too short to improve the health of the nation materially by whatever method we may apply after a boy is eighteen years of age. It is too short and too late to provide the discipline which the American home has failed to provide. It is too short to atone for the deficiencies of four years of secondary education. But it is long enough to channel the lives of millions of men away from liberal studies which are generally conceded to be the best preparation for professional progress and leadership. It is long enough to regiment young boys in the routine of a military system and thereby enfeeble them for life in a free society. There is in the system a potential threat to an adequate leadership in our great peacetime professions such as medicine, the ministry, and education.

Third: The Christian element in education is always endangered under any system of coercion. The worth of a human being and the necessary freedom to develop the power of his mind and soul are basic to the Christian conception of life and education. These ideas are the spiritual and religious concepts which feed democracy and they cannot long survive in the atmosphere of compulsion. The Christian principle of life may accept conscription in a time of national crisis, but universal conscription as a permanent peacetime policy is quite another issue. It is not clear that we can long cherish the idea of compulsion as a policy of government and yet preserve the values to which America has so long been committed. It is also impossible to forecast what effect this system would have on our democratic institutions. No nation in history has, to my knowledge, been able to escape the evils of militarism which have always accompanied universal military training.

Fourth: If we brush aside these considerations and grant the necessity and desirability of universal military training, we must still challenge the wisdom of inaugurating such a system at a time like this.

UNIVERSAL PEACTIME CONSCRIPTION [11]

If we need millions trained for defense, there is equal need of millions educated for peace. To establish and maintain peace throughout the world, America would be better prepared in the future—and peace-making is a task with a long future—if we would now plan to send thousands upon thousands of young citizens, carefully chosen, to live and study in other lands until they know what other peoples are thinking and what their problems are. We need the value of the understanding of America that this will bring to other peoples as they learn the spirit of America by actual contact with well-educated Americans. We also need millions educated in this land to understand foreign cultures and the problems of other nations, so that there will be a strong public opinion here in America to sustain a policy of wise foreign relations. We haven't the people trained now in America for establishing a peace. Too few of our thousands of national leaders have had any contact or training that they may

[11] By Albert G. Parker, Jr., President, Hanover College. *Christian Education.* 28:164-8. March 1945.

understand thoroughly the problems of other peoples which must be solved along with our own problems if a peace is to be maintained. Too many people in America have studied only vocational courses so that they are ill prepared to understand the issues which must be solved with knowledge and understanding.

We can have this training for peace at a fraction of the cost of universal military training. The American people will again be betrayed by their elected leadership or they will become the victims of a poorly enlightened public opinion if our nation does not plan to spend as much money and national effort to train a citizenry which will be able to build and sustain a wise peace as we spend for national defense.

We must have, of course, an adequate national defense. But universal military training is not adequate national defense. It would be useless without the scientists to develop new fighting tools. It would be useless without the skilled leadership that must be prepared by many years of education. It would be useless without the many kinds of skill that are necessary to wage modern war. It would be useless without doctors, nurses, dentists, scientists, officers with scientific education, and other officers with education in economics, psychology, language and many other subjects. Universal military training alone could easily become a sleeping potion to our nation. With universal military training our nation would be in danger of thinking that it had adequate defense while it lacked the more essential skills which come only through years of education, and which cannot be supplied on the spur of the moment. If we are adequately supplied with all the types of educated leadership that we need, it is quite likely that we would find that universal military training is not necessary. We may find that a limited number of men for that type of training is sufficient, and that these could be secured by voluntary enlistment.

We are not ready for any action of the Congress until the whole problem of the training for peace is faced, as well as the training for national defense. Each requires several types of training and education. All this should be thoroughly discussed and the policy of the nation embodied in one comprehensive act of Congress. Only in this way can the people of America have confidence that adequate action is being taken, both for defense and the establishment of peace.

This is not a matter of the War and Navy Departments only. Other departments of our government are concerned. It is not a matter for the military affairs committees of the Houses of Congress only. A wider base of action is necessary to formulate a comprehensive policy for defense and peace.

There are two more points I wish to make. The first is that we are dealing with a most serious matter. It is no trifling matter to be tossing around a whole year in the early life of every boy. This nation has never taken such a drastic action outside of the necessity of war. This nation has not touched any other group of its citizens in so drastic a way. Other groups are organized to protect themselves. The boys of America are not organized and they should not be made victims of ill-considered or hasty action. The age suggested for military service is a most formative age. It is the age when a boy's philosophy of life is forming, when his adult values are being set, when he is getting started in a life work or when he is entering the course of study for a profession or other skilled leadership. The more ambitious boys, on whose leadership our nation must depend for its place in the world, have years of study ahead of them and they do not wish to be delayed needlessly for a year. Already our youth are at too advanced an age when they are economically prepared for marriage and the establishing of a home. The direction of interest which a year of military training would give to many boys would be decidedly harmful; their interest could turn easily to war-making instead of to peace-making, to a secular view of life instead of to a spiritual view, to a purely vocational view instead of to a cultural view, to a view of government control of life instead of to a view of individual enterprise. The possible harmful effects appear to many of us to outweigh by a large margin the possible advantageous effects. There has to be a compelling case to justify so drastic an action as to take a year, without recourse, from every boy's life.

The final point I wish to make is that such a step toward government control of life has most serious implications. The idea of national compulsion is one that is repugnant to free

Americans. America has accepted selective service because most people have been convinced of its necessity during war. Labor has been unwilling to have its freedom limited even in wartime by a national service act. Until the American people and the boys themselves are convinced that universal military training is a national necessity it will do violence to their spirits to have this compulsion. Many of our ablest and most ambitious boys would enter life as adults with a feeling of frustration and resentment against the government, if they are delayed in their preparation for life work by government compulsion which they regard as unnecessary.

All the interest groups and all the people of America had better be aware that government compulsion once applied to one group of people is not going to be limited to that one group for long. After ten years of universal military training we would have ten million voters who had started their mature life under government compulsion, whose first experience away from their childhood home was one of having the government tell them what to do, having the government pay them and feed and clothe them. These millions of voters would be somewhat conditioned to government compulsion and control. Many might resent it for themselves but still be very ready to have it applied to others, just as now there appear to be other groups who resist government control for themselves but are quite willing to have it applied to the unorganized boys of America. Business, farming, labor, medicine, education and the press would all have to expect an increasing government control as the number of men grows who have taken their turn of government compulsion. The principle of government compulsion once invoked outside of clear military necessity will not stay limited to this group of unorganized boys. We can expect nothing else than that these boys will grow up and will extend the application of this principle of government control until our freedom has been lost.

To summarize: We need a comprehensive plan for defense and for peace; a plan which provides for all the manifold types of training and education which are needed for defense and the maintenance of peace; a plan which uses the interests, abilities and ambitions of each boy in a field for which he is qualified, and which preserves as far as possible the principle of individual choice. Only such a plan can deserve and have the whole-hearted support of the American people.

CONSCRIPTION AND PREPAREDNESS [12]

It is a fair question whether conscription was not an important cause of the fall of France. In March 1940, the French army was regarded as the finest in Europe; by July 1940, it had ceased to exist.

We know that the French army in 1940 was not equipped for the kind of war that was being fought in 1940. But M. Pierre Cot, French Minister of Aviation, has assured us that French industry, while less powerful than German industry, was supplying the French army with precisely the supplies the French military authorities asked for.

We are told that General de Gaulle developed the theory of the blitzkrieg. The French officers read de Gaulle's book; the German army applied his theories. Why?

Is not part of the answer to be found in the fact that the French army was protected by conscription from constructive criticism?

When every man has to go into the army, very few men can afford to criticize. If they have themselves completed their military service, they have sons or relatives about to undergo it. There is a tendency to soft-pedal criticism that may make for personal unpleasantness.

A military bureaucracy is like every other bureaucracy—it tends to settle down into comfortable routine, unless shaken out of its rest by emergencies. No nation is prepared to admit that it is seeking emergencies; so every nation's policy is, at least ostensibly, directed at preventing any interruption of the repose of its military bureaucracy.

When there is additional insulation against criticism provided by a system of permanent conscription, one would expect

[12] By Richard R. Wood, Executive Secretary, Friends' Peace Committee. *Commercial and Financial Chronicle.* 161:277. January 18, 1945.

a nation in which conscription is long established to be at a serious disadvantage in military efficiency when war actually occurs.

The fact of France at least suggests that this expectation is well founded and that conscription as a permanent policy is a permanent and serious threat to military efficiency.

The detrimental effect of conscription on military efficiency is aggravated by modern technical warfare.

The blitzkrieg makes possible, at least in theory, final victory in the first onset. This means that preparedness for defense must be just as total, and just as ready for instantaneous action, as preparation for attack, so long as nations seek security in their own armed power. That involves technical and industrial preparedness, organization of the whole life of the country for war, as well as more directly military preparation.

Can a military bureaucracy successfully direct such preparation when it is protected by conscription from constructive criticism? The fall of France suggests not. The war effort of the United States and Great Britain, by its effectiveness, also suggests not. Those two nations were not hampered by conscription.

Preparedness is not simply amassing armaments and supplies. That is easy; and it can make defeat certain. Besides being abundant, the armaments must be up to date. Mass production of a less up-to-date weapon gives the advantages to the nation starting a little later with more modern designs. Some Britishers claim that the Battle of Britain was really won because the British mass production of airplanes started a little later than the German, so that the British always had an advantage in quality, a slight advantage which turned out to be decisive.

This examination of the inner problem of preparedness raises serious doubts as to the possibility of achieving the sort of preparedness needed for modern war, the delicate balance between quantity and quality, unless the nation's directing forces are entirely free of the hampering traditions and bureaucratic habits inseparable from permanent conscription.

It has been said that as long as nations seek security in their own armed forces, they are doomed to total preparation for total war. It is becoming clear that even so, they cannot attain security, because each effort to increase a nation's security thereby decreases the security of some other. Total preparedness merely gives the hope of victory, it does not give the hope of security.

It has been shown that there is great doubt even that meager hope can be realized by a nation maintaining conscription as a permanent policy.

We must now ask whether permanent conscription helps or hinders the attainment of peace and security through world organization.

Here again there is grave reason to suspect the consequences of conscription. We have seen that conscription makes it unlikely that the nation having it can either prepare for war effectively or fight it successfully; but there is reason to fear that the military control of all national life inherent in a system of conscription applied to the economic and industrial preparation for modern war will be definitely unfavorable to the policies and duties of maintaining peace. Mere ineffectiveness in preparing to fight is no guarantee of effectiveness in preparing to share peacefully in an orderly community.

Again the French experience gives an instructive illustration. French military leaders browbeat and humiliated the peace-seeking German republic and tried to appease Hitler when he threatened force. This is the strongest mark of approval a nation can give to reliance on force. The French system, based on conscription, frustrated the efforts to make peace in Europe, while proving itself incapable of waging war successfully.

Conscription as a permanent policy should be seriously questioned, if for no other reason, because it seems to frustrate the effective organization of the world for peace.

It is often claimed that conscription is a means of strengthening national unity. This claim requires careful scrutiny.

Twice, in France in time of peace, the government dealt with railroad strikes by simply mobilizing the strikers. This was possible under conscription; it converted a labor dispute into mutiny against the state. One doubts whether this strengthened the sense of national unity of the workers of France.

Certainly France, just before her fall, after 150 years of conscription, was not a striking example of national unity. The disunity is commonly blamed on political corruption; but one

wonders whether permanent conscription did not contribute its
full share to the corruption.

In a country where conscription as a permanent policy, every
man has to do his military service before he can earn a living.
Now political honesty requires, not the discipline imposed by
the drill-sergeant, but the self-discipline developed in men who
follow their consciences, do what they believe to be right, and
take the consequences. Such self-discipline is not encouraged
by a system which requires every man to conform during the
formative stage of his life. After he is fullgrown is late to begin developing the independent conscience which is important
for a healthy national life. May it not be that 150 years of conscription played a part in discouraging the development of self-
discipline, and so in producing the corruption and disunity so
fatal to France?

PEACETIME CONSCRIPTION FOR MILITARY SERVICE [13]

I have introduced a resolution urging President Harry S.
Truman, Secretary of State James F. Byrnes, and the personal
representative of the President on the United Nations Organization, Edward R. Stettinius, Jr., to begin immediately efforts to
secure an agreement by the nations of the world to abandon
peacetime conscription of youth for military service.

If mutual understanding can be reached between nations and
peoples that the policy of gigantic systems of universal compulsory military service should be eliminated, it would relieve the
United States and all other nations of the necessity to assume
this great new burden at a time when we must build, reconstruct,
and readjust the world to peace.

The elimination of compulsory military service as a policy
of nations would be the greatest single act of statesmanship that
could be accomplished in the immediate present. The system
which has long been the practice of European nations has never
prevented war. It is always viewed with suspicion and fear by

[13] By Joseph W. Martin, Jr. Representative from Massachusetts. *Congressional Record.* 91: (daily) A3808. July 18, 1945.

other countries, forcing them to adopt the same policy. It becomes an insupportable burden, a constant drain on the people of the world, and a further incentive to war.

In view of the world's hope of peace and the ultimate destruction of the military power of Germany and Japan, an effort to eliminate compulsory military service as a policy of all peoples cannot come too soon. A world-wide agreement toward that end is certainly a goal no reasonable person can object to.

The text of the resolution follows:

Whereas the first concern of every American is the security of the nation; and

Whereas the American people are determined that their government shall henceforth make proper provision for the continuous maintenance of such security; and

Whereas in accordance with this firm determination, it has become necessary to consider a system of compulsory military service in the United States as a permanent part of our insurance against unpreparedness in the event of sudden war; and

Whereas compulsory military service would result in greater restrictions over the lives and activities of our people, would impose heavy burdens on them, causing greater taxes and profound changes in their way of life; and

Whereas compulsory military service has long been customary in many European states and elsewhere, but has been contrary to American tradition since the founding of our republic; and

Whereas compulsory military service has never prevented war in Europe or elsewhere, but on the contrary, causes suspicion and fears to grow between nations and inclines the rulers of men to war rather than to peace; and

Whereas 50 nations, having expressed their desire for peace, met at San Francisco and resolved to make greater efforts than ever before to abate the fear and likelihood of war in the years to come; and

Whereas the people of the United States and their leaders in all sections and parties have in good faith approved the San Francisco Charter and desire our President to take a leading part in fulfilling the great purposes for which it was formed; and

Whereas with the ultimate destruction of the military power of Germany and Japan there will never be a better time than now to secure international agreement looking to permanent peace; and

Whereas an agreement between the nations of the world to eliminate systems of compulsory military service would itself be greatly conducive to that restoration of peace which is so profoundly desired by all the plain peoples of the world, and would release their energies and resources for rebuilding their war devastated countries; and

Whereas world-wide abolition of compulsory military service in no way precludes the maintenance of national or international military forces adequate for safeguarding national or collective security: Therefore be it

Resolved, That before the United States adopts compulsory military service, the President of the United States, the Secretary of State, and the personal representative of the President on the United Nations Organization, Edward R. Stettinius, Jr., be and hereby are urged to work unceasingly for an immediate international agreement whereby compulsory military service shall be wholly eliminated from the policies and practices of all nations.

NATIONAL GUARD URGED [14]

What was it that caused us to be so unprepared? The answer is not far to seek. It was our failure to keep abreast of the technological advancements of Germany and Japan during the years that elapsed between the last World War and the beginning of this one. The fact that we did not have many tanks, for instance, might be excused due to lack of manufacturing facilities, although that is bad enough. Our situation was much worse, however. We did not know what kind of tanks we wanted. That is the inexcusable fault of our General Staff. No amount of argument can change that.

If every camp that now exists had been full of young men undergoing training at that time we would have been as ill-prepared as we were when this war actually started.

I am not so naive as to maintain that on account of our isolation we should not have a strong national defense.

The situation can best be met by expanding the National Guard.

On December 31, 1940, we had 268,564 men in the National Guard of the nation. They were divided into eighteen divisions, with some corps and army troops. By making the pay of the National Guard better and providing better means of training, better armories and better equipment, the strength of the National Guard could easily be doubled to approximately a half-million men. This force could be divided into thirty-six divisions.

[14] By William A. Smith, Justice, Supreme Court of Kansas. *New York Times.* p. 8E. July 8, 1945.

At the beginning of this war we had some National Guard divisions ready to take the field as far as they had been trained with the weapons and equipment then available. They had to be retrained because two things happened. For one thing, we no sooner entered this war than the General Staff decided that some of the National Guard divisions should be reorganized into what they called triangular divisions. They must be streamlined. I put no blame on anybody for not having done this before we were actually in the war, but that is what happened.

The other reason for retraining them at the outset of this war was the failure of the General Staff to see that they were equipped with modern weapons. These divisions had been trained in the use of the bayonet and the Springfield rifle. Their training with hand grenades was very slight, if they had been trained with them at all.

Only a few of them had ever seen the Garrand rifle. They had never seen any rifle grenades. The bazooka, which has proved to be such a marvelous weapon for the infantry against tanks in this war, was unknown to them. I merely state this by way of meeting an argument that may be made to the effect that the National Guard divisions were not ready to take the field at the beginning of this war. As far as training then available is concerned, they were on a par with the regular army divisions.

No reason appears why we should conclude that with a large group of 18-year-old men in training camps the situation would have been any better.

Now to return to my discussion. My observation is that by expanding the National Guard to twice its present size we could have half a million men divided into thirty-six divisions. It will never be necessary, however, for the United States to throw an army into the field overnight.

Here is what would happen: These thirty-six divisions would be at what we call peacetime strength—that is, there would not be as many men to a division as are required when divisions take the field in wartime. This situation could be met by filling out National Guard divisions with either selectees or volunteers. It could be accomplished in a matter of thirty days or less. The recruits could be quickly trained with men who would have had years of training in the National Guard. We would thus have approximately a million men ready within a very short time to go into action.

This is no idle dream. It is my conclusion reached after many years' observation of the National Guard and talks with officers of the regular army who have been detailed to train the National Guard. Some changes would need to be made and could readily be made in the method of selecting officers and noncoms. Arrangements could easily be made for sending officers and noncommissioned officers to service schools, such as the School of Fire at Fort Sill and the School of Musketry at Fort Benning.

In order for this plan to work it would be necessary for our General Staff to keep abreast or a little ahead of the technological progress of the rest of the world. This would be necessary also, however, under the proposed plan for universal, compulsory military training.

The beauty about the plan I suggest is that it does not involve any revolutionary change in our established military policy, such as peacetime compulsory military training would involve. We are accustomed to the National Guard and its methods of recruiting. In many communities the leaders among the young men of that locality belong to it. In many of them the National Guard organization and the armory is the social center. Many of our best officers in the regular establishment started out in it as privates and worked themselves up.

It is essentially a democratic institution. I have seen the son of the town banker or the leading lawyer serving in the ranks alongside of the son of the less prominent citizens of the community.

It has a long and distinguished lineage in our history, from the days of the Minute Men of Revolutionary times through the days of the state troops of the Civil War and later those of the First World War and intervening years.

This discussion would not be complete if I did not refer to an argument that is often made by the proponents of universal, compulsory military training for 18-year-old boys that the army training results in physical benefits.

Those who conclude that men have benefited by a session of training in an army camp by pointing out the hardihood of these men leave out of account the countless hernias, heart ailments, broken-down feet, heat prostrations and other physical weaknesses which the army training has brought out and which has caused individuals to be eliminated.

It is true that after the training at Camp Doniphan in 1917, where men trained all day in the snow with inadequate shoes, and slept at night in unheated canvas tents and went without adequate bathing or toilet facilities the next year, very few of them succumbed to the hardships of battle conditions. The reason for that, however, was that only the ones that were hardy and practically indestructible to start with came through the Camp Doniphan training. This same condition is generally true of army training. It is the last place on earth to give a young man a well-rounded physical training. Furthermore, a young man's physique is pretty well set by the time he is 18. A year at hard training would do nothing more than to make acute some latent physical weakness.

A SUBSTITUTE FOR UNIVERSAL MILITARY TRAINING [15]

In the final analysis, and perhaps in oversimplification, the proposal for universal military training is little more than project for a vast, glorified physical training program of one year's duration—and at best a poor substitute for early continued development of mind and body.

The proposed plan ignores the fundamental facts that:

1. Modern war demands well-developed physiques.
2. Modern war is technical and mechanical.

What, then, is the answer?

Physical training must be commenced, as a national policy in the elementary schools and continued through high schools.

[15] By Crandall Melvin, President, Merchants National Bank and Trust Company, Syracuse, N.Y. *Commercial and Financial Chronicle.* 161:257, 270-1. January 18, 1945.

Means must be found to carry on this training following high school, either in continuation school, college or elsewhere.

Many physical defects are discoverable early in life and can then best be corrected. The early development of the body by sound methods, calculated to improve not only muscles but a spirit of aggressiveness, team work and fair play; together with constructive measures raising the public health, will assure this country that 30 per cent of its 18-year-olds will never again be unfit for military duty. Thus inadequate physical training of one year's duration in the form of so-called universal military training with all its attendant evils will be unnecessary.

Under the proposed plan, youths could not even begin to learn during their one year's service the scientific and mechanical techniques demanded by modern war, much less keep up with them after their release.

The answer is not an "army" of ill-adapted, immature boys, torn from their normal lives for a year only to be thrown back again, dislocated and irresponsible. Instead of wasting money on such misdirected training, inducements of pay and free technical education for the scientifically and mechanically inclined form the only possible answer. And advanced training need not be so limited—other fields make their contributions to proper preparation: languages, law and medicine, for example. This type of program would obviously involve the discovery of vocational aptitudes in high school and the supplementing of customary educational curricula not only by the already suggested physical development program, but also by suitable preparatory courses. It would involve, furthermore, a great expansion of our technical schools, colleges and universities, West Point and Annapolis. (Mechanical preparedness would necessarily form a part of the over-all program.)

In this way we would be utilizing not only the economic and financial but the human resources of the country wisely—not foolishly on a year of so-called training replete with many evils. More than that, we would be preparing the youth of the nation not alone for war, but for peace.

METHODS

1. Commission.

A commission should be created by the Congress to study the entire problem thoroughly and with proper deliberation. A majority of the commission should be trained civilians drawn from all lines of endeavor; military authorities should constitute a minority on this body. After the proposal for peacetime preparedness is recommended by this commission, and public support is assured, a federal law with implementing state laws would follow.

2. Federal Law.

a. The federal act should prescribe minimum standards and requirements and provide for grants-in-aid to carry them out. But preferably the program should be handled, as traditionally, by the states and local communities.

b. Minimum standards should cover:

(1) Physical training:
  (a) Raising health of nation in other ways;
  (b) Expansion of training facilities and public health program.

(2) Technical and other training:
  (a) Discovery of individual aptitudes;
  (b) Expansion of training facilities;
  (c) Other minimum standards should cover basic literacy and citizenship; to know what we are fighting for; to know how to preserve the peace.

(3) Elementary military training;
  (a) Might possibly be added to regular high school as well as advanced curricula;
  (b) Might include military organization, equipment, tactics, basic drill, etc.

3. State Law.

They would carry out purposes of federal act, adapting them to local conditions while still conforming to minimum standards.

Conclusion

It is submitted that the suggested possible solution for peacetime preparedness is superior to the hastily contrived plan for universal military training. It will solve the problem in a better way than universal military training and avoid its admitted evils.

The proposed substitute will:

1. Prepare Us for War.
   a. By better physical development of our youth;
   b. By technical and other training demanded by modern war.

2. Prevent War.
   a. By better training than universal military training;
   b. By teaching obligations of citizenship.

3. Promote Physical Fitness.
   a. By early, continued program.

4. Be Economically Sound.
   a. By not wasting human and financial resources indiscriminately on an arbitrary program not adapted to individual skills and aptitudes.

5. Be Democratic.
   a. Because it will induce, not compel. It will seek the best potential in each individual and encourage him to develop it;
   b. Because it will avoid dangers of military domination over civilian life.

6. Weed Out the Unfit in Time.
   a. By a national screening, well in advance of the 18-year age limit. The unfit of all types would then be discovered. Rehabilitation programs would be called for. (Our crime bill is five times that for education).

7. Not Disrupt Educational, Business, Family, Moral and Physical Life of Nation, as Admittedly Universal Military Training Would.

Instead of causing the irresponsibility and dependence attendant upon a year's misdirected effort in youths' most formative years, the proposed suggestion will cause an already physically developed youth to expand—not submerge—their individual talents by offering them an American opportunity to assume their individual and national responsibilities. We will have ready for any emergency—and most of all, for peace—a physically fit, technically trained democratic reservoir of men.

EXCERPTS

The caste system as between officers and men, extending to all aspects of their lives; racial segregation; and lack of encouragement to independent thought: these are aspects of military life which still prevail to a large extent. They must be made to yield if all or some of the nation's youth are to be placed under a compulsory military regimen in peacetime. Some of these evils, it is true, are attributable to Congress and the country rather than to the armed services themselves; but that fact does not entitle the nation to fasten them upon succeeding generations.—*Ralph F. Fuchs, Professor of Law, Washington University, St. Louis. Social Science. Ap.'45. p.* 81.

More than 15,000 chemists and chemical engineers are found in the armed services doing work having no relation to their training. At the same time we have dammed up the supply of new technicians who would normally be entering technical schools and colleges. A bill has been introduced in Congress making it possible to undo some of the damage by relieving a few of the chemists from K.P. duty and scrubbing decks, and sending them back to industry, and by permitting a limited number of boys to take technical training. This appears to be about the least that must be done if we are to avoid a disastrous shortage of trained scientists in an age which every five minutes we describe as "scientific."—*"We Face a Famine of Scientists"; editorial. Saturday Evening Post. Je.* 2, '45. *p.* 96.

Seven of my children have been serving in the armed forces for some time, two of them having been in the army for 10 months prior to Pearl Harbor. Just recently I received a telegram that one of these two boys was killed in action. This young man, who was 27 years old, was obliged during his first year in the army to submit to the orders of some officers who were thoroughly incompetent and who apparently owed their positions to their political ability in civil and military life. I am afraid a large permanent military establishment would lead to a repetition of this sort of domination by men whose principal aim is their own personal advancement, and the net result of their contact with intelligent boys would be unfortunate.—*Bartholomew O'Toole, President, Pullman Trust and Savings Bank, Chicago, Commercial and Financial Chronicle. Ja. 18, '45. p. 276.*

The activities and requirements of the armed forces involve every profession, skill, and activity known in civilian life. They require the services of the doctor of medicine, the lawyer, the chaplain, the logistic expert, the chemist, the physicist, the skilled craftsman, and all the rest.

It requires a minimum of three to seven or more years of intensive study beyond high school to prepare for the practice of professions such as medicine, engineering, and others in this category. The interruption of such preparation by a year of military instruction, disassociated from the continuation of such preparation, adds a year to the time required, already long, and delays by a year the usefulness of the person to the society which made his preparation possible. The same is equally true of those preparing for other activities and responsibilities of life.—*Virgil M. Hancher and E. T. Peterson, State University of Iowa. Commercial and Financial Chronicle. F. 1, '45. p. 534.*

According to Mr. [George S.] Schuyler, [American Negro journalist], conscription would so operate as to thrust Negroes who have moved north to escape from the south's segregation system into another species of segregation even more sharply defined. "The more jimcrow institutions we have," wrote this Negro columnist, "and the more people are subjected to them, the worse the race relations will grow in this country. Compulsory military training will mean that every American boy—regardless of color or place of origin—will be drilled in the color caste system. One can imagine the effect on plastic minds." Behind this expression of fear lies the bitter experience which Negroes have had with the draft during the war. The segregation enforced in both army and navy has become a burning topic in all Negro communities. It is only natural that the same segregation would be the expected portion of Negroes in a national system of peacetime conscription.—*Editorial. Christian Century. D. 27, '44. p. 1493.*

If each of the Big Powers adopts or maintains universal conscription and an immense military establishment—and surely no one is naive enough to assume that if the United States does, the others won't—then what has become of international organization and collective security? Obviously they are sunk. What we shall have is a universal armament race on a scale not hitherto imagined. We shall be taking a huge stride away from world organization, international community, economic freedom and well-being and peace; and a huge stride toward isolationism, international anarchy, militarization, dictatorship and World War III. As President Coolidge once sagely remarked: "No amount of preparedness ever kept a country out of war or insured it victory when it came." We can have an armament race or we can have collective security; we cannot have both.—*A. J. Muste, Executive Secretary, Fellowship of Reconciliation. Independent Woman. Ap. '45. p. 98, 112.*

The strongest argument of the advocates rests upon a more intangible claim, that of training in citizenship. But I had supposed that citizenship meant, even to these advocates, the ability to function as a citizen in a democracy, and that the art of democratic living would be the necessary preparation for that. Whatever may be said of a military establishment it is not democratic, and cannot be. Discipline and unquestioning obedience to authority are its essence, for without them armies cannot be effective. The obligation to defend one's country all men accept, and compulsory military training cannot make the acceptance greater. What, then, is left to the claim of training for citizenship? The contrary argument would appear to be the stronger, that military training is opposed to democratic practice and tends to undo whatever training for democratic citizenship a youth may have had.

Surely it will be admited that education in democracy should mark our educational system from the earliest years; not only in the content of studies in history and civics but in the relationships established in the school system by the very organization of school life itself. It cannot be segregated for boys only. It should, and does in the best of our schools, mark the habits of behavior of both teachers and students from kindergarten through high school. . . . If we mean to teach democracy, we cannot confine its concept and practice to our country alone. We have the duty and high purpose to share with the peoples of the world the hopes that the human race can so order its affairs and so resolve its conflicts that conscription may everywhere be abolished, the nations disarmed, and international agencies alone exercise such policing as the world may require.—*Roger N. Baldwin, Director, American Civil Liberties Union. Educational Leadership. O. '44. p. 27-8.*

One source of confusion on the issue of peacetime conscription is the assumption that the effect of army life on young men is the same in peacetime as in wartime, whereas the exact opposite is true. When the war motive of life and death is removed, standards drop and army life tends to undermine the greatest factor in a nation's strength—its moral standards. This is shown by facts found in the reports of the Surgeon General of the U.S. Army and of the Secretary of War. For example, during each of the interwar years 1929, 1930, and 1931 crimes tried by courts martial averaged more than 18 per cent of the number of men enlisted in the army; desertions for 1929-1931 inclusive averaged 5.8 per cent. The incidence of venereal disease per 1000 in 1929—in spite of the well-known prophylactic program—was 48 in the army and 127.51 in the navy as compared with 3.24 among civilians. These are truly amazing figures and when one has made every allowance and placed the most favorable interpretation upon them they show what proved to be true in France, the possibility that conscription may actually weaken the nation. There are better means for preparedness.— *Editorial. National Education Association. Journal. Ap. '45. p. 74.*

The "Pro Committee" states that if universal military training in time of peace is adopted in the United States, a million young men will be trained each year at a cost of approximately one billion dollars. The "Con Committee" thinks these figures are inaccurate. It estimates that the annual number of trainees will be approximately 1,200,000 and will increase with the growth of population; and that the cost per trainee will be in excess of $1,500 per person, or say $1,800,000,000 per year for the entire country. This estimate is based upon a statement of General Frederick H. Osborn in his report to the President dated July 30, 1943:

> The estimated cost of maintaining an enlisted man on active duty for one year, exclusive of ordnance and overhead, is approximately $1,500.

But an initial annual cost of nearly two billion dollars is not the whole story. Three months is all that is required for the basic training of a recruit. The balance of the year is to be spent in special training with planes, ordnance and tanks and the $1,500 per trainee does not cover the cost of ordnance and overhead. Nor does the figure of $1,800,000,000 include the cost of calling trainees back to the colors for temporary training each year and it is probable that universal military training will ultimately add to the budget of the United States not less than three and possibly four billion dollars per year.—*Chamber of Commerce of the United States. Universal Military Training in Peacetime. Referendum no. 85. From comments of Committee on Negative Arguments. O. 9, '44. p. 110.*

In this stage of the world's development, and for centuries to come, there is, and there will be, no such thing as durable peace. Struggle is a part of life, wars are a part of history. Only the slow process of education and basic changes in the essential nature of man will outlaw them. And that will not be in our time, or in our children's children's children's time.

The Dumbarton Oaks plan is no insurance of peace. The preservation of tomorrow's peace depends, not upon the new League of Nations, but upon the three great powers, Britain, Russia, and the United States, and upon the agreements reached among those three great powers, *outside the framework of the Dumbarton Oaks agreement*. The police forces provided for by the Oaks agreement are *national*, not *international*, forces. They will be, essentially, ad hoc forces—that is, mixed forces composed of contingents from various member nations of the new League, mobilized for specific and temporary police purposes, not permanently organized as an international army. They will be large enough, perhaps, to prevent or suppress small wars, but they will have neither the size nor the power to prevent large wars; indeed, the Oaks agreements do not contemplate that they should be able to do this. If there is basic disagreement among the three great powers, the new League will be a façade and nothing more; if one of those three great powers commits aggression, nothing the League's "police force" can do can prevent it, or alter it.

It is clear that conscription can do little to make effective a League who effectiveness depends not upon the police forces provided for but upon the agreements, political, economic, and military, arrived at among the three great powers outside the framework of Dumbarton Oaks. It should also be clear, as we have previously seen, that no one-year *training* force could be suitable for overseas police service. The arguments of the proponents of conscription, are, therefore, dismissed on two counts. —*Hanson W. Baldwin, Writer on Military and Naval Affairs. Harper's Magazine. Mr. '45. p. 296.*

From a purely economic point of view, the hazards of compulsory military training are equally serious. They mean, of course, a very dangerous encroachment upon the national budget. To argue that the men and women under military training relieve the labor market, means to overlook that this kind of "relief" is far more expensive than almost any other kind, including even public works, to say nothing about the comparison with "normal" relief expenditures. Compulsory military training implies vast military establishments and equipment, without the generous use of which the training would be meaningless, of course. The cost of the constant flow of bigger and better equipment and of fresh munitions would constitute a very serious threat to our financial equilibrium, coming as they would on top of the astronomical cost of this war, and at times when it will be a first item on the agenda of national policy to bring the budget into balance.

Moreover, and disregarding the cost involved, it is a fallacy to assume that a large army in permanence would mean a lasting contribution toward the stabilization of employment. True, it absorbs a fraction of the working population, but does so irrespective of the cycle. In an upturn, it helps to cause labor shortage, to raise wages and to induce more malinvestment of national resources, all of which helps in turn to bring about an early reversal and to intensify the factors responsible for the subsequent depression. In other words, from the point of view of employment provision, compulsory military training is not only far too expensive, but actually worthless because it has to be operated independently of the business cycle, and because it might sharpen rather than moderate its evil effects.

Nor should we forget that if we believe in free enterprise as a cornerstone of democratic freedoms, a system that gives the government as a large-scale purchaser vast controlling powers over the markets, is an unmitigated evil only to be tolerated if compelling reasons of national security should prevail.—*Dr. Melchior Palyi, Chicago Economist. Commercial and Financial Chronicle. Should America Have Compulsory Military Training in Peacetime? Symposium. '45 p. 19.*

Universal military training for one year would also give us a yearly health inventory of our nation but too late to do much about it. A universal national service program would accomplish the same thing. It seems quite clear from the analysis of the selected service examinations that the argument that we need one year of compulsory military training for all young men in order to improve the health of the youth of our country has certain weaknesses.

It is equally clear to those who have studied these figures and health problems in this country, that we must start by considering the factors which determine the health of our youngest children: (1) heredity, which we cannot do much about; (2) environment, which we can control to great extent; (3) pre- and post-natal care; (4) food, rest, and activity, the three factors that determine normal growth and development; (5) periodic health examinations in the schools with the chief emphasis on the follow-up and correction of defects discovered, with special attention given to early detection of neuropsychiatric symptoms; (6) the inclusion of a health education program in every school, carrying through from the first grade to the high school, and a physical education program that will reach every pupil every day; (7) the establishment of clinics in all sections of the country for diagnosis and education to work in cooperation with the doctors in the community.

Such a program is not spectacular. It demands nation-wide participation and depends for its success on the cooperation of all agencies and persons working with children. It is a long-time educational program. It means increased school and medical costs but in the long run it will involve a great saving in the total taxes. Such a program would not be universal. It would not reach all boys and girls for a long time. However, it would be directed at correcting and preventing the basic causes of the large number of health defects in young people.—*J. H. Nichols, Oberlin College. Journal of Health and Physical Education. Vol. 16, no.3. Mr. '45. p.* 160.

The truth is that wars are fought by the current generation after brief training in the operation of the latest scientific equipment. And they are won by superiority of equipment, industrial resources and manpower. They are not won by goose-step training. There is no way to "prepare" a nation for modern war except to keep the entire manpower constantly in uniform, with the latest equipment. Our ships are manned by boys who never saw a ship until a few months ago. Our front-line troops are boys who had never seen a tank or shot a rifle until a few months back. France, desperately afraid of the Germans, bled herself white with universal military training. Her troops collapsed pitiably when the Germans assaulted them with superior tanks, artillery and planes. France might have held out if she had no compulsory training and had put the cost into planes and tanks. England has no compulsory training. She kept back the Germans because she had a first-class navy and a handful of Spitfires that could outfight the German planes. Training had nothing to do with it. The numskull Mussolini drilled his troops for years, pounding his chest and telling the world what they could do. They quit cold before American boys who had been small children when Mussolini started training his troops. . . .

The policies of our military leaders refute their own arguments for compulsory training. They flatly refused to let Congress pass a law to require one year of training for young boys before they were sent overseas. Thousands of our troops have gone overseas after less than a year's training, while other thousands have been kept at home after much longer training. The army does not even use the training men have already received. I have three sons. One had no military training whatever. He is now an officer, a flyer doing highly technical testing work, all of it learned since he volunteered. A second son had four years in one of the finest college R.O.T.C. units. He is an officer in the South Pacific, in service in no way connected with his four years training. He was prepared for it in 17 weeks after he left college. The third son had 1½ years in a fine R.O.T.C. unit. He is in the North Pacific doing work in no way connected with his R.O.T.C. training.

These are not exceptional cases. Any reader can cite similar instances. They merely suggest that universal training now for a war in the remote future is not an efficient or necessary method of national protection.—*Neil Carothers, Dean, College of Business Administration, Lehigh University. Commercial and Financial Chronicle. D. 14, '44 p. 2612.*

Is compulsory military service good education? The answer . . . is "No." Putting all our able-bodied boys at eighteen or nineteen into an army organization for a year is not good education. The educational results of such a program can be foreseen, and they are not pleasant to contemplate.

At the age of eighteen or nineteen, and immediately after high-school graduation for most boys, a boy would report to the army and spend the next year under the immediate direction of army sergeants, whose job would be to "make a man out of him." The boy would be put indiscriminately into a company with others who happened to appear at camp at the same time. His company would be a democratic, heterogeneous mixture of all social groups.

During most of the year he would be trained in a large army camp somewhere in Texas, Mississippi, or Alabama, where the weather permits year-round outdoor training. Here the boy would have a great deal of common experience with other American boys of all types. He would have a common experience with them in obeying orders and in handling military machines. He would share with others the experiences of "griping" and of "soldiering," which have always meant complaining about food, camp conditions, and the officers, and trying to "get by" with as little work as possible. Other common experiences that the boy would share with his company would be gambling, drinking, and other "common" forms of recreation. . . .

The thing would happen that always happens when a society of men only is created by putting all kinds of men together at random and placing them under the authority of other men who have no interest in, or preparation for, the tasks of intellectual and moral education: the lowest common denominator of intellectual, cultural, and moral life would prevail. . . .

This kind of educational experience would take the place, for thousands of boys, of a year of college or junior college. Of the boys who now go to college, a considerable fraction would never make the effort if the continuity from high school to college were broken by military training. While there is considerable question concerning the value of the academic work done by a boy who stays only a year or so in college, there is no doubt about the value to him of living in the college community. The churches have active programs for college students. The college staff is made up of men and women trained for work with young people. There is plenty of normal companionship with girls of the same social background as that of the boys.

In an effort to provide some continuing education, the army would encourage boys to take correspondence courses. A few would enroll for such courses, and a very few would stick to their studies at night while their neighbors in the barracks filled the air with noisy talk, obscenities, tobacco smoke, and the excitement of gambling.

Thus may be described the kind of "education" a boy would get in a year of compulsory military service. There are, however, some positive features. The average health of the boys would be improved, if this statement is taken to mean that most boys would gain weight and their muscles would harden and that their teeth would be filled by army dentists. But these results could be achieved at much less cost by an expanded program of physical education in the schools and a national program of dental service for adolescent boys and girls.—*Robert J. Havighurst, Professor of Education, University of Chicago; Secretary, Committee on Human Development. School Review. F. '45. p. 65-6.*

Let me point out first of all that universal compulsory military training on the part of any nation will be inconsistent with the policy of establishing an International Police Force to preserve peace and order, which many of us hope to see established after this war. In fact, it is inconsistent with any federation of the world for peace.

Universal compulsory military training or conscription has lasted on the continent of Europe for over one hundred years, and it has been called, with some justice, the key to modern European history. After trial of more than a century, it must be evident that instead of leading to peace and cooperation among the nations, it has been the active basis of their war system and of the wars of Europe. The conclusion which practically all students of European history and of social and political institutions have reached is that the universal training of large populations to the use of arms has invariably been followed in history by increased resort to armed force, both within nations and between nations. We could scarcely look for any different result if we follow the example of Europe in this matter.

In this country we rightly fear a proletarian revolution, a civil war between classes. Your committee should bear in mind that the revolutionary tribunals of Russia were Workmen and Soldiers Councils. If it had not been for the soldiers in these councils, they would have been, I believe, comparatively harmless, at least incapable of initiating and carrying through successfully a proletarian revolution. But when the whole population has been trained to the use of armed force, they naturally resort to armed force as a political method. Therefore, if there is one thing more certain than another to bring to pass in this country such an event as the Russian revolution in the future, it is universal compulsory military training.

Can one look with equanimity upon training to the use of arms of the lower elements in our own native laboring classes, both white and Negro? What will strikes become if the strikers are trained in military methods? Moreover, the growing restlessness and resentment of some elements in our Negro population makes the military training of this element a threat to the South if not to the whole nation. A population habituated to the use of arms and to military methods seldom has scruples against the use of armed force. The Russian revolution took the bloody turn it did because it occurred in a large population which had been trained to use military methods. We can scarcely hope that it will be different with us, and I think that you can see that the use of such methods will result sooner or later in the downfall of our republic.

Moreover, it is fatuous to think that the little patriotic civic instruction which might be sandwiched in with compulsory military training would suffice to stop the tendency of groups to achieve their ends by the use of the methods of armed force in which they had been instructed.

There is no argument for the adoption of such a system in the United States, because it has been adopted in Europe. If, for example, Switzerland has escaped involvement in wars and civil disturbances, we must remember that it is a small country with a small population, wonderfully united through long tradition in its political ideals. Again, Switzerland has no other means of defense, and its neutrality is guaranteed by the surrounding hostile nations. It cannot protect itself with a navy. Finally, until the present war began, its term of military training was very short.

I am not opposed to an adequate and efficient navy for this country, or to an adequate and efficient air force. Under ordinary conditions these will only be used for purposes of defense and there is little danger in them. Neither am I opposed to training military officers in our institutions of learning, nor to a small, adequately trained, mobile army for defense and to preserve internal order. But every consideration of patriotism and of political prudence would dictate that your committee should hesitate long before it enters upon an experiment which has so often proved the undoing of nations, and especially of free governments.—*From letter of Charles A. Ellwood, Professor of Sociology, Duke University, retired, to Senator Robert R. Reynolds, Chairman, Senate Military Affairs Committee. National Education Association. Journal. S. '44. p. 139.*

BIBLIOGRAPHY

An asterisk (*) preceding a reference indicates that the article or a part of it has been reprinted in this book.

BIBLIOGRAPHIES

Education for Victory. 3:5-6. F. 3, '45. Compulsory military training; annotated bibliography. S. O. Futterer, comp.
Same. Youth Leaders Digest. 7:179-82. F. '45

Higher Education. 1:8-9. Mr. 15, '45. Compulsory military training; an annotated list of selected recent references.

Higher Education. 1:6-7. Ap. 2, '45. Selected references on evaluation of army and navy training programs. R. C. M. Flynt, comp.

Lewis, Eleanor F. comp. Compulsory military training; a selected list of recent references on the desirability of one year of military training for all American young men when they reach the age of 18. 15p. H. W. Wilson Co. New York 52. '45.
Additional supplementary references. 4p. mim. '45.

Scholastic Debater. 1:6. My. '45. Bibliography on compulsory military training. Betty Paxton and others, comps.

United States. Library of Congress. Division of Bibliography. Compulsory military training; a supplementary list of references. A. D. Brown, comp. 38p mim. Washington, D.C. Ag. 20, '41.

United States. Library of Congress. General Reference and Bibliography Division. Universal military training; a selected and annotated list of references. Frances Cheney, comp. 138p. mim. Washington, D.C. Mr. 23, '45.
See also bibliographical notes under references below.

GENERAL REFERENCES

BOOKS, PAMPHLETS AND DOCUMENTS

Aly, Bower, ed. Military training; the fifteenth annual debate handbook, 1941-42. 2 vols. 220p. ea. Lucas Bros. Columbia, Mo. '41.
Bibliography, Vol. 1, p. 203-20.

Aly, Bower, ed. Peacetime military training: the nineteenth annual debate handbook. Lucas Bros. Columbia, Mo. '45.
Selected articles, bibliography and comments in brief.

American Council on Education. Summary of a poll of college presidents on universal military training. (Higher Education and National Defense. Bulletin no. 85) 6p. 744 Jackson Pl. Washington 6, D.C. Je. 8, '45.

Andrews, Marshall. Our new army. 225p. Little, Brown and Co. Boston. '42.

Association of Urban Universities. Proceedings, 1940:21-5. What colleges and universities can do in trade training to aid in the preparedness program. P. C. Nash. The Association. University of Pittsburgh. Pittsburgh. '40.

Beukema, Herman. Social and political aspects of conscription: Europe's experience. *In* Clarkson, Jesse D. and Cochran, Thomas C. eds. War as a social institution. p. 113-29. Columbia University Press. New York. '41.

Buehler, Ezra C. ed. Compulsory military service. (Annual debaters help book. Vol. 8) 422p. Noble and Noble. New York. 1941.
Bibliography, p. 389-422.

Chamber of Commerce of the United States. Universal military training in peacetime. (Referendum no. 85) 10p. The Chamber. Washington, D.C. O. 9, '44.

Debate on the proposition Resolved: That every able-bodied male citizen in the United States should be required to have one year of full-time military training before attaining the present draft age. 23p. J. W. Wadsworth, O. G. Villard, C. E. Kilbourne and J. N. Sayre. Published for the Committee on Debate Materials and Interstate Cooperation of the National University Extension Association. Artcraft Press. Columbia, Mo. N. 21, '41.

Dewey, John. Universal service as education. *In his* Education today. p. 92-100. G. P. Putnam's Sons. New York. '40.

Educational Policies Commission. Compulsory peacetime military training. 15p. The Commission. 1201 16th St. N.W. Washington 6, D.C. F. '45.
Abridged. National Education Association. Journal. 34:87-8. Ap. '45. Peacetime conscription and national security; *Summary.* Scholastic. 40:4T. Ap. 23, '45. Peacetime military training.

Educational Policies Commission. Education for all American youth. 421p. The Commission. 1201 16th St. N.W. Washington 6, D.C. '44.

Encyclopaedia of the Social Sciences. E. R. A. Seligman and Alvin Johnson, eds. Macmillan. New York. '37.
See Conscription; Military training.

Ford, Harvey S. What you should know about the army. rev. ed. 259p. W. W. Norton and Co. New York. '43.

Freeman, Harrop A. Constitutionality of peacetime conscription. 43p. Pacifist Research Bureau. 1201 Chestnut St. Philadelphia 7. '44.

Ganoe, William A. History of the United States army. 640p. D. Appleton-Century Co. New York. '42.

Governors' Conference. Proceedings, 1943:18-29. State assistance in the military training program. Ellis Arnall. The Conference. Frank Bane, Sec.-Treas. 1313 E. 60th St. Chicago 27. '43.

Harvey, Ray F. Politics of the armed services. *In* Harvey, Ray F. and others. Politics of this war. p. 217-37. Harper and Brothers. New York. '43.

Hershey, Lewis B. Establishing selective service. 19p. University of Pennsylvania Press. Philadelphia. '42.

Hilliard, Otis L. Our national draft policy. 40p. Debate Coaches Bureau. Box 284. Denison, Tex. '42.

Johnsen, Julia E. comp. Compulsory military training. (Reference Shelf. Vol. 14, no. 6) 266p. H. W. Wilson Co. New York. Ja. '41. Bibliography, p. 245-66.

Kahn, E. J. Army life. 152p. Infantry Journal. Washington, D.C. '43.

Leigh, Randolph. Conscript Europe. 308p G. P. Putnam's Sons. New York. '38.

Liddell Hart, B. H. Why don't we learn from history? [P.E.N. books] 64p. George Allen and Unwin. London. '44.

Limpus, Lowell M. How the army fights. 388p. D. Appleton-Century Co. New York. '43.

McCloskey, Burr. What attitude toward conscription; a discussion of the military draft and the proposed labor draft. 21p. mim. Independent Labor League. 84 W. Market St. Akron 8, O. '43.

Marshall, George C. Selected speeches and statements. ed. by H. A. DeWeerd. 263p. Infantry Journal. Washington, D.C. '45.

National Opinion Research Center. Compulsory military training in peacetime? (Report no. 23) 16p. mim. The Center. University of Denver. Denver 10, Colo. D. '44.

National Peace Conference. Commission on the World Community. Pros and cons of peacetime conscription. (World government series) 11p. The Conference. 8 W. 40th St. New York 18. F. '45.

National Policy Committee. Memorandum of the Washington dinner on universal military training. (Memoranda no. 35) 21p. The Committee. 1202 National Press Building. Washington 4, D.C. '44.

National Research Council. Psychology for the armed services. Edwin G. Boring, ed. 533p. Infantry Journal. 1115 17th St. N.W. Washington 6, D.C. '45.

Nickerson, Hoffman. Armed horde, 1793-1939; a study of the rise, survival and decline of the mass army. 427p. G. P. Putnam's Sons. New York. '40.

Patterson, Robert P. Selective service and the college student. 17p. University of Pennsylvania Press. Philadelphia. '41.

Pennington, Leon A. and others. Psychology of military leadership. 288p. Prentice-Hall Inc. New York. '43.

Phelps, Edith M. ed. University debaters' annual, 1940-1941: 345-88. Compulsory military training. H. W. Wilson Co. New York. '41. Bibliography, p. 382-8.

Phelps, Edith M. ed. University debaters' annual, 1941-1942: 101-48. Military training. H. W. Wilson Co. New York. '42. Bibliography, p. 140-8.

Phelps, Edith M. ed. University debaters' annual, 1944-1945: 165-200. Compulsory universal military training. H. W. Wilson Company. New York. '45. Bibliography, p. 198-200.

Rankin, E. R. comp. Universal military training; debate handbook. 102p. (Extension Bulletin. Vol. 20, no. 1) University of North Carolina. Chapel Hill. Jl. '40.

Reeve, Juliet and others. comp. Sourcebook on peacetime conscription. 52p. American Friends Service Committee. 20 S. 12th St. Philadelphia 7. N. '44.
Bibliography, p. 48-9.

*Shall we have another lost and unwanted generation of young people in the postwar period? [Suggestions resulting from discussions at the School for Executives held at Jackson's Mill, West Virginia, August 15-24, 1944.] 8p. Arthur J. Klein. College of Education. Ohio State University. Columbus 10. ['44?]

Should the United States adopt permanent military conscription? official statements of twelve important religious, educational and civic bodies. 6p. American Friends Service Committee. 20 S. 12th St. Philadelphia 7. ['44.]

Summers, Robert E. and Summers, Harrison B. comp. Universal military service. (Reference Shelf. Vol. 15, no. 2) 280p. H. W. Wilson Co. New York 52. S. '41.
Bibliography, p. 261-80.

Technocracy Inc. Total conscription; your questions answered. rev. ed. 22p. Technocracy Inc. 155 E. 44th St. New York 17. N. '43

Thomas, Norman and Weible, W. L. Should America have compulsory military training after the war? (Wake Up America. no.244) 12p American Economic Foundation. 295 Madison Ave. New York 17. '44.
Major General Walter L. Weible's discussion, revised, also appears in Army and Navy Register. p. 7. D. 9, '44.

Underhill, Garrett. We must arm. In Zero hour. p.179-213. Farrar and Rinehart. New York. '40.

United States House. Committee on Military Affairs. Extension of the Selective Training and Service Act; hearings, March 22, 1945, on H.R. 2625. 20p. 79th Congress. 1st session. Supt. of Docs. Washington, D.C. '45.

* United States. House. Select Committee on Postwar Military Policy. Universal military training; hearings, June 4-19, 1945, pursuant to H. Res. 465. 614p 79th Congress, 1st session. Supt. of Docs. Washington, D.C. '45.

Walch, John W. Complete handbook on military training. 154, 7ap. Platform News Publishing Co. 45A Free St. Portland 3, Me. '41.
Supplementary evidence file on military training; issues of Oct. 1, Nov. 15, 1941; Jan. 1, Feb. 15, 1942. Platform News.

PERIODICALS

Agricultural Education. 17:183. Ap. '45. Farm boys and military training. G. P. Couper.

America. 71:145-6. My. 13, '44. Get the record straight on permanent conscription. W. L. Lucey.

American Association of Collegiate Registrars. Journal. 20:184-6. Ja. '45. Universal military training and education. K. I. Brown.

*American Association of Collegiate Registrars. Journal. 20:186-92. Ja. '45. National needs and national service. E. H. Wilkins.

American Association of Collegiate Registrars. Journal. 20:193-6. Ja. '45. Compulsory training and technological preparedness. W. E. Wickenden.

American Association of Collegiate Registrars. Journal. 20:196-202. Ja. '45. Compulsory military training. D. J. Shank.

American Association of Collegiate Registrars. Journal. 20:272-3. Ja. '45. Plan of national service, consideration of which is endorsed in principle by the faculty of Oberlin College.

American Association of School Administrators. Official Report, 1943: 23-35. Myth of the militia. R. P. Rosengren.
Same. Texas Outlook. 27:21-6. Jl. '43.

American Association of School Administrators. Official Report, 1944: 82-8. Military training program of the army service forces. W. L. Weible.
Same condensed. Kentucky School Journal. 22:32+. Mr. '44; Montana Education. 20:20-1. Mr. '44; New York State Education. 31:422-3+. Mr. '44; Ohio Schools. 22:104-5. Mr. '44; Sierra Educational News. 40:11-12. Mr. '44; Texas Outlook. 28:38-9. Mr. '44. *Excerpts.* Pennsylvania School Journal. 92: 253-4. Ap. '44.

American Association of University Professors Bulletin. 30:487-90. [D.] '44. Shall the United States adopt universal military training? R. E. Himstead.

American Association of University Professors Bulletin. 30:508-11. [D.] '44. Petition to the President of the United States to appoint a national commission to consider proposals for compulsory military training. Committee on Youth Problems; American Council on Education.
Same. Educational Record. 26:5-8. Ja. '45.

American Defense. 2:1-3. N. '44. Think before answering; vital questions in considering military training. F. J. Brown.
Same separate. Is conscription the way to peace? 14p. American Council on Education. 744 Jackson Pl. Washington 6, D.C.

American Forum of the Air. 6, no. 36:3-14. S. 12, '44. Should we have universal military training in peacetime? J. W. Wadsworth and others.

American Forum of the Air. 6, no. 46:2-15. N. 29, '44. Should we have compulsory military training in peacetime? E. C. Johnson and others.

American Journal of Sociology. 48:331-42. N. '42. War and education in the United States. H. M. Kallen.

American Journal of Sociology. 50:271-8. Ja. '45. Problems of adjustment in army units. S. K. Weinberg.

American Magazine. 139:34-5+. Je. '45. Will compulsory military training be good or bad for our boys; poll of experts, ed. by Arthur Kornhauser.

American Observer. 14:1-3. D. 4, '44. Peacetime draft of U.S. youth debated.

American Observer. 14:1+. Je. 18, '45. Peacetime military training is debated.

American Scholar. 14, no. 1:19-32. [Ja.] '45. Design for fighting. Harlow Shapley.
    Revised. Atlantic Monthly. 176:107-14. Ag. '45.

American Teacher. 29:21-2. Ja. '45. Youth conscription, federal aid, and national security. I. R. Kuenzli.

*Annals of the American Academy. 220:29-49. Mr. '42. Training for military service. B. N. Harlow.

Army and Navy Journal. p. 8. Ja. 13, '45. Universal military training.

Army and Navy Register. p. 2. Ja. 3, '45. Compulsory military training.

*Army and Navy Register. p. 26. Ja. 20, '45. Universal military training.

Army and Navy Register. p. 8. Jl. 7, '45. Compulsory training.

Atlantic Monthly. 171:63-6. Ja. '43. Priorities in education. George Boas.

Aviation. 42:119+. Jl. '43. Split-second recognition, a new allied weapon; identification of planes, ships, and armored vehicles at speeds up to 1/100 of a second.

Banking. 37:36-8. My. '45. Keeping our powder dry. H. J. Reilly.

California Journal of Secondary Education. 20:3-4. Ja '45. Resolution on compulsory military training adopted by the California Junior College Federation.
    Same. School and Society. 61:85-6. F. 10, '45.

California Journal of Secondary Education. 20:9-15. Ja. '45. What the services teach us about P. E. C. H. Young.

Catholic Educational Review. 42:577-92. D. '44. Compulsory military training after the war? D. C. Gildea.

Catholic World. 156:140-8. N. '42. Future American army. A. R. Bandini.

Christian Century. 60:888. Ag. 4, '43. Shall we conscript women? O. G. Villard.

Christian Century. 61:1125. O. 4, '44. Are we afraid of a word?

Christian Century. 61:1373-4. N. 29, '44. President demands youth training.

Christian Education. 28:174. Mr. '45. Letter from the White House. W. D. Hassett.

Clearing House. 19:190-1. N. '44. Some questions about universal military training. H. H. Ryan.

*Commercial and Financial Chronicle. 160:1793+, 2241+, 2345+, 2458+, 2593+, 2706+, 2802+; 161:59+, 154+, 263+, 516+. O. 26, N. 23, 30, D. 7, 14, 21, 28, '44; Ja. 4, 11, 18, F. 1, '45.

Compulsory military training in peacetime for postwar America? symposium.
*p. 2824. D. 28, '44. J. T. Holdsworth; *p. 277. Ja. 18, '45. R. R. Wood.

Commercial and Financial Chronicle. 160:2273+. N. 23, '44. President Roosevelt advocates compulsory military training for youths in peacetime.

Commercial and Financial Chronicle. 161:154+. Ja. 11, '45. Congress awaits FDR message on peacetime training issue.

Commercial and Financial Chronicle. 161:199. Ja. 11, '45. Peace-time service draft drive to be directed by Colonel Jay Cooke.

Commercial and Financial Chronicle. 161:936, 966. Mr. 1, '45. Taft objects to army's action in use of 18-year-old draftees for overseas combat.

Commercial and Financial Chronicle. 161:1529. Ap. 5, '45. Defends army view on 18 yr. old fighters. G. C. Marshall.

Commonweal. 40:438-42. Ag. 25, '44. Our post-war armed forces. H. L. Binsse.

Commonweal. 41:462-4. F. 23, '45. Peacetime military training; an army private asks some questions.

Commonwealth. 18, pt. 2 (Transactions of the Commonwealth Club of California. 36, no. 4):117-52. Mr. 3, '42. Draftee physical defects —1917 and 1942. W. H. Pillsbury and others.

Congressional Digest. 20:193-224. Ag. '41. Proposed permanent policy of compulsory military service; fact material and pro and con discussion.

Congressional Digest. 24:2-32. Ja. '45. Should the United States adopt compulsory peacetime military training? background material and pro and con discussion.

Congressional Record. 91:(daily)A1723-4. Mr. 30, '45. What shall we do about compulsory military training? E. D. Thomas.

Congressional Record. 91:3771-84. Ap. 24, '45. Extension of selective training and service act of 1940.

Congressional Record. 91:(daily)A2130. Ap. 27, '45. Military service for 18-year-old soldiers. Robert Sikes.

Congressional Record. 91:(daily)A3152. Je. 19, '45. Says resistance to peacetime conscription will not be overcome quickly, if ever. Lowell Mellett.

Congressional Record. 91:(daily)A3477-8. Jl. 3, '45. Universal military training. D. P. Taylor.

Congressional Record. 91:(daily)A3628-9. Jl 10, '45. Peacetime military training. Max Schwabe.

Congressional Record. 91:(daily)A3782-4. Jl. 17, '45. Arguments for and against compulsory military training.

Current History. n.s. 7:291-6. O. '44. Conscription after the war. D. G. Redmond.

*Dartmouth Alumni Magazine. Je. '45. For military training. E. M. Hopkins.
  Same. New York Times. p. 8E. My. 6, '45.
Debater's Magazine. 1:31-7. Ja-F '45. Compulsory military service in peace time.
  Bibliography, p. 35-7. Magazine articles reviewed, p. 115-16.
Economist (London). 145:502. O. 9, '43. Skilled men for the services.
Editorial Research Reports. 1 no. 15:265-81. Ap. 15, '44. Universal service. F. P. Huddle.
Education. 63:645. Je. '43. Handwriting on the wall. C. G. Miller.
Education for Victory. 2:1+. D. 1, '43. Pre-induction needs in language communication and reading.
Education for Victory. 2:14. D. 1, '43. War Department amplifies military drill statement. H. L. Stimson.
Education for Victory. 2:9-14. Ja. 3, '44. Pre-induction training in health, sanitation, and first aid.
*Education for Victory. 3:5-7. Ja. 20, '45. Education and medicine can improve the health of the nation. L. G. Rowntree.
Education for Victory. 3:14-18+. F. 20, '45. Do we need universal military training? radio script.
Educational Forum. 9:231-6. Ja. '45. Military training and secondary education: a comparative study. A. R. Brinkman.
*Educational Forum. 9:341-8. Mr. '45. Does the probability of compulsory military training pose a problem for the public schools? L. P. Todd.
Education Leadership. 2:1-28. O. '44. We must decide . . .should we have compulsory military training for all youth after the war.
  Contents include: What are the issues? H. E. Wilson; Is permanent conscription the answer? W. C. Trow; Does national security demand it? J. M. Costello; Are we letting democracy down? Frank McCallister; Is universal training vital to world leadership? Delacey Allen; Are we being fooled by a cure-all? R. N. Baldwin.
Educational Record. 23:629-41. O. '42. Government and the colleges in wartime. S. P. Capen.
  Same. American Association of University Professors Bulletin. 28:587-99. D. '42; *Same condensed.* Education Digest. 8:1-4. D. '42.
Educational Record. 26:5-8. Ja. '45. Petition to the President of the United States to appoint a national commission to consider proposals for compulsory military training.
Educational Screen. 25:58-9+. F. '45. ABC's for GI Joe. R. E. Waggoner.
English Journal. 34:132-6. Mr. '45. Teaching the three R's in the army. P. A. Witty.
Foreign Affairs. 22:643-4. Jl. '44. War pattern of Swiss life. Werner Richter.
Fortnightly. 163 (n.s.157):98-104. F. '45. Defense and democracy. W. T. Wells.
Fortune. 30:10+. Jl. '44. Fortune survey; peacetime draft to maintain the armed forces.

Fortune. 31:269-72. Je. '45. Fortune survey: postwar armaments; what kind of force?

Frontiers of Democracy. 8:200-2. Ap. '42. Do we want military training in the high schools? F. E. Karelsen, jr.
Same condensed. Education Digest. 8:34-6. S. '42.

Harper's Magazine. 183:337-46. S. '41. Army of a democracy; a lesson from the Swiss. Charlotte Muret and Denis de Rougemont.

Harper's Magazine. 190:160-7. Ja. '45. Future defense of the U. S. A. John Fischer.

Harper's Magazine. 190:289-300. Mr. '45. Conscription for peacetime? H. W. Baldwin.
Also separate. 12p. American Friends Service Committee. 20 S. 12th St. Philadelphia 7.

Harper's Magazine. 191:97-106. Ag. '45. Odds against another war. John Fischer.

Harvard Educational Review. 14:251-9. O. '44. Education within the armed forces. C. A. Quattlebaum.

*High Points. 26:5-19. N. '44. National service and compulsory military training. S. B. Hall.
Same. *Social Science. 20:83-92. Ap. '45; *Excerpts.* Educational Digest. 10:32-3. Ja. '45.

Higher Education. 1:1-3. Mr. 1, '45. Army specialized training program. B. W. Frazier.

Hygeia. 22:258+. Ap. '44. $35,000 question. Will O'Neil.

Hygeia. 22:910-11+. D. '44. Are we fit or are we not? real meaning of the Selective Service physical examination findings. R. L. Sensenich.

Illustrated London News. 205:226, 254. Ag. 26, S. 2, '44. Post-war national service. Arthur Bryant.

Industrial Arts and Vocational Education. 31:277-80. S. '42. Preinduction training needs on the college level for enlisted men in the armed forces. R. C. Woellner.

*Information Service (Federal Council of the Churches of Christ in America) 23, no. 37:1-6. N. 11, '44. Conscrpition for peacetime military training—pro and con.

Journal of Education. 127:275-6. N. '44. Organized education and military training. W. C. McGinnis.

Journal of Education. 128:62. F. '45. Will military training be educational? W. A. Yauch.

Journal of Engineering Education. 34:326-34. D. '43. Training the ordnance soldier. H. R. Kutz.

Journal of Health and Physical Education. 12:454-5+. O. '41. Physical education for national preparedness. W. K. Streit.

Journal of Health and Physical Education. 13:516-17+. N. '42. Washington high school cadet corps. E. F. Russell.

Journal of Health and Physical Education. 14:160. Mr. '43. Military drill and the physical fitness program. A. O. Anderson.

Journal of Health and Physical Education. 15:128-9+. Mr. '44. Fit to fight. W. L. Weible.

Journal of Health and Physical Education. 15:500-1. N. '44. Recommendations of Joint Committee on Physical Fitness.

Journal of Health and Physical Education. 15:548. D. '44. On compulsory military training. D. K. Brace.

Journal of Health and Physical Education. 16:6. Ja. '45. Preparedness? Yes! but how? B. W. Miller.

Journal of Health and Physical Education. 16:7-8+. Ja. '45. Is universal military training the answer? Mabel Lee.

Journal of Higher Education. 15:440-1. N. '44. Compulsory military service.

Journal of Higher Education. 16:49-50. '45. Professional duty. R. H. Eckelberry.

Journal of Negro Education. 14:127-31. Ap. '45. Peacetime compulsory military training and the Negro's status in the armed forces. C. H. Thompson.

Ladies' Home Journal. 61:26-7+. S. '44. Why is he 4-F? J. C. Furnas.

Michigan Education Journal. 22:124-5+. N. '44. Peacetime military training; some pros and cons on universal conscription. P. W. Schulze.

Michigan Education Journal. 22:176-81+. D. '44. Many opinions on military training.

Michigan Education Journal. 22:280-1. F. '45. Education for teen-age youth or compulsory military training? W. C. Trow.

Milbank Memorial Fund Quarterly. 22:358-66. O. '44. Findings of selective service examinations. G. St.J. Perrott.

Montana Education. 21:12-15. F.; 18-20. Mr. '45. Compulsory military training and military training in high school. H. R. Douglass.
    Same. Ohio Schools. 21:102-3+. Mr. '45. *Same condensed.* Texas Outlook. 29: 8-10. Mr. '45; Viriginia Journal of Education. 38:315-16+. Ap. '45.

Nation. 160:330-2. Mr. 24, '45. Conscription between wars. C. G. Bolte.
    Same abridged. Scholastic Debater. 1:4+. My. '45.

Nation. 160:399-400; 427. Ap. 7-14, '45. Forum on peace-time conscription.

National Association of Secondary-School Principals. Bulletin. 26:5-8. My. '42. Best kind of high-school training for military service.

National Association of Secondary-School Principals. Bulletin. 28:3-12. My. '44. Legislation will affect education. P. E. Elicker.

National Association of Secondary-School Principals. Bulletin. 28:63-8. N. '44. Shall we have compulsory peacetime military training? P. E. Elicker.

National Association of Secondary-School Principals. Bulletin. 29:9-17. Ja. '45. Compulsory peacetime military training.

National Association of Secondary-School Principals. Bulletin. 29:3-6. Mr. '45. What school administrators think about peacetime compulsory military service. P. E. Elicker.

National Education Association. Journal. 33:177. N. '44. We all believe in preparedness. J. E. Morgan.

National Education Association. Journal. 33:221. D. '44. Superintendents speak out on compulsory military service. I. A. Booker.

National Education Association. Journal. 34:48+. F. '45. On permanent conscription; discussion.

*National Education Association Research Bulletin. 22:131-67. D. '44. Superintendents' opinions on compulsory youth programs. •

Bibliography. p. 157-8; Arguments for and against military training. p. 160-3. *Excerpts.* Educational Digest. 10:1-6. F. '45.

National Parent-Teacher. 39:10-12. Ja. '45. Hurrying slowly to peacetime conscription. I. A. Booker.

National Safety News. 48:14-15+. N. '43. Army's first concern; prevention of casualties, accidental and combat. R. A. Lovett.

Nation's Schools. 33:23. Ja. '44. What of compulsory military training?

Nation's Schools. 34:46. D. '44. Michigan schoolmen express opinions on military training. A. H. Rice.

Nation's Schools. 35:19. F. '45. National preparedness the issue. A. B. Moehlman.

Nation's Schools. 35:20-4. F. '45. National service for youth; 18 views.

Nation's Schools. 35:24. F. '45. What Michigan schoolmen say about compulsory military service.

Nation's Schools. 35:26-7. F. '45. Lessons from peace-time conscription in Europe. G. F. Milton.

Nation's Schools. 35:66+. F. '45. Military training controversy.

Nation's Schools. 35:27. Mr. '45. One year too long for military training. A. R. Brinkman.

New Masses. p. 3-6. Ap. 3, '45. Peacetime military training? a debate. P. M. Limbert and Carl Ross.

Also separate. 4p. American Youth for Democracy. 150 Nassau St. New York 7.

New Republic. 111:737-8. D. 4, '44. Universal service. George Soule.

New York Times. p. 1+. Jl. 17, '45. Martin proposes all nations agree to abolish conscription. C. P. Trussell.

New York Times. p. 12. Jl 3, '45. Preparedness urged now; scientists should study plans for next war. Malcolm Gillespie. •

New York Times. p. 11E. Jl. 22, '45. Military training issue quiescent but not dead. J. A. Loftus.

New York Times Magazine. p. 8-9+. Ag. 29, '43. This is how we make a soldier. E. R. Valentine.

New York Times Magazine. p. 19+. O. 22, '44. National service, yes, but what kind? L. W. Mayo.

New York Times Magazine. p. 10-11+. Jl. 29, '45. Greatest education project in history. Gladwin Hill.

*New York World Telegram. Je. 16, 18, '45. Security in training; road to security. Eleanor Roosevelt.

Newsweek. 20:46+. N. 9, '42. 8-year-old soldiers; Russian military training starts early.

Newsweek. 24:33-4. Jl. 3, '44. My boy is only 18.

Newsweek. 25:112. F. 12, '45. Conscription and the colleges. Raymond Moley.

Newsweek. 25:63. My. 7, '45. Ready for action at 18½.

Newsweek. 25:114+. Je. 11, '45. U.S. debates an ancient issue on peacetime military service.

Newsweek. 26:47. Jl. 9, '45. How the Jap learns to fight as he does. T. C. Pakenham.

Newsweek. 26:19-20. Jl. 30, '45. Road back: military deamnds will cost from 10 to 15 billions yearly.

Northwestern University on the air; The Reviewing Stand. 3, no. 19:1-11. S. 10, '44. Military training after the war. J. M. Hughes and others.

Northwestern University on the Air; The Reviewing Stand. 4, no. 14: 1-11. F. 18, '45. Universal military training. A. H. Hilgers and others.

Occupations. 23:74-6. N. '44. Salvaging illiterates in the army. Norman Kaplan.

Ohio Schools. 22:342+. N. '44. School considers universal military training.

Ohio Schools. 22:416. D. '44. What should American policy be on compulsory training plans?

Ohio Schools. 23:5. Ja. '45. Educators' answers on the compulsory military training issue.

Parents' Magazine. 19:24-5+. F. '44. They learn while they serve. L. W. Sidran.

Parents' Magazine. 19:22-3+. My. '44. Will military training be compulsory? Raymond Nathan and B. P. Brodinsky.
    Summary. School Management. 14:22. S. '44.

Parents' Magazine. 19:16-18+. N. '44. Shall we have compulsory military training after the war? symposium.
    Abridged. School Management 14:98-100. N. '44; 202-3. F. '45.

Peabody Journal of Education. 20:23-8. Jl. '42. War and the philosophy of physical education. R. T. DeWitt.

Popular Science. 145:64-71+. Ag. '44. What's being planned for our postwar strength. A. P. Armagnac.

Public Personnel Review. 5:95-100. Ap. '44. Evaluation of educational growth during military service. R. W. Tyler and Lily Detchen.

Rotarian. 66:26-8. Ja; 67:51-3. Jl. '45. Compulsory military training? symposium.

*Saturday Evening Post. 217:9-10+. D. 23, '44. General Marshall wants a citizen army. J. M. Palmer.

Saturday Evening Post. 217:96. Je. 2, '45. We face a famine of scientists.

Saturday Evening Post. 217:17+. Ja. 27, '45. How to solve our postwar defense problem. J. M. Palmer.

Scholastic. 39:12-13+. O. 20, '41. Year in the army for all young men? debate. T. A. Rousse.

Scholastic Debater. 1:4+. Ja. '45. Compulsory military training. W. N. Thompson.

Scholastic Debater. 1:1-2+. My. '45. Looking ahead at the conscription question. W. N. Thompson.

School and Society. 54:252. S. 27, '41. Does military training have broader educational values? W. I. Painter.

School and Society. 55:613-15. My. 30, '42. Outcomes of military training in schools.

School and Society. 56:116-20. Ag. 8, '42. College student and the armed forces. M. M. Chambers.

School and Society. 57:402. Ap. 10, '43. One in four 18-19-year-old selectees rejected as unfit.

School and Society. 57:674-6. Je. 12, '43. War fitness conference. Belmont Farley.

School and Society. 58:68. Jl. 31, '43. Military drill in schools and colleges. H. L. Stimson.
Same. Education for Victory. 2:19. Ag. 2, '43; California Schools. 14:188. S. '43; Journal of Health and Physical Education. 14:368. S. '43; National Education Association Journal. 32:181. S. '43; Nation's Schools. 32:19. S. '43; School Review. 51:451. O. '43.

School and Society. 58:167-9. S. 4, '43. Note on army and navy criticisms of schools and colleges. F. S. Freeman.

School and Society. 59:70-1. Ja. 29, '44. Secretary Knox's proposal for universal military training.

School and Society. 60:45-7. Jl. 15, '44. Compulsory military service? junior-college reactions. W. C. Eells.

School and Society. 60:131. Ag. 26, '44. AFT considers the problem of postwar compulsory military training.

School and Society. 60:132. Ag. 26, '44. American Council on Education studying conscription.

School and Society. 60:305-8. N. 11, '44. Should we have compulsory military service for all youth? Thomas Diamond.

School and Society. 60:309. N. 11, '44. Oberlin College faculty presents a national service plan.

School and Society. 60:371-3. D. 9, '44. Some implications of compulsory military training. L. P. Todd.

School and Society. 60:389-90. D. 16, '44. GI Joe on compulsory peacetime military training. W. C. Bagley.

School and Society. 60:412-13. D. 23, '44. Three university presidents on compulsory peacetime military training.

School and Society. 60:436. D. 30, '44. Speaks for the ACE on peacetime compulsory military training. G. F. Zook.

School and Society. 61:20. Ja. 13, '45. Educational implications of the probable adoption of peacetime training.

School and Society. 61:21. Ja. 13, '45. National Board of Managers, PTA, on compulsory military training.

School and Society. 61:44. Ja. 20, '45. Attitude of college faculties toward military training. W. C. Trow.

School and Society. 61:47. Ja. 20, '45. Minnesota group adopts resolutions on compulsory peacetime training; fifteenth annual Conference on Higher Education with Special Reference to Teachers Education, University of Minnesota.

School and Society. 61:51-2, 132. Ja. 27, Mr. 3. '45. Public-school leaders and college executives on peacetime training.

School and Society. 61:161-4. Mr. 17, '45. Function of public education in universal military service. W. W. Carpenter and A. G. Capps.

School and Society. 61:235-6. Ap. 14, '45. Comments on GI Joe's letter by a veteran of World War I.

School and Society. 61:332. My. 19, '45. Universal military training: two considerations. E. O. Sisson.

School and Society. 61:375. Je. 9, '45. New plan for compulsory military training in the USSR.

School and Society. 62:1-3. Jl. 7, '45. Conquest of illiteracy. P. A. Witty.

School Executive. 64:7-10. F. '45. Compulsory military training; should it be made a definite part of American life?

School Review. 52:73-4. F. '44. Shall we have universal military service?

School Review. 52:447-9. O. '44. Does this nation want compulsory training in peacetime?

Science Digest. 17:73-6. Ap. '45. Their first look at live bullets. Arthur Miller.

Science News Letter. 47:12. Ja. 6, '45. Maximum manpower; health and physical fitness efforts should start much earlier than proposed year of military training.

Scientific Monthly. 57:401-12. N. '43. CCC and American conservation. J. D. Guthrie.

Senior Scholastic. 43:32. D. 6, '43. Military service after war opposed by 52% of students.

Senior Scholastic. 45:44. N. 27, '44. Boys favor military training; girls against.

Senior Scholastic. 45:11-12+. D. 11, '44. Should all young men be given a year of peacetime military training.? pro and con discussion of proposed bills for universal military service.

*Social Science. 20:61-107. Ap. '45. Universal compulsory military training number.

Contents: Editorial preface; Proposal for compulsory military training in peacetime. J. W. Wadsworth; Case against compulsory military training in peacetime. C. A. Ellwood; Shall the United States adopt a plan for general compulsory military training for men as a permanent postwar policy? C. S. Collier; Some questions about compulsory military training. R. W. Tryon; Conference comment. R. F. Fuchs; I am in favor of this bill. S. P. McClenahan; *National service and compulsory military training. S. B. Hall; Military training. A. L. Cox; Compulsory military training. F. L. Lucey; Text of the bill now pending, H.R. 515, 79th Congress, 1st session; Texts of earlier bills. Introduced in the 78th Congress.

Texas Outlook. 26:25-8. Ap. '42. Texas A. & M. College blazes the trail. G. B. Winstead.

Thought. 15:623-40. D. '40. Historical background of compulsory military service. C. C. Tansill.

Time. 39:45-6. Mr. 2, '42. Military training.

Time. 43:61. Mr. 13, '44. Dwindling supply; health of the nation's young men.

Time. 44:16-17. Ag. 28, '44. Peacetime draft?

Time. 44:64. N. 20, '44. Dangerous terrain; compulsory training.

Time. 45:22. Ja. 22, '45. How the winds blow.

Time. 45:13-14. Je. 18, '45. To train or not to train.

Time. 45:16. Je. 25, '45. Combined operation.

Town Meeting (Bulletin of America's Town Meeting of the Air) 9, no. 51:3-22. Ap. 27, '44. Should we have universal military training after the war? J. M. Costello and others.

Town Meeting (Bulletin of America's Town Meeting of the Air) 10, no. 39:3-23. Ja. 25, '45. Do we want universal military training for youth? G. F. Eliot and others.

Town Meeting (Bulletin of America's Town Meeting of the Air) 11, no. 10:3-22. Jl. 5, '45. Should we have universal military training after the war? Burgess Meredith and others.

United States Naval Institute Proceedings. 71:487-97. My. '45. Obligation of freedom. F. J. Nelson.

United States News. 14:18-19. Mr. 26, '43. Human side of our army: what the U.S. soldier is like.

United States News. 16:22-3. Ja. 21, '44. Every boy in army or navy: plans for postwar training.

United States News. 17:42+. S. 15; 36+. S. 22; 34+. S. 29, '44. Should youths between 17 years of age and the early twenties in the post-war period be required to spend one year in government military, vocational or other training for their own physical upbuilding and discipline as well as for national preparedness? symposium.

United States News. 17:11-12. D. 1, '44. Draft in peacetime preview of training plan.

United States News. 18:13. Mr. 9, '45. 18-year-olds at war; army's view that youths can be trained for combat in 15 weeks.

United States News. 18:28-9. Mr. 16, '45. For the biggest army, navy, and air force in the world. David Lawrence.

United States News. 18:34-5. Je. 22; 34-6. Je. 29; 19:34+. Jl. 6, '45. Should a military training bill be enacted now, or postponed until a national military policy is established after the war against Japan is over? symposium.

*United States News. 18:13-14. Je. 29, '45. Draft after the war? our future defense needs.

University of Chicago Round Table. 349:1-26. N. 26, '44. Should we have universal military training in peacetime? Robert Hutchins and others.

Vital Speeches of the Day. 8:500-3. Je. 1, '42. American youth and the war; educating our future officers. J. B. Conant.
Same. Atlantic Monthly. 170:48-53. Jl. '42. Mobilizing American youth.

Weekly News Review. 23:1+. D. 4, '44. National debate launched on peacetime youth draft.

Weekly News Review. 23:5. D. 4, '44. Historical backgrounds of today's events.

Wilson Library Bulletin. 18:599-603. Ap. '44. Soldiers study foreign areas; ASTP and the library. F. E. Hirsch.

Woman's Home Companion. 71:14. D. '44. Should he be a soldier in peacetime? twenty-fourth Companion poll.

Wisconsin Journal of Education. 76:202. D. '43. Military drill in high school. John Holzman.

Wisconsin Journal of Education. 77:267-8. F. '45. National military training act of 1945; text of H.R. 515.

AFFIRMATIVE REFERENCES

BOOKS AND PAMPHLETS

American Legion. Answers to questions and objections regarding universal military training, combined with questions for the opponents and useful quotations. 46p. The Legion. 777 N. Meridian St. Indianapolis 6. F. '45.

American Legion. Legion called the turn. 47p. The Legion. 777 N. Meridian St. Indianapolis 6. '44.

American Legion. Material for newspaper, radio and public addresses on the subject of universal military training. 19p. The Legion. 777 N. Meridian St. Indianapolis 6. F. '45.

American Legion. Now is the time to adopt universal military training. 19p. The Legion. 777 N. Meridian St. Indianapolis 6. F. '45.

American Legion. Personal need for universal military training. 4p. The Legion. 777 N. Meridian St. Indianapolis 6. My .'45.

American Legion. Steps in legislation; answering inquiries regarding the Gurney-May bill (S.188-H.R.515) of the 79th Congress. 2p. The Legion. 777 N. Meridian St. Indianapolis 6. My. '45.

American Legion. What others have said about universal military training; a compilation of useful quotations. 8p. The Legion. 777 N. Meridian St. Indianapolis 6. Ap. '45.

American Legion. Why agriculture should support universal military training as advocated by the American Legion. 4p. The Legion. 777 N. Meridian St. Indianapolis 6. Ap. '45.

American Legion. Why educators should support universal military training as advocated by the American Legion. 4p. The Legion. 777 N. Meridian St. Indianapolis 6. Ap. '45.

American Legion. Why organized labor should support universal military training as advocated by the American Legion. 4p. The Legion. 777 N. Meridian St. Indianapolis 6. Ap. '45.

American Legion. Why the American Legion advocates universal military training. 6p. The Legion. 777 N. Meridian St. Indianapolis 6. F. '45.

American Legion. Why the Church should support universal military training as advocated by the American Legion. 4p. The Legion. 777 N. Meridian St. Indianapolis 6. Ap. '45.

Citizens Committee for Military Training of Young Men. Topic for discussion: Universal military training for young men; handbook of questions and answers on a vital subject, as revised Feb. 1, 1945. 16p. The Committee. 37 Wall St. New York 5. '45.

Citizens Committee for Military Training of Young Men. Women's Headquarters. Read what a civilian, a minister, a doctor and a college president say about military training of young men. 8p. The Committee. 660 Madison Av. New York 21.

Erskine, John. Universal training for national defense. 15p. Civilian Military Education Fund. 917 15th St. N.W. Washington, D.C. '40.
Originally prepared in 1919 as a report to General Pershing, and published in the Review of Reviews, October 1919.

Middle States Association of Colleges and Secondary Schools. Proceedings. 1944: 62-7. Universal military training from the point of view of the armed services. W. L. Weible.

Palmer, John McA. Notes on universal military training. 14p. Citizens Committee for Military Training of Young Men. 37 Wall St. New York 5. O. '44.

Read what a civilian, a minister, a doctor and a college president say about military training of young men; excerpts from panel discussion, March 14, 1945, New York. 8p. Citizens Committee for Military Training of Young Men, Inc. 9 Pine St. New York 5. '45.

Reilly, Henry J. Are our young men to have a chance? only one answer to the challenge. 24p. Civilian Military Education Fund. 917 15th St. N.W. Washington, D.C. '40.

Stimson, Henry L. Letter to Citizens Committee for Universal Military Training. 2p. The Committee. 37 Wall St. New York 5. Ag. 15, '44.

Periodicals

American Association of University Professors Bulletin. 30:491-9. [D.] '44. War Department and the program for universal military training. W. L. Weible.

American Defense. 2:1-2. Ap. '44. Role of education in universal military training. E. G. Payne.

American Defense. 2:1-3. Je. '44. Universal training for defense. J. McA. Palmer.

American Defense. 2:1-2. Ja. '45. Universal military training as I see it. J. W. Wadsworth.

American Defense. 3:1-2. Ap. '45. Approach to compulsory military training for the future of the United States. J. C. Ward, Jr.

American Magazine. 139:20-1+. Mr. '45. Tomorrow's army and your boy. H. L. Hopkins.

American School Board Journal. 110:18. Ap. '45. Universal training, a middle course. G. A. Eichler.

American Teacher. 28:14. My. '44. Compulsory military training. J. F. Landis.

American Teacher. 29:16+. N. '44. Do we need universal military training? M. D. Campbell.

Annals of the American Academy. 228:21-4. Jl. '43. Contribution of the America's to the war and to the peace. Eugenio Silva.

*Annals of the American Academy. 238:56-62. Mr. '45. Future manpower needs of the armed forces. W. F. Tompkins.

Army and Navy Journal. 82:31+. S. 9, '44. Gen. Marshall opposes large standing army.

Army and Navy Journal. 82:94+. S. 23, '44. Leaders address Legion; statements by J. V. Forrestal, G. C. Marshall, C. W. Nimitz and H. H. Arnold.

Army and Navy Register. p. 7. D. 9, '44. Universal military training. W. L. Weible.

Army and Navy Register. p. 6. Ja. 6, '45. Compulsory training or disaster.

*Army and Navy Register. p. 1-2+. Ja. 20, '45. Universal military training.

Army and Navy Register. p. 1-2+. F. 17, '45. Universal service.
    p. 2, 22 also in Cavalry Journal. 54:38-40. Ja.-F. '45.

Army and Navy Register. p. 8. Ap. 7, '45. Military training.

Army and Navy Register. p. 1+. Je. 9, '45. Universal military training; extracts from statement of Joseph C. Grew before the House Select Committee on Postwar Military Policy, June 4, 1945.

Army and Navy Register. p. 17. Je. 16, '45. Is military training necessary?

Army and Navy Register. p. 7. Je. 23, '45. Urges military training; statement before the House Postwar Military Policy Committee. D. D. Eisenhower.

Army and Navy Register. p. 8. Je. 23, '45. Overwhelming force saves lives.

*Army and Navy Register. p. 7. Jl. 14, '45. Universal military training; text of report from Select Committee on Postwar Military Policy. C. A. Woodrum.

Atlantic Monthly. 175:52-4. My. '45. Letter to twelve college presidents. McGeorge Bundy.
Discussion. Atlantic Monthly. 175:28+. Je. '45; 176:24+. Jl. '45.

*Cavalry Journal. 54:38-40. Ja.-F. '45. First requirements of a citizen army. H. S. Hawkins.
Abridged. Army and Navy Register. p. 1-2+. F. 17, '45. Universal service.

*Cavalry Journal. 54:69-71. Jl-Ag. '45. Universal military training. M. W. Curzon.

Collier's. 112:78. N. 27, '43. American blind spot.

Collier's. 113:11-12+. Ap. 29, '44. Let's train our youth now. Frank Knox.
Same. American Defense. 2:1-4. My. '44. *Same abridged.* Reader's Digest. 45:29-31. Jl. '44.

Collier's. 114:78. O. 7, '44. What kind of training?

Collier's. 114:94. N. 4, '44. Marshall on military training.

Collier's. 115:62. Ja. 6, '45. We cheated the young men.

Collier's. 115:74. Ja. 20, '45. We need a training law now.

Collier's. 115:82. F. 10, '45. Target no. 1: U.S.A.

Collier's. 115:14+. Je. 9, '45. Do we want permanent conscription? yes. J. J. McCloy.
Same. Congressional Record. 91: (daily) A2856-7. Je. 4, '45. We do not want another war.

Commercial and Financial Chronicle. 159:430-1. Ja. 27, '44. Knox proposes year's military training for youth on reaching 17 or 18 years; address before Greater Cleveland Council of Boy Scouts of America.
Same. Military service for youth. Vital Speeches of the Day. 10:230-3. F. 1, '44; New York Times. p. 9. Ja. 15, '44.

Commercial and Financial Chronicle. 160:706. Ag. 17, '44. American Legion to ask Congress for compulsory military training.

Commercial and Financial Chronicle. 160:2380. N. 30, '44. Favors foreign military service after the war. Eleanor Roosevelt.

Commercial and Financial Chronicle. 160:2477. D. 7, '44. For a formidable sea and air force, with universal military training. J. V. Forrestal.
Same. Investment Banking. 15:11-12. Ja. '45.

Commercial and Financial Chronicle. 161:1402. Mr. 29, '45. Preparedness in peace as well as in war urged. A. P. Sloan.

Commercial and Financial Chronicle. 162:191+. Jl. 12, '45. House Committee report on post-war military training.

Congressional Record. 91:(daily) A235. Ja. 22, '45. Compulsory military training. A. L. Cox.

Congressional Record. 91:(daily) A1956-8. Ap. 19, '45. Universal military training. E. N. Scheiberling.
Excerpts. Army and Navy Register. p. 2. Ap. 28, '45.

Congressional Record. 91:(daily) A2294-5. My. 7, '45. Universal military training. A. G. Thacher.

Congressional Record. 91:(daily) A2302-3. My. 7, '45. Universal training. E. M. Hopkins.

Congressional Record. 91:(daily) A2307-8. My. 8, '45. Military training—if. G. W. Stuart.

Congressional Record. 91:(daily) A2367-9. My. 10, '45. Review of The case against compulsory peacetime military training, by R. S. Conkling. Lewis Sanders.

Congressional Record. 91:(daily) A2443. My. 14, '45. Connecticut House joint resolution memorializing Congress to pass universal military legislation.

Congressional Record. 91:(daily) A2839-40. Je. 1, '45. Universal military training. Gould Lincoln.

*Congressional Record. 91:(daily) A3022-4. Je. 11, '45. Universal military training. K. T. Compton.
Same. Army and Navy Register. p. 1-2+. Je. 16, '45.

Congressional Record. 91:(daily) A3123-4. Je. 18, '45. Compulsory military training; letter from District of Columbia Department of Disabled American Veterans. F. Hendrick.

Congressional Record. 91:(daily) A3149-50. Je. 19, '45. My day— we stand to lose whole generation of scientists. Eleanor Roosevelt.

Congressional Record. 91:(daily) A3251. Je. 23, '45. Compulsory military training; statement to Select Committee on Postwar Military Policy, June 23, 1945. C. J. Nicklas.

*Congressional Record. 91:(daily) A3289-91. Je. 25, '45. Statement of Secretary of War before House Select Committee on Postwar Military Policy, June 15, 1945. H. L. Stimson.

Congressional Record. 91:(daily) A3297-8. Je. 25, '45. Statement before House Select Committee on Postwar Military Policy, June 16, 1945. G. C. Marshall.
Same. New York Times. p. 24. Je. 17, '45.

Congressional Record. 91:(daily) A3383. Je. 29, '45. Compulsory military training. Keith Holland.

Congressional Record. 91:(daily) A3828-9. Jl. 19, '45. Postwar training. Arthur Krock.

Country Gentleman. 115:80-1. My. '45. Military training for American youth; now you're talking! Ruth Hogeland.

*Dartmouth Alumni Magazine. 37:15. Je. '45. For military training. E. M. Hopkins.
Same. New York Times. p. 8E. My. 6, '45.

Education for Victory. 3:18-19. Jl. 20, '44. Universal military training favored by junior college leaders.

*Educational Record. 26:9-16. Ja. '45. Compulsory military training? Yes. Charles Seymour.

Educational Research Bulletin. 23:218-19. N. '44. Universal national service? R. H. Eckelberry.

Free World. 9:51-3. F. '45. Will peace require universal military training? Yes. J. W. Wadsworth.
Discussion. Free World. 9:8. Mr. '45.

Harper's Magazine. 190:410-13. Ap. '45. Easy chair; universal military training in peacetime. Bernard De Voto.

Harvard Educational Review. 15:2-3. Ja. '45. Compulsory military training; another point of view. H. W. Holmes.

*Horizon. 1:1-5. Ag. '41. Emergency training for philosophy. Manly Hall.

Independent Woman. 24:99+. Ap. '45. Shall we have universal military training? Yes. J. W. Castles.

Infantry Journal. 56:7. Ja. '45. Strong and healthy nation.

Journal of Health and Physical Education. 16:64+. F. '45. Is compulsory military training the answer? Yes! E. B. Degroot.

Journal of Health and Physical Education. 16:115+. Mr. '45. Physical fitness and compulsory military training. H. A. Lorenz.

Journal of Health and Physical Education. 16:181. Ap. '45. Suggested plan for military service. H. K. Jack.

Michigan Education Journal. 22:332-3. Mr. '45. Militraining? Yes! M. L. McCoy.

Nation. 160:246-7. Mr. 3, '45. Needed: a citizens' army. Irving Lipkowitz.

National Education Association. Journal. 33:179-80. N. '44. Case for peacetime conscription, developed by Civic Education Service.

National Education Association. Journal. 34:39. F. '45. Schools and the army. Ben Lear.

Nation's Schools. 32:15. D. '43. Summertime universal military training. A. B. Moehlman.

Nation's Schools. 34:26. N. '44 Should universal military training be made obligatory? H. L. Stimson.

Nation's Schools. 34:28-9. D. '44. Plus values of military training. A. R. Elliott.
  Abstract. Journal of Criminal Law and Criminology. 35:324-5. Ja. '45.

New York Herald Tribune. Je. 6, '45. History's lesson. Mark Sullivan.
  Same. Congressional Record. 91: (daily) A2934. Je. 7, '45.

New York State Education. 32:339-40+. F. '45. Peacetime military training as an instrument for peace. E. N. Scheiberling.

New York Times. p. 10E. S. 10, '44. Strong trend appears for universal training. Sidney Shalett.

New York Times. p. 1+. N. 18, '44. President [Roosevelt] presses compulsory plan of youth training.

New York Times. p. 3E. N. 19, '44. President for service by all of our youths. Arthur Krock.

New York Times. p. 7. F. 10, '45. Educators oppose delay on training; letter to President Roosevelt by heads of fourteen colleges and universities.
  Same abridged. School and Society. 61:100. F. 17, '45. Action now on conscription-training urged by 14 college executives.

*New York Times. p. 8E. My. 6, '45. Universal training. E. M. Hopkins.
  Same. Dartmouth Alumni Magazine. Je. 37:15. '45.

New York Times. p. 8E. Jl. 1, '45. Training is approved. J. H. Hildebrand.

New York Times Magazine. p. 9+. Mr. 25, '45. Soldier looks at conscription. M. D. Kirkwood.
  Discussion. New York Times Magazine. p. 12+. Ap. 15, '45.

New York Times Magazine. p. 19. Ag. 27, '44. Argument for military training. H. S. Pearson.
  Discussion. New York Times Magazine. p. 45. S. 17, '44.

Political Affairs. 24:60-8. Ja. '45. Universal military training. Carl Ross.

Progressive Education. 22:23+. F. '45. Shall America adopt postwar universal military training. Yes! Fraser Arnold.

Reader's Digest. 45:9-15. D. '44. Military essentials for our postwar safety; army, navy and air force leaders agree on proposals. T. M. Johnson.

Reader's Digest. 46:56-9. F. '45. Shall all our boys have one year's military training? T. M. Johnson.

Recreation. 37:615-18+. F. '44. Fit to fight. W. L. Weible.

Saturday Evening Post. 217:100. Ja. 27, '45. Military training for national safety. Ben Hibbs.

*Saturday Evening Post. 217:27+. My. 19, '45. Soldier's slant on compulsory training. E. J. Kahn, Jr.

Scholastic Debater. 1:4+. My. '45. Conscription between wars; military training is needed. C. G. Bolté.

School Activities. 13:61-4. O. '41. Case for compulsory military training. H. E. Gibson.

School Activities. 13:140-2+. D. '41. Affirmative rebuttal plans. H. E. Gibson.

School Activities. 14:247-8. Mr. '43. High schools should offer military training. W. W. Eubanks.

Time. 44:17. S 11, '44. Citizen soldiers; General Marshall advises a small professional army; a vast army reserve.

Time. 44:66. O. 9, '44. Last-minutemen.

Time. 45:57. Ja. 8, '45. In our homeland; reason for military training is national defense.

United States Naval Institute Proceedings. 71:275-7. Mr. '45. Compulsory military training. W. L. Brough, Jr.

United States News. 18:28-9. Mr. 16, '45. For the biggest army, navy, and air force in the world. David Lawrence.

Vital Speeches of the Day. 9:188-90. Ja. 1, '43. Let it be victory, not armistice; need for universal military training. S. F. Chadwick.

World Affairs. 108:6-10. Mr. '45. Let's look before we leap. Booth Tarkington.

School and Society. 61:173-4. Mr. 17, '45. History and hysteria. Robert Withington.

School and Society. 61:219. Ap. 7, '45. Compulsory military training. B. L. Ullman.

NEGATIVE REFERENCES

BOOKS AND PAMPHLETS

American Friends Service Committee. Peace time conscription; a problem for Americans. 14p. The Committee. 20 S. 12th St. Philadelphia 7. '44.

American Friends Service Committee. Permanent conscription. 3p. The Committee. 20 S. 12th St. Philadelphia 7. '45.

American Friends Service Committee. Universal peacetime conscription. 10p. The Committee. 20 S. 12th St. Philadelphia 7. '44.

Brumbaugh, A. J. Statement on universal military training for the House Select Committee on Postwar Military Policy. 10p. mim. American Council on Education. 744 Jackson Pl. Washington 6, D.C. Je. 6, '45.

Calhoun, Donald W. Conscription and the four freedoms. (Anvil Booklets no. 1) 10p. Plowshare Press. 5 Beekman St. New York 7. n.d.

Conkling, Roscoe S. Case against compulsory peacetime military training. 35p. Post War World Council. 112 E. 19th St. New York 3. Mr. '45.
   Abridged. Congressional Record. 91: (daily) A2197-9. My. 3, '45.

Conscription is not the American way; discussion and conclusions by eleven members of the faculty of John Carroll University, Cleveland, Ohio. 37p. America Press. New York. '45.

Fellowship of Reconciliation. What's wrong with peacetime universal military training for the United States? 2p. 2929 Broadway. New York 25. n.d.

Freeman, Harrop A. Peacetime conscription unconstitutional. 4p. Fellowship of Reconciliation. 2929 Broadway. New York 25. '45.
   Reprint from Fellowship. Ja. '45.

Freeman, Harrop A. and Freeman, Ruth S. Conscription after the war? (Forerunners studybook no. 5) 63p. Fellowship Publications. 2929 Broadway. New York 25. F. '45.

Middle States Association of Colleges and Secondary Schools. Proceedings. 1944:68-76. Universal military training from the point of view of educational institutions. H. W. Dodds.
   Same condensed. *Educational Record. 26:17-26. Ja. '45.

Muste, A. J. Conscription and conscience. 9p. American Friends Service Committee. 20 S. 12th St. Philadelphia 7. n.d.

Post War World Council. How to make a worker into a strike-breaker. 4p. The Council. 112 E. 19th St. New York 3. '44.

Socialist Party. Keys to his kingdom? 4p. The Party. 303 4th Ave. New York 10. n.d.

Stewart, Alexander. They say—but who is right? 8p. Women's International League for Peace and Freedom. 410 S. Michigan Ave. Chicago 5. '45.

Swomley, John M., Jr. Let's take a look at the facts about military training and national health. 4p. Fellowship of Reconciliation. 2929 Broadway. New York 25. '45.

*Thayer, V. T. Shall we conscript youth for peacetime service? 9p. mim. New York Society for Ethical Culture. 2 W. 64th St. New York 23. Jl. 8, '45.

Thomas, Evan W. Why we oppose military conscription. 3p. War Resisters League. 5 Beekman St. New York 7. Ja. 3, '44.

Thomas, Norman. Conscription, the test of the peace. 13p. Post War World Council. 112 E. 19th St. New York 3. '44.

Thomas, Norman. Four drafts vs. four freedoms. 3p. mim. Socialist Party. 303 4th Ave. New York 10.

Villard, Oswald G. Can peacetime conscription be justified? 2p. Fellowship of Reconciliation. 2929 Broadway. New York 25.
Reprint from Fellowship. October 1944.

War Resisters League. Should the United States adopt permanent military conscription? 6p. The League. 5 Beekman St. New York 7. '44.

War Resisters League. This must not be. 2p. The League. 5 Beekman St. New York 7. '44.

PERIODICALS

America. 71:551-3. S. 9, '44. Compulsory peacetime military training? A. P. Farrell.

America. 72:325-6. Ja. 27, '45. Serviceman on the peacetime draft. Duff Coleman.

American Association of University Professors Bulletin. 30:500-8. [D.] '44. Universal military training. A. J. Brumbaugh.

American Association of University Professors Bulletin. 31:97-102. [Mr.] '45. Universal military training; answer to Major General Weible. D. L. Bolinger.

American Federation of Labor Weekly News Service. 35:1. Je. 19, '45. Compulsory military training law opposed by AFL at public hearing.

American Teacher. 29:17-20. N. '44. Do we need universal military training? Irvine Kerrison.
Revised. Social Education. 19:26-8. Ja. '45.

Association of American Colleges Bulletin. 30:507-13. D. '44. Compulsory peacetime military training? A. P. Farrell.

Association of American Colleges Bulletin. 30:514-18. D. '44. Universal military training, a dangerous proposal. A. G. Parker, Jr.

Association of American Colleges Bulletin. 31:170-2. Mr. '45. Resolutions on compulsory military training adopted by the Association of American Colleges at annual meeting in Atlantic City on January 11, 1945.

*California Journal of Secondary Education. 20:130-5. Mr. '45. Is conscription the way to peace? F. J. Brown.

Call. 12:1+. Je. 11, '45. Socialists, labor, educators hit conscription plans at hearing.

Call. 12:1+. Je. 11, '45. Wall Street citizens whoop up militarism.

Call. 12:1. Jl. 23, '45. War Dept. campaign on conscription hit by Socialists.

Christian Century. 61:333-5. Mr. 15, '44. Conscripting youth. O. G. Villard.

Christian Century. 61:1015-16. S. 6, '44. Conscription by subterfuge.

Christian Century. 61:1056. S. 13, '44. Food for thought on conscription. M. P. Bryant.

Christian Century. 61:1190-1. O. 18, '44. Peacetime conscription?
Same abridged. Congressional Digest. 24:27+. Ja. '45.

Christian Century. 61:1372. N. 29, '44. Peacetime draft opposed by Catholic hierarchy.

Christian Century. 61:1493. D. 27, '44. Sees threat to Negroes in peacetime conscription.

Christian Century. 62:99-100. Ja. 24, '45. Permanent conscription opposed by educators.

Christian Century. 62:142-3. Ja. 31, '45. Made in Germany. R. L. Ruth.

Christian Century. 62:197. F. 14, '45. University presidents hit peacetime draft.

Christian Century. 62:299-300. Mr. 7, '45. Case against conscription. F. L. Wright.

Christian Century. 62:394-5. Mr 28, '45. Why the War Department's rush? W. P. Tolley.

Christian Century. 62:484. Ap. 18, '45. Peacetime conscription debate postponed.

Christian Century. 62:626-8. My. 23, '45. It is time to say no. W. W. Sikes.

Christian Century. 62:726-7. Je. 20, '45. Conscription hearings.

Christian Century. 62:749. Je. 27, '45. Another fellow who was for conscription: Hitler.

Christian Century. 62:854-5. Jl. 25, '45. Eisenhower on conscription.

Christian Education. 28:75-6. D. '44. Christian education and peacetime conscription.

*Christian Education. 28:160-8. Mr. '45. Universal compulsory military training in peacetime. P. H. Bowman; A. G. Parker, Jr.

Christian Education. 28:169-73. Mr. '45. Resolutions on peacetime military conscription passed by educational agencies in annual meetings held at Atlantic City.

*Collier's. 115:15+. Je. 9, '45. Do we want permanent conscription? No. R. M. Hutchins.

Commercial and Financial Chronicle. 160:2459+. D. 7, '44. Compulsory military training. H. I. Harriman.

Commercial and Financial Chronicle. 160:2625+. D. 14, '44. Peacetime conscription. G. E. Sokolsky.

Commercial and Financial Chronicle. 160:2713. D. 21, '44. Military conscription. F. J. Brown.

Commercial and Financial Chronicle. 160:2737+. D. 21, '44. Compulsory universal military training. H. W. Dodds.

*Commercial and Financial Chronicle. 161:257+. Ja. 18, '45. Substitute for universal military training. Crandall Melvin.

Commercial and Financial Chronicle. 161:424. Ja. 25, '45. Manpower conscription will impede production. Norman Thomas; Joseph Schlossberg.

Commercial and Financial Chronicle. 161:1+. Je. 14, '45. Compulsory peacetime military training.

Commercial and Financial Chronicle. 162:527. Ag. 2, '45. Compulsory peacetime military training. W. H. Weil.

Common Sense. 14:15-17. Ap. '45. Conscription of America. C. W. Mills.

Commonweal. 39:532-3. Mr. 17, '44. To maintain the peace.

Commonweal. 41:163. D. 1, '44. Universal youth service.

Commonweal. 41:219. D. 15, '44. Issue of peacetime conscription.

Commonweal. 41:284-6. D. 29, '44. CAIP on conscription.

Commonweal. 41:464-7. F. 23, '45. Peacetime military training. J. M. O'Neill.
  Same abridged. Scholastic Debater. 1:5+. My. '45.

Congressional Record. 91:(daily) A382-4. Ja. 30, '45. Let's look before we leap. Booth Tarkington.
  Same. World Affairs. 108:6-10. Mr. '45.

Congressional Record. 91:(daily) A2282-3. Mr. 7, '45. Universal military training. Emanuel Celler.

Congressional Record. 91:(daily) A2197-9. My. 3, '45. Peacetime military training. R. S. Conkling.

Congressional Record. 91:A2366-7. My. 10, '45. Post-war compulsory military training. T. W. Hunt.

*Congressional Record. 91:(daily) A2814-16. My. 31, '45. Compulsory military training in peacetime will destory government by the people. R. A. Taft.

Congressional Record. 91:(daily) A2837-8. Je. 1, '45. Will peacetime draft give United States best security? editorial from Daily Pantagraph, Bloomington, Ill.

Congressional Record. 91:(daily) A3027-9. Je. 11, '45. No military conscription needed. Josephus Daniels.

Congressional Record. 91:(daily) A3079-80. Je. 13, '45. Let's go slow on peacetime draft. P. M. Hansen.

Congressional Record. 91:(daily) A3093-4. Je. 14, '45. Statement on universal military training. E. C. Pulliam.

Congressional Record. 91:(daily) A3124-5. Je. 18, '45. Universal military training. Norman Thomas.

Congressional Record. 91:(daily) A3133-4. Je. 19, '45. Peacetime conscription. Booth Tarkington.

Congressional Record. 91:(daily) A3137. Je. 19, '45. Military conscription. W. H. Berkey.

Congressional Record. 91:(daily) A3207-8. Je. 21, '45. Let's go slow on peacetime draft.

Congressional Record. 91:(daily) A3236-7. Je. 22, '45. Peacetime military conscription—views of our boys at the front. R. F. Inger; Isadore Blumen.

Congressional Record. 91:(daily) A3279-80. Je. 25, '45. Peacetime conscription. W. H. Uphoff.

Congressional Record. 91:(daily) A3321-3. Je. 26, '45. Peacetime draft stampede. Emanuel Celler.

Congressional Record. 91:(daily) A3343. Je. 27, '45. Opposed to peace draft. G. H. Roth.

Congressional Record. 91:(daily) A3524-5. Jl. 5, '45. Universal military training. C. H. Wheatley.

Congressional Record. 91:(daily) A3588-90. Jl. 9, '45. Statement before the Select Committee on Postwar Military Policy. Norman Thomas.

Congressional Record. 91:(daily) A3718. Jl. 13, '45. Peacetime conscription. W. A. Puphal.

*Congressional Record. 91:(daily) A3808. Jl. 18, '45. Peacetime conscription for military service. J. W. Martin, Jr.

Congressional Record. 91:(daily) A3905-6. Jl. 25, '45. Compulsory peacetime military training; statement before the House Special Committee on Postwar Military Policy. C. N. Howard.

*Educational Record. 26:17-26. Ja. '45. Compulsory military training? No. H. W. Dodds.

*Foreign Affairs. 23:620-6. Jl. '45. National power and foreign policy. Grayson Kirk.

Free World. 9:47-50. F. '45. Will peace require universal military training? No. S. A. Coblentz.
  Discussion. Free World. 9:8. Mr. '45.

Harvard Educational Review. 15:1-2. Ja. '45. On compulsory military training in peace time. H. E. Wilson.

Independent Woman. 24:98+. Ap. '45. Shall we have universal military training? No. A. J. Muste.

Journal of Health and Physical Education. 16:65+. F. '45. Is compulsory military training the answer? No! J. B. Nash.

Journal of Health and Physical Education. 16:114+. Mr. '45. Health and compulsory military training. J. H. Nichols.

Journal of Health and Physical Education. 16:180+. Ap. '45. Postwar physical education or military training? C. F. Mourin.

Nation. 160:210-11. F. 24, '45. Under what banner? J. S. Nollen.

Nation. 160:315-16. Mr. 17, '45. Arms and the peace; reply to I. Lipkowitz.

*National Association of Secondary-School Principals. 28:5-7. My. '44. [Statement by Educational Policies Commission and Problems and Plans Committee.]
  Same. Parent's Magazine. 20:17+. Jl. '45. Case against compulsory military service; Abridged. National Education Association. Journal. 33:111. My. '44.

*National Catholic Educational Association Bulletin. 41:17-25. F. '45. Case against peacetime conscription. E. V. Stanford.
  Same abridged. School and Society. 61:129-31. Mr. 3, '45.

National Congress Bulletin (National Congress of Parents and Teachers). 12:4-5. Je.-Jl. '45. Questions and answers regarding peacetime military training. Mrs. W. A. Hastings.

National Education Association. Journal. 33:111. My. '44. Permanent conscription? does America want conscription as a permanent peacetime policy?

National Education Association. Journal. 33:139. S. '44. I am deeply concerned. C. A. Ellwood.

National Education Association. Journal. 33:181-2. N. '44. Case against peacetime conscriptions, developed by Civic Education Service.

National Education Association. Journal. 34:10. Ja. '45. National service year. D. G. McGarey.

National Education Association. Journal. 34:71. Mr. '45. Compulsory military training.

National Education Association. Journal. 34:74. Ap. '45. Peacetime conscription and personal standards.

National Education Association. Journal. 34:87-8. Ap. '45. Peacetime conscription and national security; abridged from pamphlet Compulsory peacetime military training, by the Educational Policies Commission.

Nation's Schools. 34:27. N. '44. Should universal military training be made obligatory? H. C. Morrison.

Nation's Schools. 34:29-30. D. '44. Case against compulsory military training. W. C. Trow.
  Abstract. Journal of Criminal Law and Criminology. 35:325-6. Ja. '45.

Nation's Schools. 35:26. Mr. '45. Military training is not preparedness. E. R. Sifert.

New Republic. 111:239. Ag. 28, '44. Compulsory military training.
  Same. School Review. 53:3. Ja. '45.

New Republic. 111:496. O. 16, '44. Compulsory military training, by a doubting GI Thomas.
  Same. School Review. 53:3. Ja. '45.

New York State Education. 32:337-8+. F. '45. Shall we require military service in peacetime? W. G. Carr.

New York Times. p. 8E. Jl. 1, '45. Conscription opposed. L. G. Brooks.

*New York Times. p. 8E. Jl. 8, '45. National Guard urged. W. A. Smith.

Newsweek. 25:81. Ja. 22, '45. Presidents say no.

Progressive. 9:1+. Ap. 30, '45. Peacetime militarism: goodby democracy. M. C. Otto.

Progressive Education. 22:2. Ja. '45. Frankly speaking. V. H. Tibbetts.

Progressive Education. 22:25+. F. '45. Shall American adopt postwar universal military training? No! Clay Coss.

Saturday Evening Post. 217:17+. Mr. 24, '45. Real case against conscription. Felix Morley.

Scholastic Debater. 1:5+. My. '45. Negative view of peacetime military training. J. M. O'Neill.

School Activities. 13:96-8. N. '41. Case against compulsory military training. H. E. Gibson.

School Activities. 13:190-2. Ja. '42. Negative rebuttal plans. H. E. Gibson.

School Activities. 16:205-7. F. '45. Should we mortgage the future of American youth? H. G. Richardson.

School Executive. 64:48-9. F. '45. Argument against compulsory military training. I. A. Booker.

School Executive. 64:34. Mr. '45. American Council petitions President Roosevelt.

School and Society. 60:117. Ag. 19, '44. Universal military training a probable source of early postwar controversy.

School and Society. 60:369-70. D. 9, '44. Compulsory military training. G. E. Snavely.

School and Society. 61:101. F. 17, '45. NASCMC on compulsory peacetime conscription.

School and Society. 61:139-41. Mr. 3, '45. Dangers of peacetime military training. W. P. Kellam.

School and Society. 61:172-3. Mr. 17, '45. Conscription-training and its alternatives. Hugh Hartshorne.

School Review. 52:328-30. Je. '44. Statement on universal military training.

School Review. 53:1-4. Ja. '45. Why the rush for compulsory military training? L. V. Koos.

School Review. 53:63-7. F. '45. Against compulsory military training in peacetime. R. J. Havighurst.

Sierra Educational News. 40:19. D. '44. Compulsory military service for 18-year-olds. C. M. Walker.

Social Service Review. 18:527-9. D. '44. Universal military training in our democracy?

*Social Studies. 36:191-6. My. '45. Post-war compulsory military training. Thomas Woody.

*Survey Graphic. 34:314-16+. Jl. '45. Why postwar conscription now? V. T. Thayer.

Vital Speeches of the Day. 6:629-31. Ag. 1, '40. Compulsory military training—for what? F. C. Smith.

Time. 44:65. N. 27, '44. Loud dissent; National Guard Association.